Great Minds in Entrepreneurship Research

"A fascinating tour through the landscape of entrepreneurship scholarship and a meditation on the scientific status of the field."
—Peter G. Klein, *W. W. Caruth Chair and Professor of Entrepreneurship, Baylor University*

"This new text, 'Great Minds in Entrepreneurship Research', is to be warmly welcomed. To revisit the seminal work of leading scholars who have contributed to establishing Entrepreneurship as a mature, complex and critical body of academic analysis offers intriguing and valuable insights into how our discipline has developed over the years. Drawing upon the work of those recognised for their contribution by the Global Award for Entrepreneurship Research, Vishal Gupta presents us with a timely evaluation of the development of critical ideas, theoretical advances and also, the contribution of entrepreneurship research to global development. I am delighted to endorse this volume and congratulate the author on his achievement."
—Susan Marlow, *Professor of Entrepreneurship, Queen's Award for Enterprise, University of Birmingham*

"Great minds in entrepreneurship, indeed! By highlighting the most significant achievements of each GAER award winner, Gupta gives us a window into the evolution of entrepreneurship research. Perhaps most importantly for today's entrepreneurship scholars, it roots out the gaps still present and provides us with the questions the rest of us still need to address."
—Andrew C. Corbett, *Paul T. Babson Distinguished Professor of Entrepreneurial Studies, Babson College*

Vishal K. Gupta

Great Minds in Entrepreneurship Research

Contributions, Critiques, and Conversations

Vishal K. Gupta
The University of Alabama
Tuscaloosa, AL, USA

ISBN 978-3-030-44124-1   ISBN 978-3-030-44125-8   (eBook)
https://doi.org/10.1007/978-3-030-44125-8

This Palgrave Macmillan imprint is published by the registered company Springer Nature Switzerland AG
The registered company address is: Gewerbestrasse 11, 6330 Cham, Switzerland

To my grandparents Ram Prakash Gupta and Chandan Devi, and Bal Krishna Goel and Swarna Lata Goel. Remembered and missed!

PREFACE

The English physicist and mathematician Sir Isaac Newton is credited with one of the most cherished metaphors for scientific advancement: If I have seen further, it is by standing on the shoulders of giants. Each generation builds on the work that already exists, seeing a little further, even as those who come in the future would, in turn, stand on the shoulders of those who are here today. Indeed, even Newton's famous turn of phrase was not entirely his own. Historians have traced the metaphor as far back as to the twelfth century, when the author John of Salisbury observed that philosopher Bernard of Chartres likened people to dwarves perched on the shoulders of giants (Merton, 1965). As BofC described it, we are able to see "more and farther than our predecessors, not because we have keener vision or greater height, but because we are lifted up and borne aloft on their gigantic stature."

At first glance, the shoulder metaphor may seem a truism, something readily obvious. Of course, we should pay attention to past ideas so we create new ones for tomorrow without reinventing the wheel. However, some believe that while "in the natural sciences, each generation stands on the shoulders of those that have gone before," the situation in the social sciences is different as "each generation steps in the face of its predecessors" (Zeaman, 1959: 167). I disagree. I see no reason to accept that social science research is less cumulative than natural science research. In my view, entrepreneurship research developed cumulatively, with each generation of scholars building on the work of those who came before them. With each iteration, we were able to see further, sometimes by a little and at other times by a lot more. No matter how unprecedented or unique recent scholarly work may seem, when you dig a little deeper, you always find them to be standing on someone else's shoulders.

As an entrepreneurship researcher, I have always had a soft spot for the oft-misunderstood 'great hero' idea that individuals can and do make a difference. Can anyone deny the impact enterprising individuals like Sam Walton, Steve Jobs, and Bill Gates have had on our lives? What is true for entrepreneurship in general is also true for academic research: progress results from the efforts of enterprising folks who make significant contributions to advancing the field, or as Sarasvathy (2002: 96) so playfully put it, the people who move us "from the world we have to live in to the world we want to live in." The popular press, of course, loves the idea of the 'great hero' entrepreneur. Consider the following description of entrepreneurs in the 2018 book *Leaders: Myth and Reality*:

> Founders are those who create. They don't tweak on the margins or incrementally improve what already exists. Instead, from whole cloth they conceive and build—simultaneously serving as both architect and engineer. Typically, it falls to them to visualize, design, and build, tasks demanding foresight, political skills, and the will to drive dream to reality (McChrystal, Eggers, & Mangone, 2018: 48).

Just as enterprising individuals are central to the entrepreneurial process, they also seem to play key roles in the introduction and growth of academic fields. The following description of the genesis of the academic field of strategy by Hambrick and Chen (2008: 32) is informative:

> In March of 1970, ten professors with interests in business policy- as the field of strategic management was then called- met in Chicago to discuss "the questions involved in defining the field… and to draw out ideas about where those of us who are interested in the field should go from here"

What is the first question that comes to mind when you read the excerpt above? For me, the question was where would the field of strategy be today if those ten professors had not decided to do something about it? I understand that not everyone who reads the above excerpt would have the same reaction, but it seems to me that the role played by a small group of players in launching a new academic field that has grown tremendously over time would be of interest to many. This focus on the 'making it happen' part of human life is also one of the "oldest bromides about what entrepreneurs do" (Sarasvathy, 2004: 519). I understand that criticism of the 'great hero' school of thought is a large and growing industry in its own right (e.g., Gartner, 1988; Vroom & Jago, 2007). Yet, I personally find it hard to see how one can refute that individual effort and aspiration are central to progress throughout history and across fields.

I grew up in India, where stories of 'great heroes' (men and women) are part of every child's daily diet. As children, my siblings and I, as also most of our friends, were glued to the idiot box when the epic stories of *Ramayan* ('the story of Rama') and *Mahabharat* ('the story of Bharat') were shown on Sunday morning prime-time.[1] There were also all the stories about Ashoka, Shivaji, Rani Laxmibai, Mahatma Gandhi,[2] the list is endless. Indian history is full of heroes (and villains!) who made a difference. After I moved to the US for graduate studies, I learned that Americans too loved their heroes. I started my American journey at Penn State, and so the first 'hero' I saw in my new country was the legendary football coach Joe Paterno, who was widely respected across the campus (at the time).[3] There, I also met people like Wendy Kopp and Bob Woodward,

---

[1] The original epics are millennia old and are pillars of Indian culture. In the 1980s, they were made into TV shows that became so popular that streets would be deserted on Sundays when they were broadcast. Karp and Williams (1998) noted that when Ramayan was on TV, it was "so popular, even with non-Hindus, that some Christian churches rescheduled Sunday services so that parishioners wouldn't miss it." These shows were back on TV during India's lockdown in the face of the global coronavirus pandemic, once again attracting hundreds of millions of viewers half of who were not born at the time of the original telecast (Bellman, 2020). The story of how a constitutionally secular country came to tune into weekly shows of these religious and cultural epics begins, as do many other such stories, with an entrepreneur. A riches-to-rags-to-riches entrepreneur, Ramananda Sagar, initially failed to raise the money he needed to bring the epic Ramayan to the TV screen, until finally his persistence paid off.

[2] Jordan and Jordan [2020] recently said this about Gandhi: He "defeated the British Empire's bayonets with a walking stick and bag of salt." We love 'great heroes' (and 'heroines,' which is what Jordan and Jordan (2020) is about), even if it sometimes means resorting to "a deft encapsulation of fiendishly complex events" in making sense of their role in shaping history (Varadarajan, 2020: A15).

[3] Coach Paterno's life also reflects a serious downside of the 'great hero' approach. At one time, Paterno was the beloved 'father figure who had won more games than any other college football coach in history. The main library on the Penn State campus bore his name. His statue outside the University's football stadium was a popular spot for alumni and their kids to take pictures. Professors, deans, and administrators lined up to

who made a strong impression on me. Over the years, I learned about *Lives*, Plutarch's widely-read book about historical Greek and Roman figures. Reading the *Lives* had long been a common practice among American leaders (Teddy Roosevelt reportedly kept a copy in his breast pocket), inspiring countless generations to aspire to the achievements of the giants who came before them.

My sense was that a 'great hero' approach to understanding scientific progress was likely out-of-fashion with many scholars. I was also not sure how to define heroes in a way that would bring some objectivity to the identification process. Put in simpler terms, I did not want them to be just people whose work I admired; I wanted them to be the key figures around which there is some consensus among my peers, the community of entrepreneurship scholars. A few years back, I read Smith and Hitt's (2005) highly informative work on theorists who originated some of the most seminal ideas in management research. Their approach embraced the 'great hero' school, but their identification of the theorists who matter was quite subjective. At some point, I also came across Waddock's (2015: 1) entertaining work on *intellectual shamans*, highly productive scholars who "become fully who they must be, and find and live their purpose, to serve the world through three capacities: healing, connecting, and sense-making, and in the process seek or come to wisdom." Directly relevant to entrepreneurship researchers is Audretsch and Lehmann's (2017: 1) work on the "makers of" the academic field of entrepreneurship, focusing on "scholars who have studied entrepreneurship," particularly "those who have set the standard and tone for thinking and analyzing entrepreneurship." Both these books focused on individual scholars, which resonated with me, but were quite subjective in their identification of the scholars selected for discussion. When Locke (2001) reviewed Pugh and Hickson's (2000) seminal *Great Writers on Organization*, the one major point

---

hear him speak on leadership and ethics. Then, the Jerry Sandusky child abuse scandal broke out, and it fundamentally altered Paterno's legacy. The coach lost his job, and the statue was taken down. For Barra (2012), Paterno, in the most important crisis of his life, failed to live up to "the ideals the coach was supposed to have cherished and lived by all his life." Marchman (2012: A15) was even more critical of "Saint Joe": "At best, Paterno was a sort of stuffed mascot, monstrously indifferent to everything around him. At worst, he orchestrated an active conspiracy…" Heroes, Crossland and Hambrick (2007: 767) observed, are "objects of celebrity and vilification….for good and for ill," perhaps far more in some cultures than in others (Crossland & Hambrick, 2011).

of criticism pertained to the decision about "which writers to include or exclude" (p. 171).

As any entrepreneurship researcher knows well, new ideas oftentimes come from thinking about possible combinations of existing elements to produce something entirely different. The problem, of course, is figuring out what to combine. In my case, I had one piece that I liked: focusing on entrepreneurship scholars who made a difference. I also knew what I lacked: an objective identification of such individuals. My *aha* moment came when it occurred to me that the missing piece—the objective identification strategy I had been looking for—would come from the work that the search committee of the *Global Award for Entrepreneurship Research* had already done in shortlisting, vetting, and deciding the award recipients. Using the awardee list of a prestigious honor that recognizes outstanding scientific contributions as a way to identify exceptional researchers is not a new idea in itself as evident from the various books that have been written about Nobel laureates over the past few decades. Indeed, books about Nobel laureates may form a literary subgenre by themselves. My original insight—if it can be called that—was in combining the 'great hero' perspective with the 'award list' approach as the bases for the present endeavor focused on a broad survey of high-quality entrepreneurship research.

I recognize that entrepreneurship research is fortunate to have had other coveted awards (e.g., *Ewing Marion Kauffman Prize Medal for Distinguished Research in Entrepreneurship*). Someone else writing a book about entrepreneurship research may have chosen to focus on other awardees (and someday someone might very well do so, making another valuable contribution to the canon). Organizational research in general is characterized by *equifinality*, so that the ultimate goal of knowledge advancement can be reached "from different initial conditions and by a variety of different paths" (Katz & Kahn, 1978: 3). As such, the present book is based on one way of understanding the progress we have made in entrepreneurship research. Alternative ways are certainly possible, and I would be among the first to welcome, and encourage, adventurers wanting to take the path(s) less traveled.

As I started discussing the idea for this book with two people who I can usually count on to give critical advice—my wife Sandra Mortal (Ph.D. in finance) and my sister Alka Gupta (Ph.D. in management)—it became apparent to me that there was some merit to what I was thinking. My informal 'elevator pitch' (the one-minute what, why, and how of the idea underlying this book) piqued their interest and they seemed genuinely interested in hearing the longer version (which doesn't happen very often!). As I elaborated my initial idea, I found myself excited by the possibility of success, but at the same time, afraid of the chances of failure. The excitement came from a growing realization that the book I had in mind could indeed capture the rich history of the entrepreneurship research through a selective focus on the scholarship of 'giants' in the field. The fear of failure stemmed from the concern that the ambitious project I had in mind may not be doable, given all other commitments of one's professional and personal life.

Academic research and popular wisdom tell us that entrepreneurs tend to be high on optimism, at least in their estimation of success at endeavors that matter to them. Entrepreneurship researchers may share the same bias toward optimism! The famous economist Alfred Marshall once observed that "young men of an adventurous disposition are more attracted by the prospects of a great success than they are deterred by the fear of failure" (Marshall, 1920: 554). Notwithstanding the gender bias in Marshall's observation, and the fact that few people who make it through the long Ph.D. journey are young by the time they get to the finish line, the rest of Marshall's words ring true for me (and I suspect many others of my ilk). Much of life, however, thrives on optimism bias. Consider Glenn's (1991: 269) observation about the state of marriage in our society: "when the probability of marital success is as low as it is in the United States today, to make a strong, unqualified commitment to a marriage … is so hazardous that no totally rational person would do it." Yet, tens of thousands of people get married every year in the US, with only about 10% of the newly married estimating that their marriage will fail (Fowers, Lyons, Montel, & Shaked, 2001: 95). The optimism bias, you could say, is fundamental to any endeavor with uncertain outcomes. The finished book we have here would not have happened if, like many others, I was not biased toward optimism, a positive illusion that because 'I think I can, I probably can.'

When I started the actual writing on this book, my father advised me to rent a cabin in the mountains, isolate myself from everyone, and simply focus on getting things done. I wish I could follow Dad's advice, but it did get me thinking about the value of minimizing distractions (of which, there were still plenty). Dad, of course, was not happy that I didn't heed his advice, but he kept me on my toes by asking regularly about the progress I was making. Many other people supported the writing of this book, directly or indirectly. Daniel Turban of the University of Missouri has been an invaluable mentor throughout my academic life. Writing for an academic audience did not come naturally to me, but he was always patient in working with me and teaching me the ropes of how to make my point clearly and succinctly (though I am still not there yet). I am fortunate to be working in a school where I have colleagues who have made a strong mark on the profession with their books: Daniel Bacharach, thanks for the simulating conversations. Unlike in history or literature, writing books is not much discussed among business professors, and so it is helpful to have colleagues who have done it themselves, value it, and are willing to share their insights.

I am very thankful to Marcus Bellenger at Palgrave Macmillan for taking a risk on an ambitious project not clearly defined in the beginning. I can only hope that the book has an impact worthy of the support from Marcus Bellenger and his Palgrave team. My sincere thanks to Hans Landstrom, professor of entrepreneurship at Lund University in Sweden for his patient advice and suggestions during the formative phase of this book. Swapnil Saurav, Ph.D. student in the Alabama management program, was my research assistant for a large part of the writing of this book and was very helpful with reading individual chapters and taking care of referencing the entire manuscript. Thanks Swapnil, I couldn't have finished this project without your help! Other Alabama Ph.D. students, namely Joshua White and Abigail Molefhi, also helped with the references for the early chapters when they were my graduate assistants. Good Ph.D. students who deliver on time the work asked of them are an invaluable resource for professors juggling multiple professional commitments and trying to meet deadlines.

Finally, there are two people who deserve special mention here. My mother instilled in me a love for reading that has allowed me to thrive in a profession filled with some of the brightest minds in the world. As I was sharing with my wife the other day, our profession is full of high-IQ people (she is definitely one of them), and my love for reading is a major reason I have been able to survive in such an intellectually charged environment. My cousin, Arvind Gupta, helped steer me onto the right path when I was getting off-track as a teenager. As a professor, I see too many students who do not seem to have had good guidance in their youth, and I am so glad he was there to advise me when I really needed it. Without a strong foundation early on, it's difficult to construct a good building later.

Forgive my digression; back to the text you now hold in your hands. Starting from 1996 and all the way through 2020, this book discusses the work of 27 GAER awardees. Fifty years have passed since the first academic conference track dedicated to entrepreneurship in 1970 (Jennings & Brush, 2013), and much has been achieved during this time (Ferreira, Fernandes, & Kraus, 2019). Looking at the works of the GAER awardees with curiosity, enthusiasm, and open-minded, akin to standing on the shoulders of giants, should help entrepreneurship research make even more progress in the years to come.

On a sunny Saturday afternoon in May 2020, when we were hunkered down at home in the face of the novel coronavirus pandemic, the wife walked into my home office to share that she sees me working all the time but there seems to be nothing to show for it. "Working, working, working," she observed, "but where is the output?" Well, this book is result of all those weekends and holidays spent at work reading and writing. I hope y'all enjoy reading it as much as I enjoyed writing it.

Tuscaloosa, USA   Vishal K. Gupta

REFERENCES

Audretsch, D. B., & Lehmann, E. E. (2017). *The Routledge companion to the makers of modern entrepreneurship*. New York: Routledge.

Barra, A. (2012, August 21). 'Paterno': A relentless, failed defense of Penn State's disgraced coach. *The Atlantic*.

Bellman, E. (2020, April 28). Coronavirus lockdown creates captive audience for '80s show. *Wall Street Journal*.

Crossland, C., & Hambrick, D. C. (2007). How national systems differ in their constraints on corporate executives: A study of CEO effects in three countries. *Strategic Management Journal, 28*(8), 767–789.

Crossland, C., & Hambrick, D. C. (2011). Differences in managerial discretion across countries: How nation-level institutions affect the degree to which CEOs matter. *Strategic Management Journal, 32*(8), 797–819.

Ferreira, J. J., Fernandes, C. I., & Kraus, S. (2019). Entrepreneurship research: Mapping intellectual structures and research trends. *Review of Managerial Science, 13*(1), 181–205.

Fowers, B. J., Lyons, E., Montel, K. H., & Shaked, N. (2001). Positive illusions about marriage among married and single individuals. *Journal of Family Psychology, 15*(1), 95–109.

Gartner, W. B. (1988). "Who is an entrepreneur?" is the wrong question. *American Journal of Small Business*, *12*(4), 11–32.

Glenn, N. (1991). The recent trend in marital success in the United States. *Journal of Marriage and the Family*, *53*(2), 261–270.

Hambrick, D. C., & Chen, M. J. (2008). New academic fields as admittance-seeking social movements: The case of strategic management. *Academy of Management Review*, *33*(1), 32–54.

Jennings, J. E., & Brush, C. G. (2013). Research on women entrepreneurs: Challenges to (and from) the broader entrepreneurship literature? *Academy of Management Annals*, *7*(1), 663–715.

Jordan, J. W., & Jordan, E. A. (2020). *The war queens: Extraordinary women who ruled the battlefield*. New York, NY: Diversion Books.

Karp, J. & Williams, W. (1998, April 22). Reigning Hindu TV gods of India have viewers glued to their sets. *Wall Street Journal*.

Katz, D., & Kahn, R. L. (1978). *The social psychology of organizations* (2nd ed.). New York: Wiley.

Locke, R. R. (2001). Book reviews: Great writers on organizations. *Business History*, *43*(2), 171–172.

Marchman, T. (2012, August 22). A sad story of Happy Valley. *Wall Street Journal*.

Marshall, A. (1920). *Principles of economics*. London, UK: Macmillan.

McChrystal, S., Eggers, J., & Mangone, J. (2018). *Leaders: Myth and reality*. New York: Portfolio/Penguin.

Merton, R. (1965). *On the shoulders of giants: A Shandean postscript*. New York: The Free Press.

Pugh, D. S., & Hickson, D. J. (2000). *Great writers on organizations*. Aldershot, UK: Ashgate.

Sarasvathy, S. D. (2002). Entrepreneurship as economics with imagination. *The Ruffin Series of the Society for Business Ethics*, *3*, 95–112.

Sarasvathy, S. D. (2004). Making it happen: Beyond theories of the firm to theories of firm design. *Entrepreneurship Theory and Practice*, *28*(6), 519–531.

Smith, K. G., & Hitt, M. A. (2005). *Great minds in management: The process of theory development*. New York: Oxford University Press.

Varadarajan, S. (2020, March 13). 'The War Queens' review: The distaff and the spear. *Wall Street Journal*.

Vroom, V. H., & Jago, A. G. (2007). The role of the situation in leadership. *American Psychologist*, *62*(1), 17.

Waddock, S. (2015). *Intellectual shamans*. Cambridge, UK: Cambridge University Press.

Zeaman, D. (1959). Skinner's theory of teaching machines. In E. Galenter (Ed.), *Automatic teaching: The state of the art* (pp. 167–176). New York: John Wiley & Sons.

CONTENTS

CHAPTER 1

Introduction

Every year, editors of leading entrepreneurship journals are invited to nominate outstanding researchers for the Global Award for Entrepreneurship Research (GAER). Informally referred to among some as the 'Nobel' for research in entrepreneurial studies, GAER is an annual prize that seeks to recognize one or more persons for producing "scientific work of outstanding quality and importance, thereby giving a significant contribution to theory-building concerning entrepreneurship and small business development, the role and importance of new firm formation and the role of SMEs in economic development" (Braunerhjelm & Henrekson, 2009: 810). Since it was first presented in 1996,[1] the GAER has gradually become the foremost recognition for academic research in entrepreneurship studies. The award winner is expected to deliver the annual prize lecture at an official ceremony in Stockholm,[2] where the award is conferred by a member of either the Swedish royal family or the Swedish cabinet.

Europe has a long history of recognizing scientific achievement through public awards. In the nineteenth century, practically every European academy of sciences had prizes for outstanding scientific results

[1] The GAER was originally the *International Award for Entrepreneurship and Small Business Research.*

[2] Starting in 2003, GAER awardees were formally requested to give a Prize Lecture. In cases where the lectures were missing, the awardees were invited in 2008 to deliver a belated Prize Lecture in the form of a publishable manuscript.

© The Author(s) 2020
V. K. Gupta, *Great Minds in Entrepreneurship Research,*
https://doi.org/10.1007/978-3-030-44125-8_1

(Monastyrsky, 1997). Many of these prizes were sometimes also awarded to foreign scholars. However, most of the prizes were either a simple one-time recognition or awarded only for a limited period of time. As a result, few prizes for scholarship and research exist that have a legitimate claim to be recognized worldwide and have a relatively long stable track record. The Fields Medal for mathematics research is one such honor. Of course, the most popular and reputed of the international awards for research is the Nobel Prize, named in honor of the entrepreneur-turned-philanthropist Alfred Nobel who willed the multi-million dollar gift that funds the award (Karier, 2010).

When Alfred Nobel died, his will stipulated five prizes for "those who, during the preceding year, have conferred the greatest benefit to humankind," with one each in physics, chemistry, medicine (or physiology), literature, and for fostering peace among nations. The first prizes were awarded in 1901 and were accompanied by a financial reward equal to the sum of the interest on Nobel's gift. In 1968, the Bank of Sweden (*Sveriges Riksbank*) persuaded the Nobel Foundation to recognize scholarly achievements in economics. Generally referred to as the Nobel Prize in economics, it became the sixth annual prize given out by the Nobel Foundation.

In many ways, the GAER mimics the Nobel prizes. Like its more illustrious Nobel counterparts, the GAER is a Sweden-based award granted every year in a glittering ceremony in Stockholm. In both cases, the award consists of a statuette and a cash award. Nominations are expected to be confidential and the deliberations of the selection committee are kept secret. Award winners tend to be researchers publishing in academic journals (rather than popular writers: think Thomas Friedman and Malcolm Gladwell). Yet, the announcement of the award is a milestone as another researcher (or two) joins the exalted ranks of the awardees and gains the respect of his or her peers.

Despite these similarities, the GAER is not actually part of the Nobel family of prizes. It is not issued by the Nobel Foundation in Sweden. Press accounts do not describe it as a Nobel. As is the case for the economics award, the GAER is not funded by the Nobel Foundation and its winners are technically not Nobel laureates. And yet, with the institution of the GAER, entrepreneurship scholars got invited to join a small, but elite, group of some of the most outstanding scientific minds in modern history. Our esteemed colleagues in physics, chemistry, economics, medicine, and even mathematics were already at the party, so we are certainly in good company with the institutionalization of the GAER.

At this point, readers who wish to learn more about GAER can read Braunerhjelm and Henrekson (2009) and Henrekson and Lundström (2009). The Website www.e-award.org is also a useful resource for those interested in learning more about the award. All three sources provide good information on the history and goals of this prestigious award, its nomination process, selection criteria, and award ceremony. When the award was being restructured in the 2000s, the *Sveriges Riksbank* was invited to join the sponsoring team as it had previously sponsored the economics prize given by the Nobel Foundation (and known officially as the *Sveriges Riksbank Prize in Economic Science in Memory of Alfred Nobel*). The bank, however, rejected the proposal stating that it could not support an award for entrepreneurship research. In a classic case of serendipity, a Swedish journalist discussed the bank's response in a national newspaper, which was seen by a high-ranking manager at the leading Swedish telecom company Telia. After a year of discussions and negotiations, Telia formally joined NUTEK (Swedish Agency for Economic and Regional Growth) and FSF (Swedish Foundation for Small Business Research) to sponsor the award for entrepreneurship research. The prize sum was enhanced, the evaluation of prospective award winners was strengthened and formalized, and the '*The Hand of God*' statuette by Swedish sculptor Carl Milles was made part of the award.[3] Currently, the partners supporting the Award are the Swedish Entrepreneurship Forum (Entreprenörskapsforum), Research Institute of Industrial Economics (IFN), Vinnova (as sponsor), and the donor Lars Backsell (Chairman of the Board of Sweden-based Recipharm AB, one of the world's largest pharmaceutical firms).[4]

IS ENTREPRENEURSHIP RESEARCH SCIENTIFIC?

The primary goal of the GAER is to honor "outstanding scientific achievement" (Brauerhjelm & Henrekson, 2009: 810). A question that immediately comes to mind then is whether entrepreneurship research

---

[3] For more such interesting information about the GAER, the interested reader can refer to the above-mentioned academic papers and the official award Web site.

[4] The donors and partner organizations have changed over the years.

is truly a scientific field of inquiry. Does scholarship in entrepreneurship deserve a similar global award for its contribution to society as is the case for the more illustrious fields of physics, chemistry, and medicine, or even the latecomer, economics? At a basic level, science is about uncovering the hidden nature of the phenomenon. The scientific method, applied relentlessly, should unravel the mysteries (usually, gradually) until basic truths emerge. During the process, theories are either confirmed or refuted, creating opportunities for new hypotheses to emerge. This basic understanding of science is also at the heart of Thomas Kuhn's masterpiece *The Scientific Revolution*, which uses examples from different academic fields to explain the progress of science.

Although 'physics envy' has long been a topic of discussion among entrepreneurship researchers (Bygrave, 1989, 2007), entrepreneurship is not 'science' in the way of physics and chemistry. Entrepreneurship is a social science dealing with human behaviors and artifacts resulting from human actions. The concepts in entrepreneurship and other social disciplines tend to be value-laden (Gergen, 1973), such that "purely factual knowledge is impossible to obtain" (Whitley, 1984: 369). Humans, as everyone knows well, are notoriously fickle and impossible to capture in fundamental equations that hold more or less independent of time and place. In contrast with laws of nature, "statistical relations among core constructs" in fields of human study are "often unstable because they are historically specific" (Davis, 2010: 699).

The GAER team seems to grasp the essentially different nature of entrepreneurship as a scientific field. Consider the following statement from the GAER committee:

A prime ambition of the Prize Committee is that over a longer time span the award-winning contributions should reflect the extraordinary width of entrepreneurship as a social science field, spanning the entire spectrum from anthropology to theoretical microeconomics, and its methodological diversity from hermeneutics to formalized deductivism via traditional hypothesis testing by means of state-of-the-art statistical methods.

Thus, the GAER committee recognizes the heterogeneity in entrepreneurship inquiry and professes to not have a preference for a particular type of research. Such theoretical and methodological plurality is a strength of entrepreneurship research, and a key reason for the phenomenal progress made by academic inquiry on entrepreneurship (Cornelius, Landström, & Persson, 2006; Davidsson, 2016).

ORIGINS

How did entrepreneurship come to be as an academic discipline? The practice of entrepreneurship is probably as old as human civilization itself. References to entrepreneurial activity—buying and selling to make a profit—are available in ancient texts such as the Vedas and the Bible. Entrepreneurs were part of everyday life in all ancient civilizations, from China to Egypt. The earliest academic reference to entrepreneurship was in the *Arthashastra* ('The Science of Money') by the third-century philosopher and statesman Chanakya (Gupta, Guo, & Ozkazanc-Pan, 2018). Modern interest in entrepreneurship as a field of study probably started with the work of the Irish-French banker Richard Cantillon (b.1680–d.1734) who discussed differences between supply and demand as a driver for buying cheaply and selling at a higher price (Cantillon, 1755). Say (1803) is credited with coining the modern term 'entrepreneur' to describe the person responsible for the production and distribution of goods in a competitive marketplace. Menger (1871) explained the entrepreneurial function as one of obtaining new information about the economic situations, especially about the value given to resources in the market, a perspective that was revitalized in Nobel laureate Friedrich von Hayek's work and came to be known as the Austrian School (Foss & Klein, 2002).

Walker (1876) brought the academic discussion of entrepreneurship to the US, where it took on a life of its own. Taussig (1915) delved into wealth creation as an essential role of the entrepreneur. Knight (1921) famously introduced the distinction between risk and uncertainty. Schumpeter (1911)'s German-language *Theory of Economic Development* was translated and published in English in 1934 after he started teaching at Harvard. It was also at Harvard that the first entrepreneurship course in the US was taught in 1947 (Katz, 2003), although entrepreneurship education in an academic setting had already originated in Japan in 1938 (Hannon, 2005). Scholarly presentations on entrepreneurship started in the 1950s (Jennings & Brush, 2013), journal papers on entrepreneurship began to appear in the 1970s, and the *Academy of Management* (AoM) accorded division status to entrepreneurship in the mid-1980s. Over the next few years, there was enough research activity for review articles to summarize developments in entrepreneurship inquiry and identify emerging challenges for researchers in the area (e.g., Low & MacMillan, 1988). By the end of the first decade of the twenty-first century, entrepreneurship was already a well-established academic discipline (Zahra & Wright, 2011). With over 2700 members, the entrepreneurship division is now one of the biggest AoM divisions (Fayolle, 2014).

RELEVANCE

If you were to present the list of GAER laureates to the general public, or even to successful practicing entrepreneurs, most (if not all) of the awardees will be unknown to them (as is also the case for other scientific disciplines, both in natural sciences and social sciences). Few awardees, such as Scott Shane and David Birch, tried to write for the general public. The vast majority of the award winners present their work in academic journals, conferences, graduate seminars, and academic texts, but generally do not engage with the broader public. When it comes to practical applications of their scholarship, many researchers suffer from the same malady as the 1991 Nobel laureate James Tobin who when asked what people could learn from his award-winning research is reported to have responded, "I guess I proved that you shouldn't put all your eggs in one basket" (Karier, 2010: 11). The challenge that researchers seem to face in being 'practically relevant' may partly be because all top-tier universities (and business schools) expect professors to produce scientific papers (Zell, 2005). Publications in top journals oftentimes require that scholars turn inward to the existing academic literature, seeing the real world as a distraction. Although the perfect scholar may be one who is able to publish research that is both scientifically rigorous and practically relevant, such individuals are few and far between in business scholarship. One estimate suggests that only about 20% of authors writing for academic journals also published in a practitioner journal (Kelemen & Bansal, 2002), and even this may be an overestimation.

Concerns about lack of relevance in academic scholarship go back decades. As far back as the 1950s, various stakeholder groups were criticizing researchers for producing irrelevant research not very useful to practitioners (Moshonsky, Serenko, & Bontis, 2019). Simon (1965) argued that organizational researchers should look to the "real world as a generator of basic research problems and a source of data" (p. 341) so as to "develop new knowledge that may be relevant to improving the operations of business" (p. 335). Beyer (1982: 588) observed that an "increasing numbers of organizational scholars have begun to express concern that organizational/administrative science has had little effect on life in organizations." In his presidential address of 1993, then AoM president Donald Hambrick noted that "our failure to present ourselves - our body of knowledge and perspective - to the world of affairs" and expressed concern about academics' proclivity to work in an "incestuous, closed loop of scholarship." A few years later, another AoM president Anne Huff lamented that researchers are "increasingly seen as 'counting angels dancing on the head of a pin' by the public" (Huff, 2000).[5] In 2001, Andrew Van de Ven accepted the "growing criticism that findings from academic and consulting studies are not useful for practitioners and do not get implemented" (Van de Ven, 2002: 178). Bennis and O'Toole (2005) charged that business schools have lost their direction, producing scholarship irrelevant to management practitioners. Gulati (2007: 775) bemoaned the 'relevance' gap in research, encouraging organizational scientists to "focus squarely on phenomena of interest to managers."

Many believe that most social scientists would like to produce knowledge that engages with and impacts managerial practice (Tranfield & Starkey, 1998), but practitioners are alienated by the writing style of academic journals. As Kelemen and Bansal (2002: 98) observed:

> Much of [the academic] research does not reach the practitioner audience because of the style in which academic research is written, a style which is significantly different from the style desired by practitioners. Thus, academic research fails to resonate with managers primarily on issues of style, not on substance. In other words, although the research topic and findings may be of interest to both researchers and practitioners, the way in which research is written and presented in academic journals has little appeal to practitioners.

Some have argued that the lack of relevance in research conducted by university professors is not just a chronic feature of academic life, but a congenital one as evident from the isolated location of many colleges, especially in the US (all but five of the GAER awardees so far are US-based).[6] As Hacker and Dreifus (2010: 18) observe:

---

[5] The expression refers to a topic of obscure intellectual inquiry of little to no value.

[6] Florida and Selingo (2020: C5) recently noted that the traditional model in American higher education was "bucolic campuses nestled in small towns and rural areas," and urban universities located in large cities "had lackluster academic reputations" (this model

Professors are often isolated not only from those outside their disciplines but also from the outside world. In the nineteenth century, when most universities and colleges were founded, the idea took hold that they should be situated far away from the sordid cities. It's a tradition that holds till this day. Hence Colby College is in Waterville, Maine (15,606), Western Oregon in Monmouth (7,741), Kenyon College in Gambier, Ohio (1,817). Even state universities are sequestered in towns like Eugene, Norman, and Tuscaloosa.

Others have argued that management research is inherently irrelevant. From this perspective, the lack of relevance is a truly unsolvable problem because the researchers and their subjects (i.e., the researched) occupy separate social systems (Kieser & Leiner, 2009). Weick (2001: S71) argued that the 'relevance gap' in business is "as much a product of practitioners wedded to gurus and fads as it is of academics wedded to abstractions and fundamentals." Finally, some—arguably, only a few—researchers argue that business scholarship is already becoming relevant as a growing number of research papers involve close collaboration between academics and practitioners with the goal of producing knowledge "that is both socially useful and academically rigorous" (Hodgkinson & Rousseau, 2009: 534).

Entrepreneurship is no exception to the problem of the rigor-relevance gap that characterizes business research in general (Frank & Landström, 2016). This is somewhat surprising as two very influential ideas have taken root since the emergence of entrepreneurship as an academic field: (a) research has to be practice-oriented, helping entrepreneurs to solve their problems, and (b) better understanding of entrepreneurship can help solve various societal problems. These two ideas, nurtured and promoted by media, policy-makers, and academics themselves, add a strong normative and advisory dimension to entrepreneurship research, making the rigor-relevance tension even more ironic. As Wiklund, Wright, and Zahra (2019: 420) explained recently:

> It was the downfall of the largest Fortune 500 firms, and the rise of new entrepreneurial firms that led to the initial systematic academic interest in entrepreneurship during the 1980s.... Scholarship at the time was

has changed over time as evident from the stellar reputations of many urban campuses in major American cities like New York University and University of Chicago, among others).

phenomenon-driven with limited attention to theory, and there was a genuine interest in understanding entrepreneurs and entrepreneurship in order to help entrepreneurs and to take entrepreneurship into the classroom. To some extent, entrepreneurship research has remained this way. Most often, this phenomenon-driven, rather than theory-driven, research has been lamented, seen as a legitimacy problem among the broader field of management .... At the same time, however, it can be an advantage when it comes to thoroughly understanding the phenomenon under study, researching relevant issues, and communicating results.

At first glance, the achievements of many entrepreneurship researchers may not come across as very important or informative. This seems to be Zahra and Wright's (2011: 68) point in characterizing much of entrepreneurship inquiry as "filling in the potholes in a well-trodden path." Some (e.g., Alvesson, 2013) argue that the vast majority of published articles across all business journals are incremental at best, tend to be narrowly defined, and based on the same assumptions, so that most research ideas and findings are already understood and part of the manager's intellectual toolkit. Starbuck (2006: 1) expresses disappointment and disillusionment with management research, noting that "years pass with negligible gains in usable knowledge; successive studies of topic appear to explain less and less" and "too much effort goes into generating meaningless research 'findings,' and the flood of meaningless 'contributions' probably obscure some discoveries that would really be useful." At the same time, research papers in entrepreneurship, like in other fields of business, may be quite incomprehensible and frustratingly difficult to understand for people not technically trained to do research (Alvesson & Sandberg, 2013). Bennis and O'Toole (2005: 99) argue that academic publishing is seen as a "vast wasteland" as far as business people are concerned.

Given the impression that much management research can be characterized by faddishness, obfuscation, and jargon (Micklethwait & Wooldridge, 1996), it is understandable that many are concerned about the value-add of our scientific enterprise (Hubbard, 2015). And yet, the reality is that entrepreneurship researchers, especially the GAER awardees, have ideas that can change the way we think and also influence public policy and classroom teaching in very substantive ways. The GAER awardees have contributed crucial intellectual capital that informs educators, thought leaders, and policy-makers. Of course, this is not to suggest that all ideas of all GAER laureates are equally important or original at all times. Some awardees and ideas may end up having little to negligible influence on the world. In these cases, academic scholarship may attract significant citations from other scholars, but will have little to show for it in terms of practice. In some cases, history may show us that an awardee may not actually have been the first to describe something, but he/she were in the right place at the right time, which is also quite important. Sometimes, the relevance of new knowledge may not be immediately evident, but have a profound impact on practice at a later stage of the scientific process (Antonakis, 2017).

ORGANIZATION OF THIS BOOK

From 1996 to 2020, a total of 27 scholars were honored with the GAER. In this book, and as summarized in Table 1.1, the 27 GAER laureates are grouped in seven chapters, from Chapters 2–8.

The classification of the awardees into different chapters is based on the GAER citation that accompanied the announcement of their award. For example, the GAER citation for the first award winner David Birch in 1996 stated the following:

For having identified the key role of new and small firms in job creation

In the classification scheme used here, Birch is categorized as receiving the award for his work on the 'small firms' and grouped with other scholars who were also honored for their work in this area (namely Zoltan Acs, David Audretsch, and John Haltiwanger). Chapter 2 focuses on the work of these four awardees (Acs and Audretsch were joint winners, and are discussed together). Chapter 3 discusses three awardees recognized for focusing on economic growth as the purpose of entrepreneurship, namely Steven Klepper, Philippe Aghion, and Boyan Jovanovic. Chapter 4 covers four awardees (namely Giacomo Becattini and Charles Sabel jointly, Maryann Feldman, and Olav Sorenson), recognized for the work related to 'geography and space in entrepreneurship.' Chapter 5 discusses four awardees (namely Howard Aldrich, William Baumol, Israel Kirzner, and Josh Lerner), honored for bringing rigorous disciplinary perspective to understand entrepreneurial activity. Chapter 6 focuses on four awardees (namely Arnold Cooper, Kathleen Eisenhardt, Shaker Zahra, and Sidney Winter), working at the interface of strategy and entrepreneurship. Chapter 7 covers five awardees (namely Ian Macmillan, William Gartner, Bengt Johannisson, the Diana Group, and Hernando de Soto Polar) for their scholarship on particular sub-domains in entrepreneurship research. Chapter 8 covers three awardees (namely David Storey,

Table 1.1 Organization of GAER awardees in this book

Year	Laureate	Country	Chapter	PhD Institution
1996	David L. Birch	US	2	Harvard University
1997	Arnold C. Cooper	US	6	Harvard University
1998	David J. Storey	UK	8	University of Warwick
1999	Ian C. Macmillan	US	7	University of South Africa
2000	Howard E. Aldrich	US	5	University of Michigan
2001	Zoltan J. Acs	US	2	The New School
2001	David B. Audretsch	US	2	University of Wisconsin
2002	Giacomo Becattini	Italy	4	Florence University
2002	Charles F. Sabel	US	4	Harvard University
2003	William J. Baumol	US	5	University of London
2004	Paul D. Reynolds	US	8	Stanford University
2005	William B. Gartner	US	7	University of Washington
2006	Israel M. Kirzner	US	5	New York University
2007	The Diana Group	US	7	Boston University (Brush); University of Nebraska (Carter), University of Georgia (Gatewood); University of Texas at Austin (Greene); Harvard University (Hart)
2008	Bengt Johannisson	Sweden	7	University of Gothenburg
2009	Scott A. Shane	US	8	University of Pennsylvania
2010	Josh Lerner	US	5	Harvard University
2011	Steven Klepper	US	3	Cornell University
2012	Kathleen M. Eisenhardt	US	6	Stanford University
2013	Maryann Feldman	US	4	Carnegie Mellon University
2014	Shaker A. Zahra	US	6	University of Mississippi
2015	Sidney G. Winter	US	6	Yale University
2016	Philippe Aghion	France	3	Harvard University
2017	Hernando de Soto Polar	Peru	7	Graduate Institute of International Studies
2018	Olav Sorenson	US	4	Stanford University
2019	Boyan Jovanovic	US	3	University of Chicago
2020	John Haltiwanger	US	2	John Hopkins University

Paul Reynolds, and Scott Shane), recognized for the strength of their overall research program in entrepreneurship.

Of course, any categorization scheme is by nature reductionist and largely subjective. As such, the classification scheme used here may give the appearance of greater intra-group similarity and higher differences between groups than is actually the case. It is fully possible that another researcher attempting to categorize the GAER awardees may come up with a different classification scheme that brings together awardees that are categorized separately here. The categorization scheme followed in this book is merely one way to organize the GAER awardees in a consistent systematic fashion. Such an approach is not uncommon in academic efforts similar to the one undertaken here. For example, Karier (2010) explores the contributions of the Nobel laureates in economics, summarizing them into 13 chapters based on the core ideas they discussed. Would another researcher looking at the same set of economists categorize them in the same way? Probably not. Such subjectivity does not undermine the value of Karier's (2010) work, which is to give readers one way to make sense of the Nobel laureates in economics and highlight the contributions already made. Of course, alternative approaches to synthesizing the works of similar awardees are possible, such as Weber's (1988) chronological consideration of Nobel laureates in physics from 1901 to 1987. The idea of organizing the awardees by the scope of their contribution based on the GAER citations is therefore one of the several alternatives that could have been pursued.

Each chapter discusses the work of the awardees, summarizes their seminal contributions, acknowledges major critiques, and identifies unresolved or open questions for future research to consider. Strengths and positive aspects of each GAER awardees' work are highlighted, and gaps or omissions in their research are discussed with an eye toward refreshing academic inquiry in the area. Many of the awardees covered in this book have made extensive contributions to entrepreneurship spanning over several years, and it would be virtually impossible to individually discuss and engage with each of their published work in a book that covers several scholars. The goal here is not to exhaustively review each author's work, but to identify important patterns and thrusts in their research and engage with dominant themes in a constructive manner.

Each of the GAER awardees is a giant in his or her area of research. Understanding the ideas they put forward, how they examined them, and the extent to which they influenced the way others thought about entrepreneurial phenomena will be useful and helpful for the continued evolution of entrepreneurship research in vibrant and productive directions. It is this constructive spirit that has guided the idea and writing of the book you now hold in your hands.

REFERENCES

Alvesson, M. (2013). Do we have something to say? From re-search to roi-search and back again. *Organization, 20*(1), 79–90.

Alvesson, M., & Sandberg, J. (2013). Has management studies lost its way? Ideas for more imaginative and innovative research. *Journal of Management Studies, 50*(1), 128–152.

Antonakis, J. (2017). On doing better science: From thrill of discovery to policy implications. *Leadership Quarterly, 28*(1), 5–21.

Bennis, W. G., & O'Toole, J. (2005). How business schools lost their way. *Harvard Business Review, 83*(5), 96–104.

Beyer, J. M. (1982). Introduction to the special issue on the utilization of organizational research. *Administrative Science Quarterly, 27*(4), 588–590.

Braunerhjelm, P., & Henrekson, M. (2009). Awarding entrepreneurship research: A presentation of the global award. *Entrepreneurship Theory and Practice, 33*(3), 809–814.

Bygrave, W. D. (1989). The entrepreneurship paradigm (I): A philosophical look at its research methodologies. *Entrepreneurship Theory and Practice, 14*(1), 7–26.

Bygrave, W. D. (2007). The entrepreneurship paradigm (I) revisited. In H. Neergaard & J. Parm Ulhoi (Eds.), *Handbook of qualitative research methods in entrepreneurship* (pp. 17–48). Cheltenham, UK and Northampton, MA: Edward Elgar.

Cantillon, R. (1755). *An essay on commerce in general.* London: Fletcher Gyle.

Cornelius, B., Landström, H., & Persson, O. (2006). Entrepreneurial studies: The dynamic research front of a developing social science. *Entrepreneurship Theory and Practice, 30*(3), 375–398.

Davidsson, P. (2016). *Researching entrepreneurship: Conceptualization and design* (2nd ed.). New York: Springer.

Davis, G. F. (2010). Do theories of organizations progress? *Organizational Research Methods, 13*(4), 690–709.

Fayolle, A. (2014). What we know and what we need to know in the field of entrepreneurship. In A. Fayolle (Ed.), *Handbook of research on entrepreneurship: What we know and what we need to know.* Cheltenham, UK: Edward Elgar.

Florida, R., & Selingo, J. (2020, May 9–10). A crisis for urban universities. *Wall Street Journal*, C5.

Foss, N. J., & Klein, P. G. (2002). *Entrepreneurship and the firm: Austrian perspectives on economic organization.* Northampton, MA: Edward Elgar.

Frank, H., & Landström, H. (2016). What makes entrepreneurship research interesting? Reflections on strategies to overcome the rigour–relevance gap. *Entrepreneurship & Regional Development, 28*(1–2), 51–75.

Gergen, K. J. (1973). Social psychology as history. *Journal of Personality and Social Psychology, 26,* 309–320.

Gulati, R. (2007). Tent poles, tribalism, and boundary spanning: The rigor-relevance debate in management research. *Academy of Management Journal, 50*(4), 775–782.

Gupta, V. K., Guo, G. C., & Ozkazanc-Pan, B. (2018). Introduction. In G. Javadian, et al. (Eds.), *Foundational research in entrepreneurship studies: Insightful contributions and future pathways* (pp. 1–13). Cham, Switzerland: Palgrave Macmillan.

Hacker, A., & Dreifus, C. (2010). *Higher education? How colleges are wasting our money and failing our kids-and what we can do about it.* New York: St. Martin's Griffin.

Hannon, P. D. (2005). Philosophies of enterprise and entrepreneurship education and challenges for higher education in the UK. *International Journal of Entrepreneurship and Innovation, 6*(2), 105–114.

Henrekson, M., & Lundström, A. (2009). The global award for entrepreneurship research. *Small Business Economics, 32*(1), 1–14.

Hodgkinson, G. P., & Rousseau, D. M. (2009). Bridging the rigour–relevance gap in management research: It's already happening! *Journal of Management Studies, 46*(3), 534–546.

Hubbard, R. (2015). *Corrupt research: The case for reconceptualizing empirical management and social science.* Thousand Oaks, CA: Sage.

Huff, A. S. (2000). 1999 Presidential address: Changes in organizational knowledge production. *Academy of Management Review, 25*(2), 288–293.

Jennings, J. E., & Brush, C. G. (2013). Research on women entrepreneurs: Challenges to (and from) the broader entrepreneurship literature? *Academy of Management Annals, 7*(1), 663–715.

Karier, T. (2010). *Intellectual capital: Forty years of the Nobel Prize in economics.* New York: Cambridge University Press.

Katz, J. A. (2003). The chronology and intellectual trajectory of American entrepreneurship education. *Journal of Business Venturing, 18*(2), 283–300.

Kelemen, M., & Bansal, P. (2002). The conventions of management research and their relevance to management practice. *British Journal of Management, 13*(2), 97–108.

Kieser, A., & Leiner, L. (2009). Why the rigour–relevance gap in management research is unbridgeable. *Journal of Management Studies, 46*(3), 516–533.

Knight, F. H. (1921). *Risk, uncertainty and profit.* New York: Augustus Kelley.

Low, M. B., & MacMillan, I. C. (1988). Entrepreneurship: Past research and future challenges. *Journal of Management, 14*(2), 139–161.

Menger, C. (1871). *Principles of economics* (J. Dingwall & Bert F. Hoselitz. Trans.). Auburn, AL: Ludwig von Mises Institute.

Micklethwait, J., & Wooldridge, A. (1996). *The witch doctors: What the management gurus are saying, why it matters and how to make sense of it*. London: Heinemann.

Monastyrsky, M. (1997). *Modern mathematics in the light of the fields medals*. Wellesley, MA: A. K. Peters.

Moshonsky, M., Serenko, A., & Bontis, N. (2019). Practical relevance of management research: The role of doctoral program graduates. In M. Jennex (Ed.), *Effective knowledge management systems in modern society* (pp. 236–265). Hershey, PA: IGI Global.

Say, J. B. (1803). *Treatise on political economy on the production, distribution and consumption of wealth*.

Schumpeter, J. A. (1911/1934). *The theory of economic development: An inquiry into profits, capital, credit, interest, and the business cycle*. Cambridge: Harvard University Press.

Simon, H. A. (1965). *The new science of management decision*. Englewood Cliffs, NJ: Prentice-Hall.

Starbuck, W. H. (2006). *The production of knowledge: The challenge of social science research*. New York: Oxford University Press.

Taussig, F. W. (1915). *Investors and moneymakers*. New York: Macmillan.

Tranfield, D., & Starkey, K. (1998). The nature, social organization and promotion of management research: Towards policy. *British Journal of Management, 9*(4), 341–353.

Van De Ven, A. H. (2002). 2001 Presidential address: Strategic directions for the Academy of Management: This academy is for you! *Academy of Management Review, 27*(2), 171–184.

Walker, F. A. (1876). *The wages question: A treatise on wages and the wages class*. New York: H. Holt.

Weber, R. L. (1988). *Pioneers of science: Nobel Prize winners in physics*. Bristol, UK: Adam Hilger.

Weick, K. E. (2001). Gapping the relevance bridge: Fashions meet fundamentals in management research. *British Journal of Management, 12*, S71–S75.

Whitley, R. (1984). The scientific status of management research as a practically-oriented social science. *Journal of Management Studies, 21*(4), 369–390.

Wiklund, J., Wright, M., & Zahra, S. A. (2019). Conquering relevance: Entrepreneurship research's grand challenge. *Entrepreneurship Theory and Practice, 43*(3), 419–436.

Zahra, S. A., & Wright, M. (2011). Entrepreneurship's next act. *Academy of Management Perspectives, 25*(4), 67–83.

Zell, D. (2005). Pressure for relevancy at top-tier business schools. *Journal of Management Inquiry, 14*(3), 271–274.

CHAPTER 2

Small Firms

Is small business and entrepreneurship the same thing? For many academics and the vast majority of laypeople, entrepreneurship and small business are interchangeable with little difference between them. Allen and Rahman (1985) discuss the role of small business incubators in providing a positive environment for entrepreneurship. Zeithaml and Rice (1987: 44) conduct a survey to "identify the state of university education in entrepreneurship/small business." Many leading entrepreneurship journals have the phrase 'small business' in their titles (Markin, Swab, & Marshall, 2017). The GAER was instituted by the Swedish Foundation for Small Business Research. Founded in 1955, the International Council for Small Business (ICSB) sought to promote the growth and development of small firms worldwide, which included focusing on entrepreneurship.

Over time, and as the field became more established, the terms entrepreneurship and small business started to be used differently. Small business research pertains to scholarship about firms that were small (though there is not 'a single, uniformly acceptable, definition of a small firm' (Beaver & Jennings, 2000: 403; Storey, 1994). Entrepreneurship research concentrates on new ventures, new entry, or a host of other phenomena related to emerging opportunities to introduce future goods and services to the market (Davidsson, 2016; Shane, 2012). A plethora of books talk about 'small business and entrepreneurship' (see, e.g., Burns (2016) and some journals include both 'small business' and

© The Author(s) 2020
V. K. Gupta, *Great Minds in Entrepreneurship Research*,
https://doi.org/10.1007/978-3-030-44125-8_2

'entrepreneurship' in their title and mission. Gradually, 'small firms' became optional for the domain of entrepreneurship research. Shepherd, Williams, and Patzelt (2015: 13) observed that "small business is not a defining characteristic of what is entrepreneurial," so that small firms are not a necessary part of entrepreneurship research (Javadian, Ellis, Gupta, Gupta, & Martin, 2020). The mission statement of AoM's entrepreneurship division makes no mention of small firms, and contemporary definitions of entrepreneurship research do not necessarily include small firms. This academic distinction between entrepreneurship and small business is inconsistent with laypersons' understanding of entrepreneurship. For the average person on the street, entrepreneurship is the story of small firms and de novo start-ups, a perspective not always shared by modern entrepreneurship researchers.

The GAER has been awarded thrice for contributions to small business research: David Birch in 1996, Zoltan Acs and David Audretsch in 2001, and John Haltiwanger in 2020.

David Birch: Small Business and Job Creation

David Birch was the first recipient of the GAER award.[1] According to the award citation, Professor Birch was honored for "having identified the key role of new and small firms in job creation." Over the years, both academic and popular press have lauded Birch's contribution to advancing our understanding about the economic contributions of small business. As Landstrom (2005: 160) wrote:

> It was Birch's systematic studies and empirical results that gave small businesses a place on the research map. Even though small businesses accounted for a large part of employment in the US, few economists before Birch had previously studied small businesses in the economy. Birch has had many followers.

Birch was arguably the most prominent evangelist for small business in the country, and to some extent in other parts of the world as well (primarily the Western, educated, industrialized, rich, and developed countries such as the UK). His ideas have shaped not only academic and

---

[1] As discussed in the previous chapter, the GAER is a direct continuation of the International Award for Entrepreneurship and Small Business Research launched in 1996.

popular discussions about small business, but also informed public policy regarding small businesses. Not bad at all for someone who started his career as an engineer and computer programmer and finished it as a naval architect restoring boats. Unlike most other GAER awardees, academic life seems to have been just one phase of Birch's long career, lasting from when he finished his doctorate at Harvard University to when he started his business consulting firm.

Birch is best known for his seminal work *The Job Generation Process*, putting forth the idea that small businesses play a critical role in new job creation. Much of the ideas presented in this limited circulation report were later elaborated in the 1987 book *Job Creation in America*. For the tremendous impact Birch had on academic and popular discourse about small business, his own publication list is quite modest as most of his published work was derived in one way or another from his 1979 report and was seldom published in peer-reviewed outlets.[2] As such to understand Birch's contribution to small business research, it seems appropriate to start with his 1979 report, which even his critics consider to be a "seminal work" in the field (Atkinson & Storey, 1994: 3). As Birch (1979: 1) noted, he had a two-pronged goal in undertaking the original research that informed his subsequent work:

> To develop an 'economic microscope' that would let us reach beneath aggregate statistics to see how the behavior of individual firms causes change and (2) to begin to draw some conclusions about what kinds of economic development policies do or do not make sense in view of what we see.

To achieve the two goals noted above, Birch (1979: 1) generated…

> …a detailed file on each of the 5.6 million business establishments over time. Knowing a fair amount about each establishment (and the firm to which it belongs) at each point along the way, we can characterize how the firm changes. By aggregating all establishments within a given location, we

---

[2] Publications that go through the "critical review" of fellow researchers and "succeed in gaining their approval" are generally considered 'certified knowledge' (Ramos-Rodriguez & Ruiz-Navarro, 2004: 982), and as such are seen as being of higher quality and reliability than works that are not peer reviewed. Case (1989) recognized that Birch "was criticized for not publishing his work in refereed economics journals, where it would be subjected to professional scrutiny before publication."

can describe the aggregate changes that place is experiencing and, most importantly, know exactly how that change took place. In the process, we can identify major generators (and destroyers) and begin to suggest which kinds of policies will foster a healthy economy and, conversely which kinds will be either a waste of time and effort or, worse, actually defeating of their intended purpose.

Birch had not actually set out to study small businesses. His original interest was in studying the dynamics of large cities, which he did by "building a huge database on every neighborhood in five US cities and analyzing what was going on" (Landstrom, 2005: 160). In trying to understand the ongoing evolution of large American cities, Birch was aware that jobs had moved away from city centers over time, which gradually channeled his research interests toward job creation as there existed little understanding at the time on how new jobs were generated. Perhaps, the fact that Birch was beginning his research program at a time of economic crisis in the country had something to do with growing focus on job creation. The 1973 oil crisis with its long lines and the subsequent stock market crash followed by the highest national unemployment levels (about 9%) since the Second World War had produced a sense of urgency about better understanding how the economy could be stimulated (Wennekers & Thurik, 1999). As Birch later recounted, "it was a time of economic recession, unemployment, all politicians needed help - from the President, the US Congress, as well as governors of different states...they were all saying 'You know where the jobs are created...help us'" (Landstrom, 2005: 161).

Birch's research was based on Dun and Bradstreet Corporation's data on individual firms, which the company used for two purposes: (a) assess the creditworthiness of each firm and (b) selling to others to use for market research and mailing lists. The company collected a large range of information about each firm, including its founding year, location, most relevant Standard Industrial Classification (SIC) Codes, number of employees, sales, to name a few. D&B wanted its data to be accurate as having wrong information about a company could, and did, result in lawsuits. While Birch (2000) acknowledged that the D&B database had some problems (e.g., clerical errors, scope of coverage, or plain misrepresentation by respondents), he also viewed it as "potentially one of the most accurate in social science history." Perhaps, an even bigger challenge Birch had to deal with was that empirical tools at the time were not developed enough to deal with 5.6 million complex records, and so the research team had to come up with new techniques suitable to analyze such large-scale datasets.

Focusing on employment growth, Birch (1979) found that:

a. The migration of business enterprises (whether the inward movement of an existing firm already located elsewhere or the outward movement of an existing firm located in the area) has a negligible, at best small, effect on the number of jobs available locally.

b. Although there are large variations in overall number of firms over time (i.e., high inter-temporal variation), deaths (when an existing firm dissolves) and contraction (when an existing firm decreases its employee base) vary little across space (i.e., inter-regional variation is low). On average, a state loses about 8% of its job base annually (or about 40% of the job base quinquennially), but this loss rate does not vary much across states.

c. Most new organizations (or births) are due to established firms starting new branches.

d. Much of the expansion (i.e., when a firm increases in size by hiring more workers) is due to independent firms, accounting for about half of all jobs (although the share of independents in job creation was found to be decreasing). Firms most likely to expand are those that survive through hard times (defined as, five consecutive years of losses), presumably because they learn from failure. Firms that expand very fast are more likely to struggle in the future (i.e., lay off employees later), suggesting that extraordinary growth may be detrimental in the long-run.

e. Interestingly, the bigger the firm, the more likely it was to contract, but the less likely it was to die. The inflection point at the time was at 20 employees, so that when a firm exceeds that size, its chances of dying are significantly reduced, whereas its chances of contracting (i.e., laying off workers) increase considerably.

Birch's (1979) findings are intriguing, but they are also constrained in their ability to cast light on the underlying processes. For example, firm growth is a major theme in entrepreneurship research (Davidsson, Delmar, & Wiklund, 2006), and Birch (1979)'s finding about high growth increasing the odds of future failure is provocative for the vast majority of scholars who generally believe 'growth is good'. The D&B data, however, did not allow for derivation of insights into why the growth-failure relationship may happen. Similarly, it is interesting that the inflection point for firm size was at 20 employees, but once again, the data do not provide insights into what explains the magic number of 20 workers.

Efforts were made to conduct Birch-like research in other countries. For example, using UK D&B files, Gallangher and colleagues argued that small firms were a major generator of new jobs in the UK (Daly, Campbell, Robson, & Gallagher, 1991; Doyle & Gallagher, 1987; Gallagher, Thomason, & Daly, 1991). Baldwin and Picot (1995) conducted similar research in Canada, contributing to the international body of evidence consistent with Birch's (1979) thesis. In this vein, Davidsson, Lindmark, and Olofsson (1998: 87) note "studies in many countries" have come to the "general conclusion that small firms are of great importance for job creation."

Birch's work also found favor with policy-makers who embraced the idea of small business as the primary creator of jobs. As Landstrom (2005: 164) observed:

> [Birch's] report was only sold in twelve copies, but its influence was enormous, not least on politicians and policy-makers around the world. The report was in line with the new political winds that had started to blow across the western world with Reagan and Thatcher as the most prominent protagonists. The report alerted both the Congress and the local economic-development officials all over the US, and it interested politicians and policy-makers not only in the US but around the world. Small business was no longer only an economic sideshow – it was the main event.

Atkinson and Storey (1994) observe a similar fascination with Birch's work among UK policy-makers, noting that:

> In 1979, the work of David Birch in the USA was extensively publicized by a newly elected UK conservative administration...There can be little doubt that the emphasis upon the small firm in government policy, most notably through an attempt to create an 'enterprise culture' ..., drew its impetus from the perceived role of small firms in creating employment...The view was widely held ... that a relaxation of the legislative constraints upon small firms would enable them to ...reduce or eliminate unemployment.

Armington and Odle (1982) was probably the first systematic attempt to cast doubt on Birch's (1979) methodological approach and question his findings about the job creation role of small business. Their primary methodological disagreement with Birch (1979) was level of analysis: establishment level in Birch's (1979) original study and enterprise level in Armington and Odle (1982). Specifically, instead of classifying firms by the numbers of employees at each location as Birch (1979) did, Armington and Odle (1982) focused on total firm size by adding up the employees at all its branches and subsidiaries.[3] The difference between establishment size and firm size is usually not a problem as the vast majority (about 90% by some estimates) of businesses are single-location firms, but multi-location companies employ a large part of the private sector workforce. Notably, many small establishments are branches or subsidiaries of large firms, so counting their employment at the establishment level rather than at the level of the firm can overestimate the job creation impact of small firms.[4]

[3] To illustrate, if the local Chipotle outlet near your campus employs 7 people, Birch (1979) would classify it as one business with 7 employees, whereas Armington and Odle (1982) consider those 7 workers to be part of Chipotle's total workforce nationwide.

[4] Whether employment should be counted at the level of the establishment or the firm may seem like a simple methodological choice that researchers make, but its practical impact was salient to many Americans during the 2020 pandemic when large companies like Shake Shack and Ruth's Hospitality Group received federal help targeted at small firms through the Payroll Protection Program (PPP). The intent of the PPP was to help struggling small businesses, which were originally defined as employing less than 500 people per establishment. The Small Business Administration (SBA), which was responsible for implementing the PPP, stipulated that firms could apply for each restaurant or hotel so long as each operated as a 'separate legal business entity' with its own employer identification number and the location doesn't have more than 500 employees. Consequently, companies like Fogo de Chão, a privately owned restaurant chain with annual revenues of $325 million across 43 restaurants, received federal aid directed at small businesses. It applied for loans for its individual restaurants and two received a total of $20 million in funding. The National Restaurant Association (NRA) lobbied to include in the stimulus legislation that "any business concern that employs not more than 500 employees per physical location of the business" and is in the restaurant, hotel and camping sector would also be covered by the loan program (Davis & Haddon, 2020). In all, hundreds of large companies, including dozens of publicly traded corporations, received PPP aid totaling upwards of $500 million (Pacheo & Francis, 2020). There was considerable public outrage when the media revealed that many large companies were receiving aid that was to help small firms. "This is outrageous," said House Small Business Committee Chairwoman Nydia Velázquez. "Multimillion-dollar companies are getting millions of dollars, it just doesn't make sense," said Sabir Mujtaba, president of Veloc Inc., a small staffing company in

The controversy over the exact impact of small business on job creation has continued over the years. Davis, Haltiwanger, and Schuh (1996a) like Birch (1979) used establishment data, but with average size definition and only for manufacturing firms, to find that there was either no relationship, or even a positive relationship, between firm size and net job creation, suggesting that either new job creation was independent of firm size or large firms created more new jobs. Using Portuguese data, Baptista, Escaria, and Madruga (2008) find that new firms have a "relatively low positive impact on employment growth in the early days of the venture," which becomes negative in the fourth-year after start-up, and turns positive again after the sixth year post start-up. Neumark, Wall, and Zhang (2011: 22) used a new longitudinal database—the National Establishment Time Series (NETS)–created from D&B data, finding that small firms "generate a disproportionate share of gross job creation (35.1%, relative to a 27.2% employment share)" as well as "also generate a disproportionate share of gross job destruction (33.9%, relative to the 27.2% employment share)." Their overarching conclusion is that "small firms (and small establishments as well) create more jobs," but the difference between small and large enterprises is considerably "smaller than Birch originally suggested" (page 27).

Other criticisms also followed: Professor George Kalidonis alleged Birch used "faulty methodology" and misinterpreted data, which caused him to make "dubious" claims about job generation (Case, 1989). There are also concerns about missing data in the D&B database as some establishments are included that should not be and some that should be included are not (Atkinson & Storey, 1994), though Birch (2000) argued that coverage is no more systematically biased than any other possible datasets that researchers may use for their investigations. Storey and Johnson (1986) questioned the extent to which the D&B dataset was appropriately 'cleaned' to address errors and mistakes, but substantial work does seem to have gone toward 'cleaning' the database (Birch, 2000; Daly et al., 1991). Some scholars believe Birch's (1979) approach

Irving, Texas, with 18 employees. The outrage forced many large companies, including Potbelly Inc. and Kara Sushi USA, to publicly declare that they were returning the stimulus money (Rudegeair, Haddon, & Simon, 2020). Large corporations getting the aid directed at small businesses "really exposed the weakness in the program," observed Tom Colicchio, a New York City restaurateur and co-founder of an advocacy group pushing Congress to change the loan program. His conclusion: "We need to quantify what a small business is" (Davis & Haddon, 2020).

of categorizing firms based on size and looking at variations in job growth across various categories is vulnerable to the 'regression fallacy' (or 'regression-to-the-mean' bias) which overestimates the role of small firms in job creation, but Davidsson et al. (1998) do not consider it a problem as they found little evidence for it in Swedish data.

Hall (1987) contends that the D&B database may be fundamentally flawed as it shows that organizational death increases with firm size, which goes against conventional wisdom that failure is more common in small firms (Ucbasaran, Shepherd, Lockett, & Lyon, 2013). Storey and Johnson (1986) argued that the D&B database, by design, is not a random sample, but is more likely to include firms that are credit-seeking as the purpose of the dataset is to assess creditworthiness. Because credit-seeking firms are more likely to be either growth-oriented or mismanaged, failure to consider this bias in the sample would cause over-estimation of the employment created by small firms. Brown, Hamilton, and Medoff (1990) are concerned that Birch (1979) does not differentiate between firm size and age, noting that:

> We have seen that small employers do not create a strikingly high share of jobs in the economy, especially if we count only jobs that are not short-lived. Most jobs are generated by new firms, which happen to be small; existing small firms have relatively high chances of failing, and when this failure rate is taken into account they do not grow faster than larger firms. Indeed, in recent years they have shrunk faster than larger firms.

Despite major concerns raised by critics about Birch's (1979) empirical approach, its popularity continued to soar. Atkinson and Storey (1994: 4) make an interesting observation in this regard:

> ...it seems that the more successful the critics were in undermining the methodology and the inferences, the greater was Birch's credibility amongst influential group of politicians.

It is a testament to the strong faith in the job creation prowess of small business in academic and public discourse that questions about the accuracy of Birch's (1979) findings had no discernable impact on the acceptance of those findings.

If one were to accept Birch's thesis of the role of small business in job creation, his research says nothing about the quality of those jobs. For many, the challenge of our times is not the "quantity of jobs [but]...the quality of jobs," especially those available to low- and- medium-skilled workers (Autor & Salomons, 2017: 45), a growing concern that has also resonated with the popular press (Vo & Zumbrun, 2016).[5] The question here is whether workers are better off working in large firms or small firms. There seems to be little doubt that employees of large firms, on average, receive greater salary, better benefits, and higher job security than their counterparts in smaller firms (Oi & Idson, 1999; Wagner, 1997).[6] On the other hand, it is possible that employees in smaller firms experience greater job satisfaction than those in larger firms (Idson, 1990; Kruse, 1992), though the jury is still out on this issue. Furthermore, despite constant calls for public policy on job creation to focus on small firms, it has yet to be demonstrated that marginal public investment in employment generation has a bigger impact when directed at small firms rather than larger firms (Brown et al. 1990). These concerns do not directly question Birch's (1979) findings, but pertain more to the scope of his research.

ZOLTAN ACS AND DAVID AUDRETSCH: SMALL BUSINESS AND INNOVATION

In 2001, two good friends and economists, Zoltan Acs and David Audretsch, were honored for their work on the relationship between small firms and innovation. The official citation recognized the two scholars for "research on the role of small firms in the economy, especially the role of

---

[5] Writing for *The New York Times*, Desmond (2018) contends that "Americans want to believe jobs are the solution to poverty [but] they're not" because for those with little education, the jobs that are available "do not pay enough to live on." The noted American author Barbara Ehrenreich's book Nickel and Dimed memorably depicted the difficult life of those working in low-tier minimum-wage jobs (e.g., in retail and restaurant industries), bringing the issue of job quality center-stage in public imagination. Academic research seems to have lagged public interest when it comes to quality of jobs created.

[6] Professor James Medoff of Harvard and other economists have revealed that "large companies pay higher wages and provide better benefits than small ones. And at least some studies suggest that larger businesses are more stable employers" (Case, 1989). At the onset of the 2020 Coronavirus pandemic, Weber (2020) noted that "a pandemic can be a good time to work for a big company...as... many small businesses operating with little cushion are laying off employees."

small firms in innovation." Landstrom (2005: 205) is more descriptive in his commentary on the two economists:

> Zoltan Acs and David Audretsch are two of the most prolific researchers within the entrepreneurship and small business field. Both jointly and individually they have published a considerable amount of scientific articles and books and have made a number of significant contributions in the area of small business economics...Apart from their own empirical work, Zoltan Acs and David Audretsch have made important contributions to the open and critical assessment and discussion of the role of small firms in the economy, including organizing several high class conferences and editing books. However, their single most important contribution is the establishment of the *Small Business Economics* journal as a high quality outlet for small business research.

Acs and Audretsch were not the first to talk about the innovative role of small firms. The credit for linking small firms with innovative activities goes to the famed economic thinker Joseph Schumpeter (Hagedoorn, 1996). Not surprisingly, most researchers who study innovation refer to Schumpeter and his pioneering role in fostering academic interest in innovation (Godin, 2008). For many scholars (e.g., Becker, Knudsen, & Swedberg, 2012), Schumpeter is a sort of patron saint of those interested in innovation. While in his later years Schumpeter advocated that large monopolistic firms were the primary driver of innovative activity in society (Ahuja, Lampert, & Tandon, 2008), his early years as a scholar were marked by an emphasis on the role of entrepreneurial firms in introducing new innovations (Goss, 2005). For some (e.g., Freeman, 1982; Nelson & Winter, 1977), there are two Schumpeters: the early-Schumpeter (or Schumpeter I) who saw entrepreneurial small firms as the driver of innovative activity and late Schumpeter (or Schumpeter II) who believed that large firms were responsible for most new innovations.[7] As Acs and Audretsch (1988a) wrote:

---

[7] Langlois (2003) does not believe that Schumpeter changed his opinion on innovation with time, attributing the apparent tension in his work to ignorance of the economic process where entrepreneurs bring innovations to life and monopoly formalizes the innovative process for superior benefits (Hong, Oxley, Mccann, & Le, 2016: 5381). de Jong and Marsili (2006: 215) write: "In the "Schumpeter Mark I" (SM-I or "entrepreneurial") pattern, innovation was mainly generated by the entrepreneurial activity and creativity of small and new firms. In the "Schumpeter Mark II" (SM-II or "routinised") pattern, innovation originates in the formal R&D activity of large and established firms."

Who innovates more-the large or the small firm? This question has generally been the essential focus of the Schumpeterian debate.

Using a new measure of innovative activity (total innovations per employee), Acs and Audretsch (1988b) were able to directly compare Schumpeter's conflicting views about firm size and innovation. Their results are revealing: the relationship between firm size and innovation is U-shaped, where both small and large firms are conducive to innovation. They also found that over the full range of firm size in their data, innovative activity was associated with large firms, but monopoly power deterred innovation. Around the time their paper examining Schumpeter's conflicting hypotheses about innovation and firm size came out, Acs and Audretsch published several other papers related to innovation and small firms. Acs and Audretsch (1988a) relied on the SBA's data on number of innovations in each four-digit SIC industry recorded in 1982 to identify the antecedents of innovative activity. Their findings show innovation in the industry is negatively related to concentration and unionization, and positively related to R&D, skilled labor, and the degree to which large firms comprise the industry. They also found that the greater the extent to which an industry is composed of large firms, the higher the innovative activity. Notably, the increased innovative activity will tend to emanate more from small firms than from large firms.

The findings about the innovative role of small firms were consistent with what Acs (1979) had learned about the US steel industry during his doctoral dissertation (Acs, 1979). Small firms in the steel industry—'mini mills—were able to successfully compete with the large corporations by using innovative production technologies and organizing themselves in innovative ways (Landstrom, 2005). These small companies seemed quite Schumpeterian in their approach. Recall that Schumpeter (1934) viewed innovations as 'new combinations'—of products, production techniques, markets, supply sources, or organizational forms.[8] The innovative role of

---

[8] Over the years, a number of scholars have noted that for Schumpeter the concept of innovation referred to "the carrying out of new combinations" interpreted in a broad sense (Langlois, 2003). These new combinations "cover the following five cases: (1) The introduction of a new good -- that is one with which consumers are not yet familiar -- or of a new quality of a good. (2) The introduction of a new method of production, that is one not yet tested by experience in the branch of manufacture concerned, which need by no means be founded upon a discovery scientifically new, and can also exist in a new way of handling a commodity commercially. (3) The opening of a new market, or going into

small steel mills in bringing about technical change in the American steel industry was the focus of Acs (1988).

Interestingly, Acs and Audretsch (1987a) had shown that the market environment most conducive to innovation is quite similar for large and small firms (except for R&D, which they found to be more important for large firms). Acs and Audretsch (1987b) argued that the relationship between firm size and innovativeness was contingent on the market environment. Larger firms were more innovative in industries that were capital-intensive, concentrated, highly unionized, and produce a differentiated offering, while smaller firms had advantage in industries that were highly innovative, utilize a large component of skilled labor, and comprised of a higher proportion of large firms. Thus, the conclusions of Acs and Audretsch (1987a) and Acs and Audretsch (1987b) appear to be at odds with each other. Other researchers (e.g., Koeller, 1995) have found that innovative activities of large and small firms respond differently to economic and technological conditions, which seems consistent with Acs and Audretsch (1987b). Koeller (1995) also found that high industry concentration and capital intensity appear to have greater depressing effects on small-firm innovation than on large-firm innovation, which also seems (at least partly) in line with Acs and Audretsch (1987b).

So, who is more innovative: small firms or large firms? As the above discussion shows, Acs and Audretsch's research is mixed on this issue, which is consistent with Schumpeter's conflicted views. Using the same 1982 SBA data on innovation, they had used earlier, Acs and Audretsch (1988c) find that:

1. large firms in manufacturing introduced 2608 innovations, whereas small firms contributed 1923 innovations.
2. Because small-firm employment was only about half as much as large-firm employment, the average small-firm innovation rate was 0.322 compared to large-firm innovation rate of 0.225.

a market into which the particular branch of manufacture of the country in question has not previously entered, whether or not this market has existed before. (4) The conquest of a new source of supply of raw materials or half-manufactured goods, again irrespective of whether this source already exists or whether it has first to be created. (5) The carrying out of the new organisation of any industry, like the creation of a monopoly position (for example through trustification) or the breaking up of a monopoly position" (Schumpeter, 1934: 66).

3. Innovation rate is higher for large firms in the tires, chemicals, industrial machinery, and food machinery industries, whereas innovation rate is higher for small firms in the scales and balances, computing equipment, control instruments, and synthetic rubber industries.
4. Of the industries covered by the SBA (based on four-digit SIC codes), small firms were more innovative in 156 (slightly more than one-third) industries and large firms were more innovative in 122 (slightly more than one-quarter) industries.

Based on their findings, Acs and Audretsch (1988c: 205) conclude that "the answer to the Schumpeterian hypothesis and the general debate regarding which firm size is the most conducive to innovation is that it depends on the particular industry." They also favorably cite Scherer's warning (1980: 4181) that "the search for a firm size uniquely and unambiguously optimal for invention and innovation is misguided." Acs and Audretsch (1988c: 197) also advise policy-makers to "create environments which are conducive to small-firm innovation as well as large-firm innovation." More recent research on the issue of firm size and innovation (e.g., Vaona & Pionta, 2008: 295) have found that the relationship between firm size and innovation is also contingent on type of innovation, arguing that "innovation policies should explicitly identify their major objective and target group of firms."

Small firms are seen as more innovative because they tend to be more flexible and less bureaucratic, have quick decision-making due to clear chain of command and less resistance to change and adapt. Large firms may be more innovative because of their bigger resource portfolio, ability to spread the risk of failure over a larger base due to economies of scale, deeper market penetration, and attractiveness to capital and skilled labor. Both theoretical arguments have found some traction in the literature: Empirical studies have found evidence for a positive relationship between size and innovation (e.g., Dewar & Dutton, 1986; Sullivan & Kang, 1999) and a negative relationship (Aldrich & Auster, 1986), as well as no relationship between the two (Aiken, Bacharach, & French, 1980). When theoretical research provides no clear guidance and empirical evidence is mixed, meta-analysis can be an effective tool to identify the general trend of research in a particular area (Aguinis, Pierce, Bosco, Dalton, & Dalton, 2011). Damanpour (1992: 384) meta-analyzed 36 correlations from 20 empirical studies on firm size and innovation, finding a mean positive correlation of 0.32 ($p < 0.05$) between size and innovation. A later, and larger, meta-analysis of 87 correlations from 53 studies found a considerably smaller, but still positive and statistically significant, mean correlation between size and innovation ($r = 0.15$, $p < 0.05$). Thus, it seems efforts to consolidate the empirical literature on size and innovation reveal that, on the whole, larger firms may be more innovative than smaller firms.

Three other observations are worth making here. First, some have argued that the effect of size on innovativeness may be contingent on type of innovation (Ettlie & Rubenstein, 1987): small firms prefer investing in product innovation which are considered a better means of new entry and rapid growth (Fritsch & Meschede, 2001), while large firms emphasize process innovations which can yield larger benefits because of greater economies of scale (Cohen & Klepper, 1996). Damanpour (2010)'s meta-analysis of 20 published studies, however, finds no evidence to support the idea that organizational size is differently related to process and product innovation. Interestingly, Damanpour (1992) also did not find support that innovation type moderated the relation between firm size and innovativeness. Second, it is common knowledge that innovation is difficult to capture. More than half a century ago, Kuznets (1962) noted that the absence of reliable measures of innovative activity is a major obstacle to advancing our knowledge about innovation, an observation that remains true to this day. In their work, Acs and Audretsch (1988a, 1988b, 1988c) employed innovativeness per employee as an indicator of innovation, but several other measures for innovation also exist (e.g., R&D, patents), and there is no consensus regarding anyone of them. Finally, the majority of researches, including Acs and Audretsch (1991), measure firm size using number of employees, but alternative measures of size are possible too (e.g., total asset base, market value of equity). Given the increasing tendency toward automation, outsourcing and subcontracting, and heightened pace of globalization, number of employees may not always be a good indicator of firm size, particularly in knowledge-based industries. Research on firm size and innovation may benefit from greater consideration of non-traditional and less-common measures of firm size (Damanpour, 2010).

JOHN HALTIWANGER: YOUNG FIRMS AND NET JOB CREATION

The 2020 GAER awardee, John Haltiwanger, was recognized for "pioneering research advancing our understanding of job creation and destruction, productivity growth, and the role of small business and entrepreneurial firms in economic development." There are two different, albeit related, research streams pertaining to entrepreneurship in Haltiwanger's work: young firms (Decker, Haltiwanger, Jarmin, & Miranda, 2016) and churning in the labor market (e.g., Davis & Haltiwanger, 1992, 2001). Haltiwanger's research challenges the popular position that small firms are responsible for much of the job creation in the American economy. Instead, Haltiwanger (2015) suggests that researchers should pay attention to firm age more than firm size. Haltiwanger also distinguishes between job creation and destruction (Davis & Haltiwanger, 2001) to argue that researchers should consider net job creation (difference between jobs created and job destroyed) and not just gross job creation (total jobs created without accounting for job lost). Public discourse about job creation, Haltiwanger's research reminds us, rarely distinguishes between the small business share of gross job creation and its share of net job creation.

Davis et al. (1996a) examine job creation and destruction in the US manufacturing sector using the Longitudinal Research Database (LRD) at the Center for Economic Studies in the US Bureau of the Census. The LRD contains longitudinally linked plant-level data from the Censuses and Annual Surveys of Manufactures (Davis, Haltiwanger, and Schuh, 1996b). About 160,000 manufacturing establishments were sampled in the Annual Survey of Manufacturers between 1972 and 1986. Accounting for ninety-nine percent of manufacturing employment in the country, the LRD sampling frame covers all US manufacturing establishments with five or more employees. Over the years, a large and successful research program has been carried out using the LRD (for reviews, see Bartelsman & Doms 2000; Caves 1998). Nevertheless, empirical research using the LRD found problems with broken longitudinal linkages that lead to spurious establishment births and deaths (Jarmin & Miranda, 2002).

Davis et al. (1996a) define a job as an employment position filled by a worker, so that no distinction is made between part-time, full-time, and overtime employment positions. This information is used to assess plant-level changes in the number of filled employment positions over 12-month periods, or net job creation. Davis et al. (1996a) find that firms with at least 500 employees account for more than 50% of net job creation and the survival rate for new jobs is higher at larger firms than smaller firms. Interestingly, small firms exhibit a high rate of gross job creation, but they also lose a high rate of jobs, so that at an aggregate level, net job creation is not associated with firm size. Davis and Haltiwanger (1992) are interested in job reallocation, defining it as the rate at which employment positions are reallocated across establishments (not firms). They find that job reallocation rate is inversely related to business cycles (countercyclical correlation) and is typically associated with movement of workers across employers in the same economic sector and long-term joblessness. Quarterly job creation and destruction rates during sample period are about 5%, with job destruction being much more sensitive than job creation to business cycles (Caballero, Engel, & Haltiwanger, 1997).

Baldwin, Dunne, and Haltiwanger (1998) compare job creation and destruction in US and Canada during the 1972–1993 time period, finding significant cross-national similarities in the pattern and magnitude of jobs created and lost when industry is conceived at the 2-digit SIC level. For both countries, they find more volatility in job destruction than job creation, a negative correlation between job creation and destruction, and countercyclical trends in job reallocation, with the trends more prominent in the US than in Canada. Studies in two Eastern European countries during the post-reforms time period in the 1990s show that after an initial spurt in job destruction, the labor market stabilized with job creation and job destruction at about 10% (Haltiwanger & Vodopivec, 1999) and job flows, but not worker flows, approaching rates observed in the developed countries (Haltiwanger & Vodopivec, 2003).

Baily, Bartelsman, and Haltiwanger (2001) use the Annual Survey of Manufactures (ASM) portion of the LRD for the years 1972 through 1989 to distinguish aggregate labor productivity from plant-level productivity in the US. They decompose change in aggregate productivity into within-plant and between-plant components for continuing plants and for plant entry and exit. Updating the LRD data to 1992, and combining it with monthly Bureau of Labor Statistics (BLS) data on accessions, layoffs, and exits from 1947 to 1981, Davis and Haltiwanger (1999) document that increases in job destruction accompany every major economic contraction in the post-World War II period covered in their sample. They also find that allocative shocks are the main driving force for cyclical movements in job reallocation, but their contribution to employment fluctuations is contingent on the identification assumptions researchers make.

Conventional wisdom posits that small firms are the primary creators of jobs in an economy (Neumark et al. 2011). Haltiwanger (2012) explains that business start-ups contribute much to job creation, and start-ups—by definition, are small. Thirty-eight percent of employment from start-ups are from firms that startup with less than 10 employees—and more than 70% of employment from startups are at firms that startup with less than 50 employees. Young firms exhibit an "up or out" dynamic—they either grow fast on average or they exit. Using data from Census Bureau's Business Dynamics Statistics and Longitudinal Business Database (LBD), Haltiwanger, Jarmin, and Miranda (2013) find that the significant relationship between firm size and growth disappears after controlling for firm age. Unlike the LRD, which covers only manufacturing, the LBD covers nearly all the non-farm private economy, as well as some public sector activities (Jarmin & Miranda, 2002). Start-ups contribute about 20% of US gross (total) job creation, while high-growth businesses (which are disproportionately young) are responsible for almost 50% of gross job creation (Decker, Haltiwanger, Jarmin, & Miranda, 2014). Start-ups and young firms are therefore important contributors to job creation and productivity growth in the US, but most start-ups fail. Among surviving young firms, a relatively small share of very high-growth firms contributes substantially to job growth (Haltiwanger, 2015). Decker et al. (2014) encourage researchers to study new businesses, shifting attention toward firm age rather than size, and de novo start-ups instead of new establishments of existing firms. Using LBD data from 1976 to 2011, Decker et al. (2016) report that the aggregate US economy has seen a decline in young firm activity in the post-2000 period.

While much of Haltiwanger's work on labor market churning has focused on manufacturing establishments and firms, the retail sector has also drawn some attention. Foster, Haltiwanger, and Krizan (2006) used data from the Census of Retail Trade (CRT), which is based on a survey of retail trade establishments every five years that collects data on establishments concerning the kind of business, physical location, sales in dollars, and employment for the pay period including March 12. For any new cohort of entrants, many of the new establishments fail, and those that fail are substantially less productive than incumbents. For successful entrants, they exhibit more rapid productivity growth in the first five years after entry than incumbents over that same period, suggesting learning by doing, a large gap between the productivity of entering establishments of national chains and the productivity of exiting single-unit establishments. Exiting establishments are substantially less productive than incumbents (by approximately 25%), and entering establishments exhibit about the same productivity as incumbents at the point of entry. Much of the contribution of net entry to overall productivity growth is associated with the displacement of single-unit establishments by the entry of highly productive establishments from national chains. Haltiwanger, Jarmin, and Krizan (2010) used the LBD to examine if large chains displace more retail employment than they create and how they affect the level of economic activity in retail markets. Large chains are defined as retailers operating in 15 or more states and small chains operate in 14 or less states. They find a substantial negative impact of large retailer entry and growth on employment growth at both single-unit and especially smaller chain stores—but only if the large retailer is in the immediate area and in the same detailed industry (6-digit SIC and 8-digit NAICS).

Summary

This chapter discusses the work of four GAER honorees, namely David Birch, Zoltan Acs and David Audstresch, and John Haltiwanger, all of who were interested in the role of small firms. On average, small firms comprise about half of all business enterprises in the US (the focus of the research of scholars discussed in this chapter), contributing about half of private sector jobs in the country. Birch's seminal insight that 'small firms are responsible for most job creation' drew favorable positive attention to small businesses, to which Acs and Audretsch added that small firms were also a locus of innovation in society. Yet, as Haltiwanger suggested, it may not be small firms per se, but young firms that were responsible for the positive outcomes for which small firms were getting credit. The importance, and precise contribution, of small and young firms to the economy of a country thus remains an open question, in need of more systematic inquiry, in the US and in other countries.

References

Acs, Z. J. (1979). *Price behavior and the theory of the firm in competitive and corporate markets* (PhD thesis). New York: New York University.

Acs, Z. J. (1988). Innovation and technical change in the US steel industry. *Technovation, 7*(3), 181–195.

Acs, Z. J., & Audretsch, D. B. (1987a). Innovation in large and small firms. *Economics Letters, 23*(1), 109–112.

Acs, Z. J., & Audretsch, D. B. (1987b). Innovation, market structure, and firm size. *Review of Economics and Statistics, 69,* 567–574.

Acs, Z. J., & Audretsch, D. B. (1988a). Innovation in large and small firms: An empirical analysis. *American Economic Review, 78*(4), 678–690.

Acs, Z. J., & Audretsch, D. B. (1988b). Innovation and firm size in manufacturing. *Technovation, 7*(3), 197–210.

Acs, Z. J., & Audretsch, D. B. (1988c). Testing the Schumpeterian hypothesis. *Eastern Economic Journal, 14*(2), 129–140.

Acs, Z. J., & Audretsch, D. B. (1991). R&D, firm size and innovative activity. *Innovation and Technological Change, 98*(2), 451–456.

Aguinis, H., Pierce, C. A., Bosco, F. A., Dalton, D. R., & Dalton, C. M. (2011). Debunking myths and urban legends about meta-analysis. *Organizational Research Methods, 14*(2), 306–331.

Ahuja, G., Lampert, C. M., & Tandon, V. (2008). Moving beyond Schumpeter: Management research on the determinants of technological innovation. *Academy of Management Annals, 2*(1), 1–98.

Aiken, M., Bacharach, S. B., & French, J. L. (1980). Organizational structure, work process, and proposal making in administrative bureaucracies. *Academy of Management Journal, 23*(4), 631–652.

Aldrich, H., & Auster, E. R. (1986). Even dwarfs started small: Liabilities of age and size and their strategic implications. *Research in Organizational Behavior, 8,* 165–198.

Allen, D. N., & Rahman, S. (1985). Small business incubators: A positive environment for entrepreneurship. *Journal of Small Business Management, 23*(3), 12–22.

Armington, C., & Odle, M. (1982). Small business: How many jobs? *The Brookings Review, 1*(2), 14–17.

Atkinson, J., & Storey, D. J. (1994). Small Firms and Employment. In J. Atkinson & D. J. Storey (Eds.), *Employment, the small firm and the labour market* (pp. 1–27). London, UK: Routledge.

Autor, D., & Salomons, A. (2017, June). Does productivity growth threaten employment? "Robocalypse now"? *Proceedings of the European Central Bank Annual Conference, Sintra, Portugal, 27.*

Baily, M. N., Bartelsman, E. J., & Haltiwanger, J. (2001). Labor productivity: Structural change and cyclical dynamics. *Review of Economics and Statistics, 83*(3), 420–433.

Baldwin, J., Dunne, T., & Haltiwanger, J. (1998). A comparison of job creation and job destruction in Canada and the United States. *Review of Economics and Statistics, 80*(3), 347–356.

Baldwin, J., & Picot, G. (1995). Employment generation by small producers in the Canadian manufacturing sector. *Small Business Economics, 7*(4), 317–331.

Baptista, R., Escária, V., & Madruga, P. (2008). Entrepreneurship, regional development and job creation: The case of Portugal. *Small Business Economics, 30*(1), 49–58.

Bartelsman, E. J., & Doms, M. (2000). Understanding productivity: Lessons from longitudinal microdata. *Journal of Economic Literature, 38*(3), 569–594.

Beaver, G., & Jennings, P. (2000). Editorial overview: Small business, entrepreneurship and enterprise development. *Strategic Change, 9*(7), 397–403.

Becker, M. C., Knudsen, T., & Swedberg, R. (2012). Schumpeter's theory of economic development: 100 years of development. *Journal of Evolutionary Economics, 22*(5), 917–933.

Birch, D. L. (1979). The job generation process. In *MIT program on neighborhood and regional change*. Cambridge: MIT Press.

Birch, D. L. (2000). The job generation process. *Small Business: Critical Perspectives on Business and Management, 2*, 431–465.

Brown, C., Hamilton, J. T., & Medoff, J. L. (1990). *Employers large and small.* Boston, MA: Harvard University Press.

Burns, P. (2016). *Entrepreneurship and small business.* New York: Palgrave Macmillan.

Caballero, R., Engel, E. M. R. A., & Haltiwanger, J. (1997). Aggregate employment dynamics: Building from microeconomic evidence. *The American Economic Review, 87*(1), 115–137.

Case, J. (1989, January 1). The disciples of David Birch. Inc. Accessible at https://www.inc.com/magazine/19890101/5491.html.

Caves, R. E. (1998). Industrial organization and new findings on the turnover and mobility of firms. *Journal of Economic Literature, 36*(4), 1947–1982.

Cohen, W. M., & Klepper, S. (1996). Firm size and the nature of innovation within industries: The case of process and product R&D. *Review of Economics and Statistics, 78*(2), 232–243.

Daly, M., Campbell, M., Robson, G., & Gallagher, C. (1991). Job creation 1987–89: The contributions of small and large firms. *Employment Gazette, 99*(11), 589–596.

Damanpour, F. (1992). Organizational size and innovation. *Organization Studies, 13*(3), 375–402.

Damanpour, F. (2010). An integration of research findings of effects of firm size and market competition on product and process innovations. *British Journal of Management, 21*(4), 996–1010.

Davidsson, P. (2016). A "business researcher" view on opportunities for psychology in entrepreneurship research. *Applied Psychology, 65*(3), 628–636.

Davidsson, P., Delmar, F., & Wiklund, J. (2006). *Entrepreneurship and the growth of firms.* Cheltenham, UK: Edward Elgar.

Davidsson, P., Lindmark, L., & Olofsson, C. (1998). The extent of overestimation of small firm job creation–An empirical examination of the regression bias. *Small Business Economics, 11*(1), 87–100.

Davis, B. & Haddon, H. (2020, April 6). Big restaurants, hotel chains won exemptions to get small business loans. *Wall Street Journal.*

Davis, S. J., & Haltiwanger, J. (1992). Gross job creation, gross job destruction, and employment reallocation. *Quarterly Journal of Economics, 107*(3), 819–863.

Davis, S. J., & Haltiwanger, J. (1999). On the driving forces behind cyclical movements in employment and job reallocation. *American Economic Review, 89*(5), 1234–1258.

Davis, S. J., & Haltiwanger, J. (2001). Sectoral job creation and destruction responses to oil price changes. *Journal of Monetary Economics, 48*(3), 465–512.

Davis, S. J., Haltiwanger, J. C., & Schuh, S. (1996a). Small business and job creation: Dissecting the myth and reassessing the facts. *Small Business Economics, 8*(4), 297–315.

Davis, S. J., Haltiwanger, J. C., & Schuh, S. (1996b). *Job creation and destruction.* Cambridge: MIT Press.

de Jong, J. P., & Marsili, O. (2006). The fruit flies of innovations: A taxonomy of innovative small firms. *Research Policy, 35*(2), 213–229.

Decker, R. A., Haltiwanger, J., Jarmin, R. S., & Miranda, J. (2014). The role of entrepreneurship in US job creation and economic dynamism. *Journal of Economic Perspectives, 28*(3), 3–24.

Decker, R. A., Haltiwanger, J., Jarmin, R. S., & Miranda, J. (2016). Where has all the skewness gone? The decline in high-growth (young) firms in the US. *European Economic Review, 86,* 4–23.

Desmond, M. (2018, September 11). Americans want to believe jobs are the solution to poverty. They're not. *The New York Times.*

Dewar, R. D., & Dutton, J. E. (1986). The adoption of radical and incremental innovations: An empirical analysis. *Management Science, 32*(11), 1422–1433.

Doyle, J., & Gallagher, C. (1987). Size-distribution, growth potential and job-generation contribution of UK Firms, 1982–84. *International Small Business Journal, 6*(1), 31–56.

Ettlie, J. E., & Rubenstein, A. H. (1987). Firm size and product innovation. *Journal of Product Innovation Management: an International Publication of the Product Development & Management Association, 4*(2), 89–108.

Foster, L., Haltiwanger, J., & Krizan, C. J. (2006). Market selection, reallocation, and restructuring in the US retail trade sector in the 1990s. *The Review of Economics and Statistics, 88*(4), 748–758.

Freeman, C. (1982). *The economics of industrial innovation.* Cambridge: MIT Press.

Fritsch, M., & Meschede, M. (2001). Product innovation, process innovation, and size. *Review of Industrial Organization, 19*(3), 335–350.

Gallagher, C. C., Thomason, J. C., & Daly, M. J. (1991). The growth of UK companies and their contribution to job generation, 1985–87. *Small Business Economics, 3,* 269–286.

Godin, B. (2008). In the shadow of Schumpeter: W. Rupert Maclaurin and the study of technological innovation. *Minerva, 46*(3), 343–360.

Goss, D. (2005). Schumpeter's legacy? Interaction and emotions in the sociology of entrepreneurship. *Entrepreneurship Theory and Practice, 29*(2), 205–218.

Hagedoorn, J. (1996). Trends and patterns in strategic technology partnering since the early seventies. *Review of Industrial Organization, 11*(5), 601–616.

Hall, B. H. (1987). The relationship between firm size and firm growth in the US manufacturing sector. *Journal of Industrial Economics, 35,* 583–606.

Haltiwanger, J. C. (2012). Job creation and firm dynamics in the United States. *Innovation Policy and the Economy, 12*(1), 17–38.

Haltiwanger, J. C. (2015). Job creation, job destruction, and productivity growth: The role of young businesses. *Annual Review of Economics, 7*(1), 341–358.

Haltiwanger, J. C., Jarmin, R. S., & Krizan, C. J. (2010). Mom-and-pop meet big-box: Complements or substitutes? *Journal of Urban Economics, 67*(1), 116–134.

Haltiwanger, J. C., Jarmin, R. S., & Miranda, J. (2013). Who creates jobs? Small versus large versus young. *Review of Economics and Statistics, 95*(2), 347–361.

Haltiwanger, J. C., & Vodopivec, M. (1999). Gross worker and job flows in a transition economy: An analysis of Estonia. *Labour Economics, 9*(5), 601–630.

Haltiwanger, J. C., & Vodopivec, M. (2003). Worker flows, job flows and firm wage policies: An analysis of Slovenia. *Economics of Transition, 11*(2), 253–290.

Hong, S., Oxley, L., McCann, P., & Le, T. (2016). Why firm size matters: Investigating the drivers of innovation and economic performance in New Zealand using the Business Operations Survey. *Applied Economics, 48*(55), 5379–5395.

Idson, T. L. (1990). Establishment size, job satisfaction and the structure of work. *Applied Economics, 22*(8), 1007–1018.

Jarmin, R. S., & Miranda, J. (2002). *The longitudinal business database* (CES Working Paper No. 02–17). Available at https://ssrn.com/abstract=212 8793.

Javadian, G., Dobratz, C., Gupta, A., Gupta, V. K., & Martin, J. (2020). Qualitative research in entrepreneurship studies: A state-of-science. *Journal of Entrepreneurship, 29*(2), 1–36.

Koeller, C. T. (1995). Innovation, market structure and firm size: A simultaneous equations model. *Managerial and Decision Economics, 16*(3), 259–269.

Kruse, D. L. (1992). Profit sharing and productivity: Microeconomic evidence from the United States. *The Economic Journal, 102*(410), 24–36.

Kuznets, S. (1962). Inventive activity: Problems of definition and measurement. In *The rate and direction of inventive activity: Economic and social factors* (pp. 19–52). Princeton, NJ: Princeton University Press.

Landstrom, H. (2005). *Pioneers in entrepreneurship and small business research.* New York: Springer.

Langlois, R. N. (2003). Schumpeter and the obsolescence of the entrepreneur. *Advances in Austrian Economics, 6,* 283–298.

Markin, E., Swab, R. G., & Marshall, D. R. (2017). Who is driving the bus? An analysis of author and institution contributions to entrepreneurship research. *Journal of Innovation & Knowledge, 2*(1), 1–9.

Nelson, R. R., & Winter, S. G. (1977). Simulation of Schumpeterian competition. *American Economic Review, 67*(1), 271–276.

Neumark, D., Wall, B., & Zhang, J. (2011). Do small businesses create more jobs? New evidence for the United States from the National Establishment Time Series. *Review of Economics and Statistics, 93*(1), 16–29.

Oi, W. Y., & Idson, T. L. (1999). Firm size and wages. In O. Ashenfelter & D. Card (Eds.), *Handbook of labor economics: Vol. 3.* (pp. 2165–2214). Amsterdam: Elsevier.

Pacheo, I., & Francis, T. (2020, April 22). Public companies got $500 million in small business loans. *Wall Street Journal.*

Ramos-Rodríguez, A. R., & Ruíz-Navarro, J. (2004). Changes in the intellectual structure of strategic management research: A bibliometric study of the Strategic Management Journal, 1980–2000. *Strategic Management Journal, 25*(10), 981–1004.

Rudegeair, P., Haddon, H., & Simon, R. (2020, April 23). Ruth's Chris to repay loan amid outcry over rescue program. *Wall Street Journal.*

Scherer, F. M. (1980). *Industrial market structure and economic performance* (2nd ed.). Chicago, IL: Rand McNally College Pub. Co.

Schumpeter, J. A. (1934). *The theory of economic development: An inquiry into profits, capital, credit, interest, and the business cycle.* Boston, MA: Harvard University Press.

Shane, S. (2012). Reflections on the 2010 AMR decade award: Delivering on the promise of entrepreneurship as a field of research. *Academy of Management Review, 37*(1), 10–20.

Shepherd, D. A., Williams, T. A., & Patzelt, H. (2015). Thinking about entrepreneurial decision making: Review and research agenda. *Journal of Management, 41*(1), 11–46.

Storey, D. J. (1994). *Understanding the small business sector.* London: Routledge.

Storey, D. J., & Johnson, S. (1986). Job generation in Britain: A review of recent studies. *International Small Business Journal, 4*(4), 29–46.

Sullivan, P., & Kang, J. (1999). Quick response adoption in the apparel manufacturing industry: Competitive advantage of innovation. *Journal of Small Business Management, 37*(1), 1–13.

Ucbasaran, D., Shepherd, D. A., Lockett, A., & Lyon, S. J. (2013). Life after business failure: The process and consequences of business failure for entrepreneurs. *Journal of Management, 39*(1), 163–202.

Vaona, A., & Pianta, M. (2008). Firm size and innovation in European manufacturing. *Small Business Economics, 30*(3), 283–299.

Vo, L. T., & Zumbrun, J. (2016, November 5). Just how good (or bad) are all the jobs added to the economy since the recession? *Wall Street Journal.*

Wagner, J. (1997). Firm size and job quality: A survey of the evidence from Germany? *Small Business Economics, 9*(5), 411–425.

Weber, L. (2020, March 22). During coronavirus crisis, big companies display largess—but for how long? *Wall Street Journal.*

Wennekers, S., & Thurik, R. (1999). Linking entrepreneurship and economic growth. *Small Business Economics, 13*(1), 27–56.

Zeithaml, C. P., & Rice, G. H., Jr. (1987). Entrepreneurship/small business education in American universities. *Journal of Small Business Management, 25*(1), 44–50.

CHAPTER 3

Purpose

Perhaps more than their counterparts in other academic fields, entrepreneurship researchers have been concerned about the purpose of their inquiry for a long time. More than three decades ago, Low and Macmillan (1988: 141) argued in their seminal article:

> Because of the range of approaches available for entrepreneurship research, some common ground is needed upon which to synthesize the insights of diverse approaches of inquiry. At the broadest level, there is a need for an overall, common purpose that will forge some unity among entrepreneurship researchers.

Since then, identifying a unique purpose for scholarly inquiry in their field has been an important issue for many entrepreneurship researchers (Shane, 2012; Venkatraman, 1997). Some may wonder why there is such a strong emphasis on identifying a distinctive purpose for entrepreneurship inquiry. Hambrick and Chen (2008: 35), building on Merton's (1973) important work, argued that new academic fields are launched when "early advocates...claim that some important phenomena fall outside the scope of existing disciplines."[1] The logic here is that there needs to be some issue(s) or phenomena unique to the domain claimed

---

[1] A field of study that gains legitimacy and has its own community of experts is a discipline (Nissani, 1997). From this perspective, a discipline can have several academic fields, each with its own unique purpose not covered by other fields. Disciplines have disciples

© The Author(s) 2020
V. K. Gupta, *Great Minds in Entrepreneurship Research*,
https://doi.org/10.1007/978-3-030-44125-8_3

by the emerging field that is not adequately explained by existing fields. If a new field lays claim to issue(s) already covered in sufficient depth by existing fields, then the incumbent will prevail over the emergent player. Over the years, several researchers have noted that scholarly calls about how existing academic fields are unable or unwilling to address a critical issue or important phenomena play an important role in the successful ascendance of new fields of study (Coviello, McDougall, & Oviatt, 2011; Fagerberg & Verspagen, 2009).

Conceptualizing entrepreneurship as "creation of new enterprise," Low and Macmillan (1988) called for research that "explains and facilitates the role of new enterprise in furthering economic progress." Economic growth has long captured the imagination of entrepreneurship researchers. Discourse analysis of foundational texts reveals that economic growth often appears as "*the* legitimate reason for entrepreneurship research" and entrepreneurship is seen as "something positive, leading to improvement" in the economy, which is "both valued and expected" (Ahl, 2006: 602). Schoonhoven and Romanelli (2001: xi) contend that "we study entrepreneurship because we believe it is essential to creation and renewal of economic wealth and well-being."

The citations for the GAER laureates reveal that this prestigious award has, on three occasions, been given to scholars for their contributions toward a better understanding of the purpose of entrepreneurship research: Steven Keppler in 2011, Philippe Aghion in 2016, and Boyan Jovanovic in 2019.

Steven Klepper: New Firm Entry, Innovation, and Growth

Steven Klepper, the 2011 awardee, was recognized by the GAER committee for "significant contributions to our understanding of the role of new firm entry in innovation and growth." Of the 100+ papers he

---

(e.g., university faculty and students) trained in specific thought systems and specialization areas with their own tools and vocabulary (Macinnis & Folkes, 2010). Marketing is considered a discipline, whereas consumer behavior and international marketing are fields of study within marketing. Researchers have also talked of transdisciplinary fields, which draw from different disciplines to examine their subject matter (Gray, 2010), although it is interesting that research communities aspiring for field status generally benefit from positioning themselves "at the intersection of multiple existing fields" (Hambrick & Chen, 2008: 36).

published in his productive career, Klepper (1996) is his most cited work. By the time of this writing, it had accumulated about 950 Web of Science (WoS) citations, which is remarkable for an academic paper published more than twenty years back.[2] Klepper (1996) examines evolution of industries, building on a rich literature on the topic of product life cycle (PLC; Cao & Folan, 2012).[3] Agarwal, Buenstorf, Cohen, and Malerba (2015: 741) observed that the theoretical insights presented in Klepper (1996) were instrumental in establishing "his reputation as one of the world's leading researchers on industry evolution."

Originally proposed in the marketing literature (Klepper, 1997), PLC is modeled on the immutable biological cycle of birth-growth-maturity-death which is characteristic of all living organisms (the "evolutionary pattern"; Klepper, 1996: 562). Smallwood (1973) considered PLC to be a fundamental marketing concept akin to the periodic table of elements in the physical sciences, although other researchers (e.g., Wood, 1990) consider it to have economic origins in the work of Schumpeter (1934).[4] Most researchers, including Klepper (1997), trace back the PLC concept to Dean (1950: 45) who observed that "new products have a protected distinctiveness which is doomed to progressive degeneration from competitive inroad," presenting the "cycle of competitive degeneration":

[2] Some estimates suggest that less than 15% of AER articles receive more than three citations per year (Durden & Ellis, 1993). AER articles aged twenty years or more are considered 'highly cited' if they attract 8 cites or higher per year, 'classics' if they receive 24 cites or higher annually, and 'super classics' for 48 cites or higher per year. Based on this criterion, Klepper (1996) may be considered at least a 'classic', and possibly a 'super classic'. In the entrepreneurship literature, Wales, Gupta, and Mousa (2013) consider articles with 10+ citations per year as a 'classic' and 25+ citations annually as 'super classic'.

[3] It is worth mentioning here that Birch and his colleagues had already concluded, based on their research at the firm-level using the D&B database, that there was "not a great deal of support for a strong life cycle model of corporate evolution" in the US economy (Birch & MacCracken, 1981: 9).

[4] Despite the explicit Schumpeterian emphasis in Klepper's research (Braunerhjelm & Carlsson, 2011), Klepper (1997: 145) locates the origins of PLC in the marketing literature when he records that "originally proposed in the marketing literature, the product life cycle has been become [sic] a rallying point for how a number of different disciplines view the evolution of new industries…"

The invention of a new marketable specialty is usually followed by a period of patent protection when markets are still hesitant and unexplored and when product design is fluid. Then comes a period of rapid expansion of sales as market acceptance is gained. Next the product becomes a target for competitive encroachment. New competitors enter the field, and innovations narrow the gap of distinctiveness between the product and its substitutes ...

Forrester (1958) and Patton (1959) elaborated the PLC ideas, but it was Levitt (1965) who breathed new life into the concept which he first described as "a seemingly unemployable piece of professional baggage." Nevertheless, and despite his limited focus, Dean's (1950) articulation of the cycle was "explicit enough to be seen as the origin of the" PLC concept (Cao & Folan, 2012: 646). The classic PLC model is an S-shaped curve—a simple parabola that can be represented by the equation: $Y = a + bX + cX^2$ (Cox, 1967)—divided into four segments around which a consensus had developed: introduction, growth, maturity, and decline. The PLC framework, thus, posits four common stages that all industries go through over time.

Abernathy and Utterback (1978), which Klepper (1996: 562) considered to be the "most influential" early work in the area, proposed that PLC is driven by how new technologies evolve based on their research on the automobile industry. Specifically, they stated:

1. In the beginning, there is considerable uncertainty about user tastes and preferences (even among users themselves). Consequently, many firms offering different versions of the product enter the market. Product innovation is paramount.
2. Users try out different versions of the product and producers learn how to improve the product. Gradually, opportunities to improve the product are depleted and a clear product standard, called a 'dominant design', emerges. Producers who are unable to efficiently produce the dominant design leave the industry, contributing to a decrease in the number of producers. Product innovation decreases.
3. The establishment of a dominant design reduces the pace of technological change in the industry, which allays producers' fears about risking investment in improving their production processes. Producers invest in capital-intensive methods of production, which increases the minimum size for efficiency in the industry.

Klepper (1996) identified several problems with Abernathy and Utterback's (1978) view of PLC:

1. The logic of dominant design may not apply to all new products, particularly those for which consumer tastes are heterogeneous. It is also an "imprecise" idea that does not readily lend itself to operationalization.
2. The logic that product and process innovation are sequentially linked such that producers will not invest in process innovation until product innovation has stabilized does not fit what is observed in the real world where production processes are often vastly improved before a particular product configuration becomes dominant.
3. The influence of demand-side factors is ignored as the incentive to innovate is simply attributed to the deletion of new opportunities for product innovation and the establishment of a dominant design.

The major accomplishment of Klepper (1996: 579–580) was to "shore up" the "logical foundations" of PLC by "showing how a simple model could explain all the central features of the PLC" by building on two key insights: (a) the ability to appropriate the returns to process R&D depends centrally on firm size, and (b) firms differ in the expertise they possess, causing them to emphasize different forms of product innovations. The initial differences between firms are amplified as firms become bigger, which advantages early entrants and subsequently causes a decline in the number of firms and the rate of product innovation in the industry—the shakeout phase (although the term 'shakeout' first showed up in Klepper and Graddy (1990)). How important is Klepper (1996)? Agarwal et al. (2015: 741)'s comment on Klepper (1996) is informative in this regard:

> "Solving" the problem of giving an endogenous account of the industry life cycle in Klepper (1996), this article could have been Klepper's final word on this issue. Instead, the article provided the starting point of an even more detailed inquiry into the dynamics of evolving markets that would occupy Klepper for the rest of his life.

Klepper (1997) scans the academic literature for evidence on the evolution of new industries to examine the extent to which PLC applies to industry evolution, concluding that before foreign firms made inroads beginning in the 1960s, the American automobile industry "would appear to merit its status as an exemplar of the PLC" (page 160). Similar trends were observed for other industries: automobile tires, televisions, picture tubes, penicillin, typewriters, and commercial aircraft for trunk carriers. To establish generalizability of PLC-consistent industry evolution, Klepper (1997) looked toward Gort and Klepper (1982), Klepper and Graddy (1990), Klepper and Miller (1995), and Agarwal and Gort (1996), observing that major features of the PLC seem widespread: entry into the industry is more frequent in the early days, early entrants tend to dominate, product innovation is at its highest early on, output growth slows down with time, and shakeouts are common in industries. Interestingly, many of the departures from PLC are also quite common across several industries, such as rise in innovations after shakeouts and surprising endurance of many late entrants.

One of Klepper's (1997: 168) intriguing observations was that a sizable proportion of industries examined showed patterns markedly different from PLC, suggesting the "possibility of alternative life cycle paths." Consistent with the PLC logic, these industries had high early growth in output that slowed over time. Perhaps more importantly, in a significant departure from PLC, deviant industries experienced continual entry, shakeouts were either avoided or reversed, early entrants did not enjoy stable first-mover advantage, and initial leaders lost market share to domestic challengers.

Based on Klepper (1997), PLC-deviant industries can be categorized into three groups: one group includes the petrochemical, disposable diaper, and zipper industries, characterized by the emergence of firms specializing in production-related innovations about 20–30 years after commercialization of the core product. For example, about 20 years after disposable diapers were introduced (Joseph, 1990), several firms began to offer up-to-date manufacturing equipment, with about half of them providing integrated production solutions using state-of-the-art technology (Elzinga & Mills, 1994). Another group, which includes diagnostic imaging products (nuclear imaging, ultrasonic, computed tomographic, magnetic resonance imagining (MRI) instruments, and X-ray) and automatic teller machines (ATM), was characterized by a division of labor between technical specialists and marketing/manufacturing firms, with the former being initial innovators specializing in product innovation and the latter being late entrants. For instance, ATMs were commercialized by de novo companies, and once the market for ATMs began to expand, firms with prior experience selling related products entered the new industry (Lane, 1989). A third group, which includes business jets and lasers, was characterized by specialization based on product submarkets. The business jet industry, for example, comprises of aircrafts that differ on size, speed, distance, and maneuverability as buyers differ in the value they place on each of these attributes and sellers offer only a limited range of aircraft types (Phillips, Phillips, & Phillips, 2012).

Another important area in which Klepper made significant contributions (e.g., Holbrook, Cohen, Hounshell, & Klepper, 2000; Klepper, 2002a, 2002b; Klepper & Simons, 2005; Klepper & Simons, 2000a, 2000b) involves historical analysis of industry evolution, focusing on the role, origin, and experiences of new firms that shaped the industry. For many scholars (e.g., Chiles, Bluedorn, & Gupta, 2007: 484), historical analysis is the preferred research approach toward entrepreneurship as it can cast light on "the emergence and evolution of higher-level, complex social phenomena, including organizations, markets, and industries, resulting from lower-level entrepreneurial action and interaction occurring over time and within a particular institutional context." Despite growing interest in understanding how organizations and industries come to be (Sarasvathy, 2009), entrepreneurship research (and management scholarship in general) has been slow to adopt history analyses as part of their toolkit. Jones and Wadhwani (2006) noted that there is "little traction behind using historical research to seek broader theoretical conceptualizations of entrepreneurship." The truth is that few historical analyses papers make it to top journals in management,[5] so that Klepper's success in getting his work accepted at major journals is quite impressive.

The work of Klepper and colleagues (e.g., Holbrook et al., 2000; Klepper & Simons, 2000a) on historical evolution of industries seems to build on his original interest in the PLC model. Klepper and colleagues focused their historical analyses on industries where a small number of

---

[5] What is generally referred to as 'organizational science' actually combines "many different disciplines" (Ferris, Ketchen, & Buckley, 2008: 742). Mahoney (1985: 15) argues that the "so-called organizational sciences encompass scholarship in the more traditional social sciences of economics, sociology, psychology, political science, and related disciplines." Consequently, organizational science is a "multidisciplinary field" characterized by varied methodologies (though dominated by variance-focused studies that "embed a small set of well-developed variables in a nomological net and use statistical techniques to test predicted relationships between variables" (Streb & Gupta, 2011: 262) at various levels of analysis and using an amazing diversity of theories and concepts (Ferris et al., 2008).

firms dominated at some point, namely automobiles, tires, televisions, and penicillin (Klepper & Simons, 2005) and semiconductors (Holbrook et al., 2000). Consider the US tire industry, where the first 25 years were characterized by steady growth in the number of participating firms, and the next 14 years saw drastic shakeout with the number of firms declining by over 80% (Klepper & Simons, 2000a). The authors find that older and larger firms survived longer, and firms near around the geographic center of the industry (Akron, Ohio) were also found to be more technologically progressive. Why was this the case? Contrary to Christensen's (1997) provocative insight that in the face of technological change established incumbents will be outcompeted by new players, Klepper and Simons (2000a) find that older and larger firms, as well as those near the geographical center, were much more likely to be at the technological frontier, which allowed them to dominate over the later entrants. Klepper and Simons (2000b) found similar evidence for the US television receiver industry, where experienced firms that produced radios before TVs were more likely to enter TV manufacturing, had higher innovation rates, which eventually resulted in greater market share and longer survival. Once again, their findings challenged Christensen's (1997) provocative thesis that incumbents are seldom able to withstand the innovative efficacy of new entrants.

Focusing on the US automobile industry between 1895 and 1966, Klepper (2002a) found that among the 725 firms to enter during this period, those that already had experience in related industries outperformed de novo entrants. An original insight from this work was that when start-ups were launched by individuals with prior work experience at the established firms, they were able to outcompete rivals. In effect , founders needed to have work histories upon which to build their entrepreneurial endeavors (Holbrook et al., 2000). Why this is the case, however, is not very clear. On the one hand, Klepper (2001) finds some evidence that founders of high-tech spin-off firms build on the prior experience of their functional position rather than the specific technologies of the parent firm. On the other hand, Klepper and Sleeper (2005) find that in the laser industry, spin-off founders leveraged targeted knowledge gained from the parent firm, and not the general knowledge. Klepper (2002b) considered four different industries (automobiles, tires, televisions, and penicillin), and once again found that prior experience and early entry provided substantive advantage, especially in the face of technological change. Looking at the same four industries, Klepper and

Simons (2005) show that the innovativeness of the early entrants was the driver behind their longevity. Holbrook et al. (2000), examining four early entrants into the US semiconductor industry, argued that established firms enter new domains to leverage intangible assets that were originally developed for other purposes.

Braunerhjelm and Carlsson (2011) note that Klepper's contributions to entrepreneurship are primarily in the area of industrial dynamics, which focuses on processes of change and the causes and consequences of the evolutionary processes (Carlsson, 1987). For Dahmén (1984: 25), scholars working in industrial dynamics are primarily interested in "causal chains outside the scope of macroeconomic growth analyses, namely in disequilibria and chain effects created inter alia by entrepreneurial activities, market processes and competition as a dynamic force." Klepper's entrepreneurship-related work fits in this area as it discusses firm entry, exits, spin-offs, and innovation to cast light on the evolution and transformation of industries over time (Braunerhjelm & Carlsson, 2011).

Much of the literature on industrial dynamics, as does Klepper's work, builds on Schumpeter's insights into the transformative effects of innovative activities. Schumpeter was also an advocate for detailed research into historical growth processes. Schumpeter (1939: 13), for example, observed that "general history (social, political, and cultural), economic history, and more particularly industrial history are not only indispensable but really the most important contributors to the understanding of our problem… all other materials and methods, statistical and theoretical, are only subservient to them and worse than useless without them." Schumpeter would likely have been proud of Klepper's "systematic longitudinal empirical analyses with the massive, detailed collections and analyses of historical data on firm entry, exit, size, location, distribution networks, and technology choices" in several industries over time (Braunerhjelm & Carlsson, 2011: 132).

The PLC model, which informs a large part of Klepper's entrepreneurship research, has come under strong criticism from many quarters. Critics argue that there is no clear consensus about the level of analysis in PLC studies (Wood, 1990), so that there is considerable confusion as to whether PLC provides a better explanation at the industry level (see Klepper's work discussed above), product forms (Polli & Cook, 1969; Tellis & Crawford, 1981), product classes (Dhalla & Yuspeh, 1976), or brands (Enis, La Garce, & Prell, 1977). Researchers have also found that unlike in the biological life cycle that is the inspiration for PLC, decline does not necessarily follow maturity in the industrial world as companies can rejuvenate product offerings (Cox, 1967; Tellis & Crawford, 1981). The classic S-curve characterized by four or five sequential phases may actually apply to less than a quarter of cases in the real world (Polli & Cook, 1969), with countless other variations possible for industries in the real world. Notably, Levitt's (1965) original premise was that PLC helps managers manage the life cycle, but the industry-level work in this area does not really speak to how management can influence the life cycle. In other words, for it to be a useful business concept, PLC should be a sort of dependent variable, which is not the case in much of the academic literature.

Klepper's work focused largely on concentrated industries (e.g., American automobile industry; Klepper (2002b)), where a small number of competitors—each with sizable market share—prevail. Consider the following description from Klepper (2002b) for the American automobile industry, which he studied from 1895 to 1966. The start date of 1895 is understandable as it marked the time when George Selden received the first patent for the automobile in the US and the Chicago Herald-Tribune sponsored the first automobile race in America. The 1966 end-point seems arbitrary though, except that Klepper (2002b) identified entrants into the industry based on Smith (1968) which had previously used the same end-date. Given that much happened in the American automobile industry in the more than three decades between Smith (1968) and Klepper (2002b), one is left puzzled as to why data from the intervening time period were not used as it would show considerable new entry by foreign players such as Honda and Toyota. Well-established incumbents gradually lost market share to new entrants (which were established car companies overseas), with a substantive shift over time away from oligopoly. Further, there are also fragmented industries (as opposed to concentrated) and it would be interesting to track entry into and exits from such industries. For example, the US restaurant industry, estimated at $800 billion in 2017, is highly fragmented with rival firms differing along several important facets such as type of food served, price, level of service, dining ambience, and geographic reach. It is unclear whether Klepper's approach to examining industry evolution is constrained to concentrated industries, or can be readily extended to fragmented industries where a large number of firms are in play at any given time. It seems relevant to examine evolution trajectories in fragmented industries generally typified by several small competitors with no dominant players in particular.

PHILIPPE AGHION: FIRM INNOVATION, ENTRY AND EXIT, AND ECONOMIC PRODUCTIVITY

In 2016, the GAER committee recognized Philippe Aghion, one of the "most prolific...economists of his generation" worldwide (Acs, Braunnerhjelm, & Karlsson, 2017: 2). The GAER citation highlighted his "outstanding analyses of the relationship between, on the one hand, firm-level innovation, entry and exit and, on the other hand productivity and growth." Aghion is an economist by training, and his published works rarely include the term 'entrepreneurship', preferring to focus on 'new entry' instead (Acs et al., 2017). This is notable because many scholars consider new entry to be what entrepreneurship "is all about" (Wennekers & Thurik, 1999: 33). As Lumpkin and Dess (1996: 136) note:

> The essential act of entrepreneurship is new entry. New entry can be accomplished by entering new or established markets with new or existing goods or services. New entry is the act of launching a new venture, either by a start-up firm, through an existing firm, or via "internal corporate venturing" (Burgelman, 1983). New entry is thus the central idea underlying the concept of entrepreneurship.

Acs et al. (2017) identified six broad streams of research in Aghion's scholarship: growth theory (Aghion, Akcigit, & Howitt, 2014), innovation (Aghion, Bloom, Blundell, Griffith, & Howitt, 2005), firm entry (Aghion & Bolton, 1987), finance (Aghion, Bacchetta, & Banerjee, 2004), regulation (Aghion, Algan, Cahuc, & Schleifer, 2010), and industrial policy (Aghion, 2011). Most relevant to our purpose here is Aghion's research on developing a new theory of economic growth based on Schumpeter's work (Aghion, 2017), generally referred to as Schumpeterian Growth Theory (SGT; Aghion, Akcigit, & Howitt, 2015). Schumpeterian growth is a particular form of economic growth based on the notion of creative destruction (Dinopoulos & Sener, 2007). The idea of creative destruction—defined simply as the process through which advancements make existing ideas and structures obsolete—is Schumpeter's landmark contribution to entrepreneurship studies (Metcalfe, 1998).[6] Dinopoulos and Sener (2007) credit four papers with the initial

---

[6] Reinert and Reinert (2019: 386) trace the idea of 'creative destruction' back to Friedrich Nietzsche, who they argue, got it, via his *erzieher* (educator) Arthur Schopenhauer, from Hinduism which provides "one of the most complex and certainly one

development of SGT, namely Romer (1990), Segerstrom, Anant, and Dinopopulos (1990), Grossman and Helpman (1991), and Aghion and Howitt (1992).[7] SGT differs from conventional neoclassical growth models by emphasizing that economic growth is an endogenous outcome of the economic system, not the result of external forces originating from outside the system (Romer, 1994). The growth model developed by Aghion and Howitt (1992), which borrowed "directly from the theoretical IO and patent race literatures" (Aghion et al., 2014: 517), built on three core ideas derived from Schumpeter's work:

1. Innovations drive long-run growth (without sustained technological progress, long-run growth is not possible);
2. Innovations are a result of investments made by entrepreneurs responding to economic incentives stemming from policies and institutions.
3. Old technologies are replaced by new innovations, so that there is always a conflict between the old and the new. At a basic level, the replacement of old technologies by new ones is what Schumpeter (1942) famously referred to as the process of creative destruction.

of the richest cosmological illustrations of the dynamics of creation and destruction." Perelman (1995) credits the US economist David Wells with anticipating Schumpeter's idea of creative destruction in his book Wells (1889). Nightingale (2015: 70) believes that Schumpeter's ideas may have been inspired by the German theologian Adolf von Harnack who "outlined a history of Christianity that was structured around a dynamic theory of historical change driven by charismatic innovators, revolutions and the creative destruction of old orders." Scott (2006: 1–2) attributes Schumpeter's famous phrase to Karl Marx, observing that Marx viewed "the notion of capitalism as a turbulent scene of production and exchange, gripped by the forces of competition in an endless process of self-transformation." It seems there is growing academic interest in the origins of Schumpeter's thesis of creative destruction (Nightingale, 2015), but there is no consensus yet on it.

[7] Per WoS, of the four foundational papers, Romer (1990) is the most cited with 3812 citations since publication, compared to 2298 citations for Aghion and Howitt (1992). Interestingly, Romer (1994: 3) makes no mention of Aghion and Howitt (1992) in his account—which he calls the "scholarly equivalent to creation myths"—of the origins of a Schumpeterian-based endogenous theory of economic growth. Aghion et al. (2015: 558) recount the development of SGT somewhat differently: work on SGT "was initiated in the fall of 1987 at MIT, where Philippe Aghion was a first-year assistant professor and Peter Howitt was a visiting professor on sabbatical from the University of Western Ontario. During that year they wrote their 'model of growth through creative destruction' … which was published as Aghion and Howitt (1992)." While Aghion et al. (2015) acknowledge parallel works to formalize Schumpeterian growth theory, they consider only Corriveau (1991) and Segerstrom et al. (1990) as relevant.

Aghion's work on Schumpeterian growth theory 'operationalizes' the concept of creative destruction. If a key benefit of formal models is that they congeal oral notions to confront them with data, Aghion and his colleagues' work was instrumental to the crystallization of Schumpeter's idea of creative destruction. This occurred in two major ways as Aghion et al. (2015: 558) observed:

> First, it has led to models based on creative destruction that shed new light on several microeconomic aspects of the growth process: in particular, the role of competition, firm dynamics, and cross-firm and cross-sector reallocation. Second, it makes use of rich micro data, in particular on entry, exit, and firm size distribution, to confront predictions, which distinguishes it from other growth theories.

Where Schumpeter's creative destruction was about the replacement of the old with the new, Aghion's work revealed that competition and productivity display an inverted U-relationship (Aghion et al., 2005). When starting from an initially low level of competition, increasing rivalry fuels innovation and growth, but when starting from a high level of initial competition, greater competition may be less positively—or even nega-tively—related to innovation and productivity growth. For incumbent firms, innovation and productivity growth are stimulated by competi-tion and new entry, in particular when the firm is near the technology frontier or in intense rivalry with competitors. As a result, Aghion and colleagues encouraged the liberalization of product-market competition and entry as a way to obtain innovation benefits and productivity growth by established firms, particularly when they are more advanced in their industry. Patent protection supports the effect of product-market rivalry on encouraging investments in R&D and innovation.

A major part of Aghion's scholarship was based on theoretical modeling (Acs et al., 2017), which involves starting with specific assumptions to construct an environment in which the actions to be explained take place (Moorthy, 1993). Such modeling is uncommon in entrepreneurship research, but it offers some benefits not available other-wise. First, models require clearly specifying key assumptions and deriving specific propositions from them, which lays out an 'audit trail' that can distinguish between logical propositions and groundless claims (Saloner, 1991). Second, theoretical models tend to be high on internal validity as, at least when done well, modeling essentially leaves no question about the cause–effect relationships involved (Moorthy, 1993). Good models deliberately eliminate distracting forces—other 'causes'—that may affect the phenomenon in question, which increases internal validity (but at the expense of external validity). Finally, theoretical models are pedagogical in their orientation, so that their main purpose is to teach us how the real world works by providing a common language that serves as the basis for cumulative knowledge development.

Acemoglu, Aghion, and Zilibotti (2006) relates to research on "technology frontier" (Caselli and Coleman, 2006), which refers to the "set of all efficient techniques available in the given state of the arts (the famous 'book of blue prints')" (Sato, 1974: 354). Researchers in this area often talk of 'distance from frontier', or its inverse 'proximity to frontier' (Vandenbussche, Aghion, & Meghir, 2006), and conceive it at the level of the firm or the country. Frontier is defined in terms of highest total factor productivity (Griffith, Redding, & van Reenen, 2004). For the firm level, Acemoglu, Aghion, Lelarge, Van Reenen, and Zilibotti (2007: 1764) operationalize proximity to frontier as "ratio of the firm's value added per hour to the value added per hour of the firm at the 99th percentile of the distribution in the same four-digit industry." At the country level, Acemoglu et al. (2006: 40) operationalize proximity to frontier as total factor productivity (TFP) "in industry i in country c at time t divided by the highest TFP in industry i at time t in the sample." Notably, the level of per-worker productivity in the US has always been high enough to put the US at the forefront of the world technology frontier (Henderson & Russell, 2005), although there is also substantial within-country heterogeneity with some American states using production factors more efficiently than others (Growiec, 2012). Acemoglu et al. (2006) found that developing countries (those further from the technology frontier) have an investment-based strategy, relying on existing firms and managers to boost investment, and developed countries (those closer to the technology frontier) have an innovation-based strategy with younger firms and more stringent selection of firms and managers. R&D is more important when distance to the technology frontier is low. Interestingly, barriers to competition were found to have limited costs (or even benefits) in countries further from the technology frontier, but become much more costly in proximity to the frontier.

An interesting feature of modern organizational research is that while much work has been done on between-country comparisons, research on within-country comparisons remains uncommon (Gupta & York, 2008).

Aghion, Burgess, Redding, and Zilibotti (2008) look at interstate variations within one country (in this case, India) to understand the differential
effects of industrial deregulation (or alleviating licensing requirements)
on manufacturing output. Using data from the 1980 to 1997 period,
these researchers find that industries located in states with pro-employer
labor market institutions grew more quickly than those in pro-worker
environments. Because India has a federal structure, labor market regulations differ across states, and so these scholars build on prior research
(Besley & Burgess, 2004) to code each Indian state as neutral, pro-
worker, or pro-employer. The effects of lifting regulatory requirements
around industrial licensing were different across states with different
labor market regulations. While the notion that 'too much regulation
is bad' is not new (Nichols, Hendrickson, & Griffith, 2011; Weisman,
1994), Aghion et al. (2008)'s contribution was to identify a staggered
exogenous shock—delicensing of industries over an 18-year period—
to compare manufacturing before and after delicensing. Such studies
where the methodological set-up centers around an exogenous shock are
referred to as a difference-in-differences (D-in-D) model in economics
(Angrist & Pischke, 2008) and an untreated control group design with
pre- and post-test in psychology (Shadish, Cook, & Campbell, 2002).
The logic of D-in-D models is to observe the effect of an exogenous
'shock' on a 'treatment' group, where the treatment effect is the difference between the treated group and a comparable control group across
time (Antonakis, Bendahan, Jacquart, & Lalive, 2010).

Aghion (2017: 11) noted that when he started, the dominant framework in economics was based on neoclassical assumptions, which he first
challenged and then refined over a series of paper. One refinement seems
relevant to mention here. The original Aghion and Howitt (1992) growth
model predicted that increasing competition is detrimental to growth as it
reduces monopoly rents from innovative activity as well as entrepreneurs'
incentives to invest in innovation. When empirical research by other
scholars did not support this prediction, Aghion and colleagues found
that firms react differently to greater competition depending on how
close they are to the technology frontier. Firms closer to the technology
frontier innovate even more to rise above competition, and firms further
from the frontier innovate less because heightened rivalry will demoti-
vate them (Aghion et al., 2005). Subsequently, Aghion, Blundell, Griffith,
Howitt, and Prantl (2009) use UK data to examine whether entry of
technologically advanced players (defined as greenfield entry of foreign

firms) spurs innovation among incumbents (in the form of productivity and patenting). Using an instrumental variable approach (instrumenting greenfield foreign entry using major policy reforms aimed at changing entry costs), Aghion et al. (2009) find that technologically advanced entry spurs innovativeness in sectors proximal to the technology frontier as successful innovation allows incumbents to survive the threat. The same technologically advanced entry, however, discourages innovation in laggard sectors (those further away from the technology frontier), where the threat of new entry seems to reduce the expected rents that accrue to innovation.

Gustavsson and Poldhal (2003) use firm-level data to examine Aghion et al.'s (2005) prediction regarding the inverted U-shaped relation between competition and R&D (or innovation). These scholars measure competition using two indicators: Herfindahl index and price cost margin. Results revealed that competition proxied by Herfindahl index had an inverted U-shaped relationship with R&D, but no relationship existed when competition was proxied by price cost margin. Clearly, more research is needed to identify boundary conditions of the curvilinear relationship between competition and innovation suggested by Aghion et al. (2005).

As has been noted earlier, Aghion's work rarely refers to entrepreneurship as he focuses generally on 'entry', either by start-ups or incumbents. Yet, scholars have recognized that "firms and entrepreneurs play a big role" in Aghion's scholarship on economic growth (Acs et al., 2017: 3).

Boyan Jovanovic: Competitive Dynamics of New Ventures

The 2019 GAER awardee was Boyan Jovanovic, recognized for his "pioneering research that advances our understanding of the competitive dynamics between incumbent firms and new ventures, entrepreneurial learning and selection processes, and the importance of entrepreneurship for the economy." Minniti et al. (2019) identify Jovanovic as providing "original and significant contributions" to entrepreneurship research in three areas: the importance of entrepreneurship for the economy (e.g., Benhabib & Jovanovic, 1991; Greenwood & Jovanovic, 1999; Hobijn & Jovanovic, 2001), why some people become entrepreneurs (e.g., Evans & Jovanovic, 1989; Jovanovic & Moffitt, 1990) and the competitive dynamics between incumbent firms and new entrants (e.g., Jovanovic, 1982; Jovanovic & Rousseau, 2014).

Looking back at the last century, Jovanovic and Rousseau (2003) identify two technological revolutions that generated the most creative destruction: (a) introduction of electricity and internal combustion, and (b) rise of microcomputer and information technology. Conventional wisdom suggests that when new technologies come about, they are embraced most keenly by new firms. There are three reasons why technological breakthroughs favor new firms: managers of old firms do not have the awareness or skill to benefit from new technologies, human and physical capital of old firms is tied to their current practices, and may not readily convert to the new technology, and management and workers in older firms may resist a new technology because it devalues their experience (Greenwood & Jovanovic, 1999). The arrival of a major new technology thus destroys old firms by making workers, machines, and managers obsolete. Major technological change, however, favors young, small firms—companies that tend to have a flatter organizational structure, fewer unionized, or entrenched workers, and more new up-to-date management practices (Jovanovic, 2001).

When investors foresee a technological shift on the horizon, they anticipate how established firms and new firms will react, which depresses stock prices of large firms (Hobijn & Jovanovic, 2001). Interestingly, the IT revolution did not create lasting value for the young firms that went public at the time and instead benefitted large firms (Jovanovic & Rousseau, 2003). Yet, Jovanovic (2001) contends that we are entering the era of young firms as they benefit from faster adoption of new technologies and speedier introduction of new products.[8]

Jovanovic's doctoral dissertation was on the topic of job-matching and turnover (published as Jovanovic, 1979a), where he develops a mathematical model to explain that a mismatch between a worker and the employer leads to lower wages and early separation. When the quality of the match is held constant, more specific capital investment in the match is associated with lower likelihood of match termination in the future (Jovanovic, 1979b). Mincer and Jovanovic (1981) contend that job mobility declines with age, and even more sharply with tenure. Jovanovic (1984a) considers

[8] Interestingly, Jovanovic and Rousseau (2001: 336) show that firms "that first listed at the close of the 19th century were as young as the companies that are entering the NYSE, AMEX, and NASDAQ stock exchange today."

job-matching as the major cause for job-change, arguing that even when a decline in demand for the firm's offerings leads to layoffs, it is the poorly matched employees who are terminated first from their job. As such, these studies explain job turnover and unemployment as a function of a mismatch between the employee and employer, rather than a result of changing composition of product demand and a changing technology (Dagsvik, Jovanovic, & Shepard, 1985). Jovanovic (1984b) proposes that workers move into and out of the labor market because of changes in the perceived value of their market opportunities. The discretion workers have in moving to jobs that are a better match for them contributes between 6 and 9% of gross national product (Jovanovic & Moffitt, 1990).

Jovanovic has contributed much to job turnover and labor mobility, but very few of these papers are directly relevant to entrepreneurship research. Evans and Jovanovic (1989) examine whether entrepreneurs must finance themselves and bear the risk of failure (as Frank Knight suggests) or capitalists bear the risks for entrepreneurs who focus on identifying opportunities (the position attributed to Joseph Schumpeter). Using data from the National Longitudinal Survey of Young Men, Evans and Jovanovic (1989) conclude that wealthier people are more inclined to become entrepreneurs as capital is essential for starting a business so that those with insufficient funds at their disposal are excluded from entrepreneurship. Jovanovic (1994) discusses that when workers' skills differ from managers' skills, the best talents may not flow into entrepreneurship (as he says is the case for professional sports). When people can choose between wage work and managerial work, the output gains are U-shaped (Eeckhout & Jovanovic, 2012): International labor mobility raises output by more in the rich and the poor countries, and by less in the middle-income countries. Jovanovic and Nyarko (1996) find that accumulation of human capital may be inversely related to new technology adoption. Agents rich in human capital may prefer to avoid switching to new technologies, which will hamper their future growth, but agents lacking in human capital may be willing to switch technologies repeatedly because they have no attachment to a particular skill, which will help them achieve higher growth in output. Skills, educational achievement, and experience are generally seen as a positive input to technology adoption (Gupta, Niranjan, Goktan, & Erikson, 2015; Lee, Kozar, & Larsen, 2003), but Jovanovic and Nyarko (1996) challenge this positive view to propose investment toward human capital as an overall impediment to adopting new technologies.

Jovanovic's most cited work is in the area of competitive dynamics between firms in an industry (Jovanovic, 1982), which lays out a mathematical model to explain firm entry, exit, and growth as a function of 'noisy' selection based on efficiency as efficient firms will survive and grow, while inefficient firms decline and fail. Jovanovic and Lach (1989) were interested in the diffusion of a new innovation, which tends to follow an S-shaped path such that the proportion of potential users who adopt an innovation is an increasing function of time (from the first adoption) which is initially convex but later becomes concave (Jensen, 1982). Jovanovic and Lach (1989) show that innovation diffusion is S-shaped when identical, atomless potential entrants can benefit from learning by doing realized by earlier entrants. The first-mover advantage for early entrants is from higher revenues per unit of output because of lack of competition, but late entrants have the advantage of lower production costs as they learn from the experiences of early entrants. For Jovanovic and Rob (1989), a key ingredient to the growth and diffusion of technological knowledge in an industry and society is the ease of communicating with and copying someone else's ideas. Jovanovic and Rob (1990) distinguish between extensive search (which seeks major breakthroughs) and intensive search (which attempts to refine past breakthroughs), suggesting that there is a tendency for the importance of the product improvements to gradually decline with time as each successive intensive search is made from a distribution with a smaller variance.

Jovanovic and Macdonald (1994a) are interested in the non-monotonicity of the number of firms over the lifecycle of an industry. Prior research (e.g., Gort & Klepper, 1982; Klepper & Graddy, 1990) finds that in the early days of a new industry there are a few firms commanding high prices. The high profits attract new entrants and encourage higher production, which increases output and lowers price, which then leads to a 'shakeout' as some firms must exit from the industry. Firms that are technological leaders rely on innovations to reduce their costs and become more efficient, whereas the laggards rely more on imitation which causes technology to spread from the leaders to the followers and forces technological convergence among firms as the industry matures (Jovanovic & Macdonald, 1994b). Gort and Klepper (1982) argued that shakeouts are preceded by new innovations that dampen the profitability of laggards who are unable to imitate the leaders from among the existing firms. Jovanovic and Macdonald (1994a) contend that the rise in innovation that precipitates a shakeout is a response to an invention developed outside the industry in question. Firms try to implement the new invention, so that the winners of the implementation race increase their output and remain in the industry, while the laggards exit from the industry. Thus, new industries originate from a basic invention and shakeouts are the result of a major refinement to the original invention.

Most readers will be familiar with Intel co-founder Gordon Moore's prediction that the processing power of computers will increase exponentially every couple of years. Jovanovic and Rousseau (2002) argue that the so-called Moore's Law is a special case of the efficiency that occurs among producers of any good as a by-product of their experience with making and selling it (generally described as learning curve in the literature). Assuming that the law would continue to operate forever,[9] Jovanovic and Rousseau (2002) find that incumbent firms are losing ground faster today than they did before and predict that growth in the coming decades would be even faster. Jovanovic and Rousseau (2014) distinguish between capital investment by entering and young firms (which they label 'extensive investment') and by older and listed firms (which they call 'intensive investment'). Extensive investment is more elastic than intensive investment to changes in Tobin's Q, and when aggregate Q increases, new and young firms increase their investment, but older established firms lower their investment.

Jovanovic (2019) emphasizes that the entrepreneur is a bearer of risk who makes a specific employment choice. Often, entrepreneurship does not pay enough to compensate people for the risk that it entails, which shows up as a discount in the earnings of those who engage in entrepreneurial activities. New and young firms are agents of technological change, helping in diffusion of knowledge that accelerates industry dynamics and facilitates economic growth (Minniti et al., 2019). Jovanovic also has other publications that cast light on specific parts of the entrepreneurship literature (e.g., Jovanovic, 2014; Jovanovic & Szentes, 2013; Prat & Jovanovic, 2014) as well as work unrelated to entrepreneurship (e.g., Benhabib & Jovanovic, 2012; Jovanovic & Yatsenko, 2012). A

---

[9] For some time now, experts have been talking about the eventual demise of Moore's Law (Merritt, 2013). At the minimum, it seems that Moore's Law is gradually slowing down, noticeably aging, getting cranky and hard to manage, though Intel disagrees with this position (Clark, 2015).

common theme across his wide-range of work is the emphasis on mathematical modeling as a powerful methodology for advancing theory and research on complex phenomena.

SUMMARY

The purpose of research has long been a key concern for entrepreneurship scholars. Low and Macmillan (1988) lay down the gauntlet when they stipulate that explaining and facilitating economic growth in the key purpose of entrepreneurship research. At the time, the idea that new ventures drive economic growth and power modern economies went against the historical emphasis on large, well-established corporations in American society (Gupta & Gupta, 2015). As Galbraith (1968: 13–14) noted:

> Seventy years ago the corporation was confined to those industries- railroading, steam boating, steel making, petroleum recovery and refining, some mining- where, it seemed production had to be on a large scale. Now it also sells groceries, mills grain, publishes newspapers and provides public entertainment, all activities that were once the province of the individual proprietor or the insignificant firm.

Atkinson and Lind (2018: 6–7) observed:

> Bigness was seen as the ultimate achievement, while small firms were seen as ones that failed to become big...Small firms were looked down on as a second-class group characterized by lower wages, lower management quality, and higher insecurity...America's large corporations...provided stable jobs, supported the arts, encouraged employees to become involved in their communities, and assumed leadership positions in civic organizations. There was a widely shared sense that the corporation was committed to the local community, that the corporation's goals, the worker's, and the community's were in sync.

The historical fascination with big business may surprise us today, but it was in keeping with the central position large corporations had in the economy of the time. By linking entrepreneurial endeavors to economic growth, Low and Macmillan (1988) were trying to elevate entrepreneurship to a higher status in academic and public discourse, at least equal to, if not higher than, the large corporations that were so highly visible in the research literature and everyday life. For many scholars today, the linkage between "entrepreneurship and economic growth is critically important to understand the micro-drivers of growth and to design policies conducive to societal prosperity" (Acs et al., 2017: 4). The focus of this chapter was on three scholars, namely Steven Klepper, Phillipe Aghion, and Boyan Jovanovic, who contributed novel insights into how entrepreneurship played an instrumental role in economic growth.

REFERENCES

Abernathy, W. J., & Utterback, J. M. (1978). Patterns of industrial innovation. *Technology Review, 80*(7), 40–47.

Acemoglu, D., Aghion, P., & Zilibotti, F. (2006). Distance to frontier, selection, and economic growth. *Journal of the European Economic Association, 4*(1), 37–74.

Acemoglu, D., Aghion, P., Lelarge, C., Van Reenen, J., & Zilibotti, F. (2007). Technology, information, and the decentralization of the firm. *Quarterly Journal of Economics, 122*(4), 1759–1799.

Acs, Z. J., Braunerhjelm, P., & Karlsson, C. (2017). Philippe Aghion: Recipient of the 2016 Global Award for Entrepreneurship Research. *Small Business Economics, 48*(1), 1–8.

Agarwal, R., & Gort, M. (1996). The evolution of markets and entry, exit and survival of firms. *The Review of Economics and Statistics, 78*(3), 489–498.

Agarwal, R., Buenstorf, G., Cohen, W. M., & Malerba, F. (2015). The legacy of Steven Klepper: Industry evolution, entrepreneurship, and geography. *Industrial and Corporate Change, 24*(4), 739–753.

Aghion, P. (2011). Some thoughts on industrial policy and growth. In O. Falck, C. Gollier, & L. Woessmann (Eds.), *Industrial policy for national champions* (pp. 13–30). Cambridge, MA: MIT Press.

Aghion, P. (2017). Entrepreneurship and growth: Lessons from an intellectual journey. *Small Business Economics, 48*(1), 9–24.

Aghion, P., & Bolton, P. (1987). Contracts as a barrier to entry. *American Economic Review, 77*(3), 388–401.

Aghion, P., & Howitt, P. (1992). A model of growth through creative destruction. *Econometrica, 60*(2), 323–351.

Aghion, P., Akcigit, U., & Howitt, P. (2014). What do we learn from Schumpeterian growth theory? In S. Durlauf & P. Aghion (Eds.), *Handbook of economic growth* (Vol. 2, pp. 515–563). New York: Elsevier.

Aghion, P., Akcigit, U., & Howitt, P. (2015). The Schumpeterian growth paradigm. *Annual Review of Economics, 7*(1), 557–575.

Aghion, P., Algan, Y., Cahuc, P., & Shleifer, A. (2010). Regulation and distrust. *Quarterly Journal of Economics, 125*(3), 1015–1049.

Aghion, P., Bacchetta, P., & Banerjee, A. (2004). Financial development and the instability of open economies. *Journal of Monetary Economics, 51*(6), 1077–1106.

Aghion, P., Bloom, N., Blundell, R., Griffith, R., & Howitt, P. (2005). Competition and innovation: An inverted-U relationship. *Quarterly Journal of Economics, 120*(2), 701–728.

Aghion, P., Blundell, R., Griffith, R., Howitt, P., & Prantl, S. (2009). The effects of entry on incumbent innovation and productivity. *Review of Economics and Statistics, 91*(1), 20–32.

Aghion, P., Burgess, R., Redding, S. J., & Zilibotti, F. (2008). The unequal effects of liberalization: Evidence from dismantling the license Raj in India. *American Economic Review, 98*(4), 1397–1412.

Ahl, H. (2006). Why research on women entrepreneurs needs new directions. *Entrepreneurship Theory and Practice, 30*(5), 595–621.

Angrist, J. D., & Pischke, J. S. (2008). *Mostly harmless econometrics: An empiricist's companion*. Princeton: Princeton University Press.

Antonakis, J., Bendahan, S., Jacquart, P., & Lalive, R. (2010). On making causal claims: A review and recommendations. *The Leadership Quarterly, 21*(6), 1086–1120.

Atkinson, R. D., & Lind, M. (2018). *Big is beautiful: Debunking the myth of small business*. Cambridge, MA: MIT Press.

Benhabib, J., & Jovanovic, B. (1991). Externalities and growth accounting. *American Economic Review, 81*(1), 82–113.

Benhabib, J., & Jovanovic, B. (2012). Optimal migration: A world perspective. *International Economic Review, 53*(2), 321–348.

Besley, T., & Burgess, R. (2004). Can labor regulation hinder economic performance? Evidence from India. *The Quarterly Journal of Economics, 119*(1), 91–134.

Birch, D. L., & MacCracken, S. (1981). Corporate evolution: A micro-based analysis. In *MIT program on neighborhood and regional change*. Cambridge, MA: MIT Press.

Braunerhjelm, P., & Carlsson, B. (2011). Steven Klepper: Recipient of the 2011 Global Award for Entrepreneurship Research. *Small Business Economics, 37*(2), 131.

Burgelman, R. A. (1983). A process model of internal corporate venturing in the diversified major firm. *Administrative Science Quarterly, 28*(2), 223–244.

Cao, H., & Folan, P. (2012). Product life cycle: The evolution of a paradigm and literature review from 1950–2009. *Production Planning & Control, 23*(8), 641–662.

Carlsson, B. (1987). Reflections on 'industrial dynamics': The challenges ahead. *International Journal of Industrial Organization, 5*(2), 135–148.

Caselli, F., & Coleman, W. J. (2006). The world technology frontier. *American Economic Review, 96*(3), 499–522.

Chiles, T. H., Bluedorn, A. C., & Gupta, V. K. (2007). Beyond creative destruction and entrepreneurial discovery: A radical Austrian approach to entrepreneurship. *Organization Studies, 28*(4), 467–493.

Christensen, C. M. (1997). *The innovator's dilemma: When new technologies cause great firms to fail.* Boston, MA: Harvard Business School Press.

Clark, D. (2015, July 16). Intel rechisels the tablet on Moore's Law. *Wall Street Journal.*

Corriveau, L. (1991). *Entrepreneurs, growth, and cycles* (Unpublished doctoral dissertation). University of Western Ontario, ON, Canada.

Coviello, N. E., McDougall, P. P., & Oviatt, B. M. (2011). The emergence, advance and future of international entrepreneurship research: An introduction to the special forum. *Journal of Business Venturing, 26*(6), 625–631.

Cox, W. E. (1967). Product life cycles as marketing models. *The Journal of Business, 40*(4), 375–384.

Dagsvik, J., Jovanovic, B., & Shepard, A. (1985). A foundation for three popular assumptions in job-matching models. *Journal of Labor Economics, 3*(4), 403–420.

Dahmén, E. (1984). Schumpeterian dynamics: Some methodological notes. *Journal of Economic Behavior & Organization, 5*(1), 25–34.

Dean, J. (1950). Pricing policies for new products. *Harvard Business Review, 28*(6), 45–53.

Dhalla, N. K., & Yuspeh, S. (1976). Forget the product life cycle concept. *Harvard Business Review, 54*(1), 102–112.

Dinopoulos, E., & Sener, F. (2007). New directions in Schumpeterian growth theory. In *Elgar companion to neo-Schumpeterian economics.* Cheltenham, UK: Edward Elgar.

Durden, G. C., & Ellis, L. V. (1993). A method for identifying the most influential articles in an academic discipline. *Atlantic Economic Journal, 21*(4), 1–10.

Eeckhout, J., & Jovanovic, B. (2012). Occupational choice and development. *Journal of Economic Theory, 147*(2), 657–683.

Elzinga, K. G., & Mills, D. E. (1994). Trumping the Areeda-Turner test: The recoupment standard in Brooke group. *Antitrust Law Journal, 62*(3), 559–584.

Enis, B. M., La Garce, R., & Prell, A. E. (1977). Extending the product life cycle. *Business Horizons, 20*(3), 46–56.

Evans, D. S., & Jovanovic, B. (1989). An estimated model of entrepreneurial choice under liquidity constraints. *Journal of Political Economy, 97*(4), 808–827.

Fagerberg, J., & Verspagen, B. (2009). Innovation studies: The emerging structure of a new scientific field. *Research Policy, 38*(2), 218–233.

Ferris, G. R., Ketchen, D. J., Jr., & Buckley, M. R. (2008). Making a life in the organizational sciences: No one ever said it was going to be easy. *Journal of Organizational Behavior, 29*(6), 741–753.

Forrester, J. W. (1958). Industrial dynamics: A major breakthrough for decision makers. *Harvard Business Review, 36*(4), 37–66.

Galbraith, J. K. (1968). *The new industrial state.* New York: The New American Library.

Gort, M., & Klepper, S. (1982). Time paths in the diffusion of product innovations. *Economic Journal, 92*(367), 630–653.

Gray, R. (2010). A re-evaluation of social, environmental and sustainability accounting. *Sustainability Accounting, Management and Policy Journal, 1*(1), 11–32.

Greenwood, J., & Jovanovic, B. (1999). Information-technology revolution and the stock market. *American Economic Review, 89*(2), 116–122.

Griffith, R., Redding, S., & Reenen, J. V. (2004). Mapping the two faces of R&D: Productivity growth in a panel of OECD industries. *Review of Economics and Statistics, 86*(4), 883–895.

Grossman, G. M., & Helpman, E. (1991). Quality ladders in the theory of growth. *Review of Economic Studies, 58*(1), 43–61.

Growiec, J. (2012). The world technology frontier: What can we learn from the US States? *Oxford Bulletin of Economics and Statistics, 74*(6), 777–807.

Gupta, V. K., & York, A. S. (2008). The effects of geography and age on women's attitudes towards entrepreneurship: Evidence from the state of Nebraska. *International Journal of Entrepreneurship and Innovation, 9*(4), 251–262.

Gupta, V., & Gupta, A. (2015). The concept of entrepreneurial orientation. *Foundations and Trends in Entrepreneurship, 11*(2), 55–137.

Gupta, V. K., Niranjan, S., Goktan, B. A., & Erikson, J. (2015). Individual entrepreneurial orientation role in shaping reactions *to new technologies. International Entrepreneurship and Management Journal, 12*(4), 935–961.

Gustavsson, P., & Poldhal, A. (2003). *Determinants of firms R&D: Evidence from Swedish firm level data* (Working Paper No. 178). Stockholm School of Economics, The European Institute of Japanese Studies.

Hambrick, D. C., & Chen, M. J. (2008). New academic fields as admittance-seeking social movements: The case of strategic management. *Academy of Management Review, 33*(1), 32–54.

Henderson, D. J., & Russell, R. R. (2005). Human capital and convergence: A production-frontier approach. *International Economic Review, 46*(4), 1167–1205.

Hobijn, B., & Jovanovic, B. (2001). The information-technology revolution and the stock market: Evidence. *American Economic Review, 91*(5), 1203–1220.

Holbrook, D., Cohen, W. M., Hounshell, D. A., & Klepper, S. (2000). The nature, sources, and consequences of firm differences in the early history of the semiconductor industry. *Strategic Management Journal, 21*(10–11), 1017–1041.

Jensen, R. (1982). Adoption and diffusion of an innovation of uncertain profitability. *Journal of Economic Theory, 27*(1), 182–193.

Jones, G., & Wadhwani, R. D. (2006). *Entrepreneurship and business history: Renewing the research agenda* (HBS Working Paper, No. 07-007).

Joseph, L. E. (1990, September 23). The bottom-line on disposables. *New York Times.*

Jovanovic, B. (1979a). Job matching and the theory of turnover. *Journal of Political Economy, 87*(5), 972–990.

Jovanovic, B. (1979b). Firm-specific capital and turnover. *Journal of Political Economy, 87*(6), 1246–1260.

Jovanovic, B. (1982). Selection and the evolution of industry. *Econometrica, 50*(3), 649–670.

Jovanovic, B. (1984a). Wages and turnover: A parametrization of the job-matching model. In G. R. Neumann & N. Westergård-Nielsen (Eds.), *Studies in labor market dynamics* (pp. 158–167). Berlin: Springer.

Jovanovic, B. (1984b). Matching, turnover, and unemployment. *Journal of Political Economy, 92*(1), 108–122.

Jovanovic, B. (1994). Firm formation with heterogeneous management and labor skills. *Small Business Economics, 6*(3), 185–191.

Jovanovic, B. (2001). New technology and the small firm. *Small Business Economics, 16*(1), 53–56.

Jovanovic, B. (2014). Misallocation and growth. *American Economic Review, 104*(4), 1149–1171.

Jovanovic, B. (2019). The entrepreneurship premium. *Small Business Economics, 53*(3), 555–568.

Jovanovic, B., & Lach, S. (1989). Entry, exit, and diffusion with learning by doing. *The American Economic Review, 79*(4), 690–699.

Jovanovic, B., & MacDonald, G. (1994a). The life cycle of a competitive industry. *Journal of Political Economy, 102*(2), 322–347.

Jovanovic, B., & MacDonald, G. M. (1994b). Competitive diffusion. *Journal of Political Economy, 102*(1), 24–52.

Jovanovic, B., & Moffitt, R. (1990). An estimate of a sectoral model of labor mobility. *Journal of Political Economy, 98*(4), 827–852.

Jovanovic, B., & Nyarko, Y. (1996). Learning by doing and the choice of technology. *Econometrica, 64*(6), 1299–1310.

Jovanovic, B., & Rob, R. (1989). The growth and diffusion of knowledge. *Review of Economic Studies, 56*(4), 569–582.

Jovanovic, B., & Rob, R. (1990). Long waves and short waves—Growth through intensive and extensive search. *Econometrica, 58*(6), 1391–1409.

Jovanovic, B., & Rousseau, P. L. (2001). Why wait? A century of life before IPO. *American Economic Review, 91*(2), 336–341.

Jovanovic, B., & Rousseau, P. L. (2002). Moore's law and learning by doing. *Review of Economic Dynamics, 5*(2), 346–375.

Jovanovic, B., & Rousseau, P. L. (2003). Two technological revolutions. *Journal of the European Economic Association, 1*(2–3), 419–428.

Jovanovic, B., & Rousseau, P. L. (2014). Extensive and intensive investment over the business cycle. *Journal of Political Economy, 122*(4), 863–908.

Jovanovic, B., & Szentes, B. (2013). On the market for venture capital. *Journal of Political Economy, 121*(3), 493–527.

Jovanovic, B., & Yatsenko, Y. (2012). Investment in vintage capital. *Journal of Economic Theory, 147*(2), 551–569.

Klepper, S. (1996). Entry, exit, growth, and innovation over the product life cycle. *The American Economic Review, 86*(3), 562–583.

Klepper, S. (1997). Industry life cycles. *Industrial and Corporate Change, 6*(1), 145–182.

Klepper, S. (2001). Employee startups in high-tech industries. *Industrial and Corporate Change, 10*(3), 639–674.

Klepper, S. (2002a). The capabilities of new firms and the evolution of the US automobile industry. *Industrial and Corporate Change, 11*(4), 645–666.

Klepper, S. (2002b). Firm survival and the evolution of oligopoly. *RAND Journal of Economics, 33*(1), 37–61.

Klepper, S., & Graddy, E. (1990). The evolution of new industries and the determinants of market structure. *RAND Journal of Economics, 21*(1), 27–44.

Klepper, S., & Miller, J. H. (1995). Entry, exit, and shakeouts in the United States in new manufactured products. *International Journal of Industrial Organization, 13*(4), 567–591.

Klepper, S., & Simons, K. L. (2000a). The making of an oligopoly: Firm survival and technological change in the evolution of the US tire industry. *Journal of Political Economy, 108*(4), 728–760.

Klepper, S., & Simons, K. L. (2000b). Dominance by birthright: Entry of prior radio producers and competitive ramifications in the US television receiver industry. *Strategic Management Journal, 21*(10–11), 997–1016.

Klepper, S., & Simons, K. L. (2005). Industry shakeouts and technological change. *International Journal of Industrial Organization, 23*(1–2), 23–43.

Klepper, S., & Sleeper, S. (2005). Entry by spinoffs. *Management Science, 51*(8), 1291–1306.

Lane, S. J. (1989). *Entry and competition in the ATM manufacturers' market* (Working Paper). Boston University School Management.

Lee, Y., Kozar, K. A., & Larsen, K. R. (2003). The technology acceptance model: Past, present, and future. *Communications of the Association for Information Systems, 12*(1), 752–780.

Levitt, T. (1965). Exploit the product life cycle. *Harvard Business Review, 43*, 81–94.

Low, M. B., & MacMillan, I. C. (1988). Entrepreneurship: Past research and future challenges. *Journal of Management, 14*(2), 139–161.

Lumpkin, G. T., & Dess, G. G. (1996). Clarifying the entrepreneurial orientation construct and linking it to performance. *Academy of Management Review, 21*(1), 135–172.

MacInnis, D. J., & Folkes, V. S. (2010). The disciplinary status of consumer behavior: A sociology of science perspective on key controversies. *Journal of Consumer Research, 36*(6), 899–914.

Mahoney, T. A. (1985). Journal publishing and the organizations sciences: An analysis of exchanges. In L. L. Cummings & P. J. Frost (Eds.), *Publishing in the organizational sciences*. Homewood, IL: Richard D. Irwin.

Merritt, R. (2013, August 27). Moore's law dead by 2022, expert says. *EE Times*.

Merton, R. K. (1973). *The sociology of science: Theoretical and empirical investigations*. Chicago, IL: University of Chicago Press.

Metcalfe, J. S. (1998). *Evolutionary economics and creative destruction* (Vol. 1). London: Psychology Press.

Mincer, J., & Jovanovic, B. (1981). Labor mobility and wages. In S. Rosen (Ed.), *Studies in labor markets* (pp. 21–64). Chicago: University of Chicago Press.

Minniti, M., Andersson, M., Braunerhjelm, P., Delmar, F., Rickne, A., Thorburn, K., et al. (2019). Boyan Jovanovic: Recipient of the 2019 Global Award for Entrepreneurship Research. *Small Business Economics, 53*(3), 547–553.

Moorthy, K. S. (1993). Theoretical modeling in marketing. *Journal of Marketing, 57*(2), 92–106.

Nichols, M. W., Hendrickson, J. M., & Griffith, K. (2011). Was the financial crisis the result of ineffective policy and too much regulation? An empirical investigation. *Journal of Banking Regulation, 12*(3), 236–251.

Nightingale, P. (2015). Schumpeter's theological roots? Harnack and the origins of creative destruction. *Journal of Evolutionary Economics, 25*(1), 69–75.

Nissani, M. (1997). Ten cheers for interdisciplinarity: The case for interdisciplinary knowledge and research. *Social Science Journal, 34*(2), 201–216.

Patton, A. (1959). Stretch your product's earning years: Top management's stake in the product life cycle. *Management Review, 48*(6), 9–14.

Perelman, M. (1995). Retrospectives: Schumpeter, David Wells, and creative destruction. *Journal of Economic Perspectives, 9*(3), 189–197.

Phillips, A., Phillips, A. P., & Phillips, T. R. (2012). *Biz jets: Technology and market structure in the corporate jet industry*. New York: Springer.

Polli, R., & Cook, V. (1969). Validity of the product life cycle. *The Journal of Business, 42*(4), 385–400.

Prat, J., & Jovanovic, B. (2014). Dynamic contracts when the agent's quality is unknown. *Theoretical Economics, 9*(3), 865–914.

Reinert, E., & Reinert, H. (2019). Creative destruction in economics: Nietzsche, Sombart, Schumpeter (with Hugo Reinert). In R. Kattel (Ed.), *The visionary realism of German economics: From the thirty years' war to the cold war* (pp. 385–412). London: Anthem.

Romer, P. M. (1990). Endogenous technological change. *Journal of Political Economy, 98*(5, Part 2), 250–281.

Romer, P. M. (1994). The origins of endogenous growth. *Journal of Economic Perspectives, 8*(1), 3–22.

Saloner, G. (1991). Modeling, game theory, and strategic management. *Strategic Management Journal, 12*(S2), 119–136.

Sarasvathy, S. D. (2009). *Effectuation: Elements of entrepreneurial expertise*. Cheltenham, UK: Edward Elgar.

Sato, K. (1974). The neoclassical postulate and the technology frontier in capital theory. *The Quarterly Journal of Economics, 88*(3), 353–384.

Schoonhoven, C. B., & Romanelli, E. (2001). *The entrepreneurship dynamic: Origins of entrepreneurship and the evolution of industries*. Stanford, CA: Stanford University Press.

Schumpeter, J. A. (1934). *The theory of economic development: An inquiry into profits, capital, credit, interest, and the business cycle*. Boston, MA: Harvard University Press.

Schumpeter, J. A. (1939). *Business cycles*. New York: McGraw-Hill.

Schumpeter, J. A. (1942). *Capitalism, socialism and democracy*. New York: Harper & Brothers.

Scott, A. J. (2006). Entrepreneurship, innovation and industrial development: Geography and the creative field revisited. *Small Business Economics, 26*(1), 1–24.

Segerstrom, P. S., Anant, T. C., & Dinopoulos, E. (1990). A Schumpeterian model of the product life cycle. *The American Economic Review, 80*(5), 1077–1091.

Shadish, W. R., Cook, T. D., & Campbell, D. T. (2002). *Experimental and quasi-experimental designs for generalized causal inference*. Boston, MA: Houghton Mifflin.

Shane, S. (2012). Reflections on the 2010 AMR decade award: Delivering on the promise of entrepreneurship as a field of research. *Academy of Management Review, 37*(1), 10–20.

Smallwood, J. E. (1973). The product life cycle: A key to strategic marketing planning. *MSU Business Topics, 21*(1), 29–35.

Smith, P. H. (1968). *Wheels within wheels: A short history of American motor manufacturing.* New York: Funk & Wagnalls.

Streb, C., & Gupta, V. K. (2011). Methodology of entrepreneurship research in a radical subjectivist paradigm. In M. Raposo, D. Smallbone, K. Balaton, & I. Hortovanyi (Eds.), *Entrepreneurship, growth and economic development: Frontiers in European entrepreneurship research* (pp. 51–84). Cheltanham, UK: Edward Elgar.

Tellis, G. J., & Crawford, C. M. (1981). An evolutionary approach to product growth theory. *Journal of Marketing, 45*(4), 125–132.

Vandenbussche, J., Aghion, P., & Meghir, C. (2006). Growth, distance to frontier and composition of human capital. *Journal of Economic Growth, 11*(2), 97–127.

Venkatraman, S. (1997). The distinctive domain of entrepreneurship research. *Advances in Entrepreneurship, Firm Emergence and Growth, 3*(1), 119–138.

Wales, W., Gupta, V. K., & Moussa, F. (2013). Empirical research on entrepreneurial orientation: An assessment and suggestions for future research. *International Small Business Journal, 31*(4), 357–383.

Weisman, D. L. (1994). Why less may be more under price-cap regulation. *Journal of Regulatory Economics, 6*(4), 339–361.

Wells, D. A. (1889). *Recent economic changes and their effect on the production and distribution of wealth and the well-being of Society.* New York: Appleton.

Wennekers, S., & Thurik, R. (1999). Linking entrepreneurship and economic growth. *Small Business Economics, 13*(1), 27–56.

Wood, L. (1990). The end of the product life cycle? Education says goodbye to an old friend. *Journal of Marketing Management, 6*(2), 145–155.

CHAPTER 4

Geography

There is considerable academic interest in spatial aspects of entrepreneurship (Sternberg, 2009). Researchers in this area operate at the interface of entrepreneurship and geography (Backman & Lööf, 2015), a seemingly fertile area of inquiry that has begun to attract the attention of scholars and policy-makers (Rubén, Isabel, & Coro, 2017; Steyaert & Katz, 2004). A recent survey of 'expert' entrepreneurship researchers revealed that they considered 'geography' to be one of the most important areas for academic inquiry (Kuckertz & Prochotta, 2018).[1] At first glance, the connection between entrepreneurship and geography seems self-evident, especially when one considers that the goal of entrepreneurial activity is economic growth (as discussed in the previous chapter). As Acs and Varga (2005: 324) wondered, "if economic growth arises from the creation of new recipes to rearrange things, might not entrepreneurship and geography play some role in this transformation?" For Plummer and Pe'er (2010: 520), there seems no doubt that "entrepreneurship is, and always has been, both a cause and an outcome of the geographic distribution of economic activity." Researchers working at the interface of entrepreneurship and geography research bring together the actor (individual or organizational) and the place (where the action takes

---

[1] These scholars defined 'expert' researchers as those who published at least one research over the course of the period 2014–2016 in one or more of the premier field journals in entrepreneurship. Based on a survey of 225 'expert' researchers, the topic of geography was seen as having the most academic potential in entrepreneurship research.

© The Author(s) 2020
V. K. Gupta, *Great Minds in Entrepreneurship Research*,
https://doi.org/10.1007/978-3-030-44125-8_4

place), so that entrepreneurial endeavors are driven by people and the environmental conditions around them (Thornton & Flynn, 2003).

Plummer and Pe'er (2010) identify two major schools of thought at the interface of entrepreneurship and geography. The majority view, they argue, views geography as a proxy for local contexts, so that the form, function, and outcomes of entrepreneurial processes vary based on the specific conditions of the time and place in which entrepreneurship takes place (Zahra, Wright, & Abdelgawad, 2014). The minority view, Plummer and Pe'er (2010: 522) argue, posits "entrepreneurship as an inherently spatial process," where local frictions manifest in the positioning of entrepreneurs and touch upon all aspects of the entrepreneurial process (Andersson, 2005). Additionally, there are also those who believe that when it comes to entrepreneurial activity, geography is now dead as "location is not an impediment to entrepreneurial success—you can start your firm in any location regardless of tax rates, living conditions, or other touted advantages" (Kirchhoff, 1997: 472).

The citations for the GAER laureates suggest that the award has been given thrice—to four researchers—for work advancing scholarly understanding of spatial aspects of entrepreneurship: the 2002 award to Giacomo Beattini and Charles Sabel, in 2013 to Maryann Feldman, and in 2018 to Olav Sorenson.

CHARLES SABEL AND GIACOMO BECATTINI: ENTREPRENEURIAL ACTIVITY IN DISTRICTS

The GAER has been shared twice by two scholars: Acs-Audretsch in 2001 (discussed in a previous chapter) and Sabel-Becattini in 2002 (discussed here). The official citation for the GAER award to Giacomo Becattini and Charles Sabel recognized them for "revitalizing Alfred Marshall's century-old ideas regarding the competitive advantages of geographical agglomerations of specialized small firms in so-called industrial districts."

Before proceeding further, it would be useful to understand what the phrase 'industrial districts' means. For some, industrial districts are "webs of inter-organizational networks mostly composed by small and medium firms localized in a limited territorial area and specialized in the same economic sector" (Sammarra & Biggiero, 2001: 61).[2] Goodman (1989: 21) defines industrial districts as "a territorial system of small- and medium-sized firms producing a group of commodities whose products are processes which can be split into different phases." Sforzi (1989: 154) views an industrial district as a "system of small industrial firms involved in different phases of the same production process, closely linked to the population, spatially concentrated, and sharing a relatively restricted geographical area." As with most concepts in the organizational literature, multiple definitions of 'industrial districts' can be found in the literature (Belussi & Sedita, 2019), with most—though not all—researchers building on the seminal work of the English economist Alfred Marshall.

The critical Marshallian insight that the GAER citation recognizes, and that Sabel and Beattini benefited from in their work, was the idea that manufacturing facilities can be organized along two lines: (a) under one roof of a large enterprise, or (b) small factories operating in locations specializing in a particular industry. During Marshall's time, the dominant view among economists was that the most efficient factory system was one where all relevant processes were concentrated in one place with high vertical integration. In observing economic activity around him in nineteenth-century England—which some have called "the promised land of classical economic laws" (Becattini, 2001: 85)—Marshall observed two efficient manufacturing systems, particularly when he looked at cutlery works in Sheffield and metal trade in Birmingham. In his 1879 work *The Economics of Industry*, Marshall wrote[3]:

> We shall find that some of the advantages of division of labor can be obtained only in very large factories, but that many of them, more than at first sight appears, can be secured by small factories and workshops, provided there are a very great number of them in the same trade. ... The manufacture of commodity often consists of several distinct stages, to each of which a separate room in the factory is devoted. But if the total amount

---

[2] As is common in social science research, other labels are sometimes used, such as "system areas" (Garofoli, 1991) and "small enterprise spatial system" (Bianchi, 1996: 199).

[3] This is the only work that Marshall officially co-wrote with his wife Mary Paley, a renowned economist in her own right (Cicarelli & Cicarelli, 2003). For various reasons, Alfred Marshall considered this work to be unworthy, and inferior to *The Principles of Economy*, deciding not to invest in publishing it further. It remains unclear why Mary Marshall did not pursue the 1879 book further or wrote another book based on it.

of the commodity produced is very large, it may be profitable to devote separate small factories to each of the steps....But small factories, whatever their number, will be at a great disadvantage relative to large unless many of them are collected together in the same district. ... in these districts a further division of specialisation has grown up, and separate trades have sought separate localities. ... Those that work in wool do not generally live among the Lancashire cotton workers, but are collected together in Yorkshire; and they themselves are divided into the "woollen trade" and the "worsted trade".

Scholars believe that these writings formed the bases for Marshall's (1890) later work on 'external and internal economies,' so that the rationale for industrial districts rests on the logic of agglomeration economics which refers to the idea that economies may be external to the firm but internal to the area for a group of firms (Landstrom, 2005). For Marshall, industrial districts offered both economic and non-economic (or social) benefits to firms that located there. The former were the result of localization economies resulting from the geographical agglomeration of enterprises in the same industry; the latter resulted from the norms and values that arose from the indivisibility of industry and local society. In terms of economic benefits, Marshall proffered the following:

1. Proximity of business provided benefits such as reduced transaction and transportation costs. Proximity also made it easier to access inputs such as specialized labor and technical know-how.
2. The 'division of labor' between firms in the same locality allowed individual firms to specialize in a given task or production stage, and sell its products to a large group of customers. In effect, industrial districts generated 'economies of variety' as the final product could be made in different ways using inputs from multiple sources, yet benefited from 'economies of scale' that came from task specialization.
3. When an area focused on a particular industry, there was a constant flow of new spin-offs and entrepreneurial activity, encouraged by the presence of market opportunities vital for the survival of new ventures.

In terms of the social benefits of industrial districts, Marshall considered the following:

1. The routine interdependence, social familiarity, and face-to-face contacts helped foster mutual knowledge and trust, which reduced friction in interactions between firms and facilitated the flow of information.
2. Firms that violated local norms were readily sanctioned by others in the community without recourse to expensive legal channels.
3. The 'industrial atmosphere' that resulted from the involvement of the whole community in a common sphere provided support and resources for small firms. The notion of the 'industrial atmosphere' seems important to the concept of Marshallian districts. Because skilled workers are concentrated in industrial districts, the puzzles of the business are "no mysteries; but are, as it were, in the air, and children learn many of them unconsciously" (Marshall, 1890: 287).

Interestingly, Marshall's ideas on industrial districts had little influence on economic thinking over much of the twentieth century as economists focused on the advantages of large-scale manufacturing and economies of scale. The Marshallian concept was later rediscovered in the Italian context by Sabel and Becattini, both of whom noticed intriguing patterns in parts of the Italian economy. As Landstrom (2005: 242) wrote of what Sabel and Becattini discovered:

In several Italian regions, both the agricultural sector and large firms were declining, but parts of the industries were growing, and the structures of these growing industries were agglomerations of small firms strongly connected to international markets. The researchers realized that high productivity in a manufacturing process could not only be achieved by investing in means of production but was related to the physical contiguity of firms – economies that were external to any one firm, but internal to an industrial sector or territorial group of firms.

Both Sabel and Becattini discovered interesting phenomena in the Italian economy, but their work appeared largely independent of each other. Sabel wrote in English and Becattini in Italian. The first publication, considered the starting point for modern research on industrial districts, was Becattini (1979), which was originally in Italian and later translated into English and published as Becattini (1989).[4] Given the profound impact of this article on subsequent research in the area of industrial districts, a brief discussion about it seems appropriate before moving forward. For Becattini (1989), the starting point for research on industrial districts is Marshall's distinction between internal and external economies. The former arose from the "resources of the industrial houses of business engaged in it, on their organization and the efficiency of the management," while the latter accrue from "the general development of the industry." Becattini (1989) considered the advantage of industrial districts to be that they allowed firms to benefit from both internal and external economies. Furthermore, Marshall did not constrain his definition of industrial districts to small- or medium-sized enterprises (Bellandi, 1989). Becattini (1989), however, considered SMEs as essential to industrial districts, and he drew on Marshall (1919: 196–197)'s work:

> The advantages of production on a large scale can in general be as well attained by the aggregation of a large number of small maters into one district as by the erection of a few large works....With regard to many classes of commodities it is possible to divide the process of production into several stages, each of which can be performed with the maximum of economy in a small establishment....If there exist a large number of such small establishments specialized for the performance of a particular stage of the process of production, there will be room for the profitable investment of capital in the organizing of subsidiary industries adapted for meeting their special wants.

Becattini (1991) also argued that industrial districts should be regarded as a 'creative milieu', suggesting that an industrial district is not really one unless it is creative. For a territorially defined environment (aka the industrial district) to be a source of creativity, different competencies need to coexist. Yet, mere coexistence of various competencies is not sufficient for creativity to prosper—there is also a need for a 'linking primer' that connects various competences, fostering dynamic interactions between them and encouraging dialogue between actors. Overall, the coexistence

---

[4] The acknowledgments section of Becattini (1989: 133) notes that it is "a new version of" Becattini's original book published in 1979 in Italian. A future bilingual reexamination would do well to consider the extent to which Becattini's views evolved, or not, over the 10-year period regarding the meaning and significance of industrial districts.

of competencies and the presence of catalysts will produce a creative milieu where random spurs to recombine knowledge are anticipated and promoted (as opposed to left to chance).

For various reasons, Becattini's research, and other works on Italian industrial districts, did not attract much attention internationally until Sabel published *The Second Industrial Divide* in 1984 (co-authored with Michael Piore). The central concept of the book is the idea of 'industrial divides', which refers to historical moments at which important choices are (inadvertently) made that then determine the future trajectory of technological development (Brody, 1985). Per Piore and Sabel (1984: 19), the first industrial divide was characterized by the domination of mass production, wherein the guiding mantra was that "the cost of making any particular good could be dramatically reduced if only machinery could be substituted for the human skill to produce it." The emphasis here was on disaggregating tasks done by hand into its simpler parts, each of which would then be undertaken faster and more accurately by a machine. Mass production, therefore, entailed high-volume manufacturing of standardized goods by customized machines operated by low-skilled or semi-skilled workers (e.g., Ford's Model T). Piore and Sabel (1984) argued in favor of an alternative form of technological development, which they called flexible specialization, wherein general-purpose machine tools were to be used for customized production that allowed for faster introduction of novel products. In doing so, these scholars were inspired by the success of the Japanese in coordinating and improving production by quality circles, high skill levels, and other factors that facilitated flexibility and low costs. Piore and Sabel (1984) discuss Emilia Romagna—one of the richest regions in Italy where wage rates at the time were twice the national average and per capita income was second in the nation (Harrison, 1992)—as a model for flexible specialization. Piore and Sabel (1984) argued that the distinguishing features of industrial districts were flexibility, skilled labor, and social values that put a premium on cooperation between firms specializing in different activities.

For its proponents (e.g., Harrison, 1992: S108), the concept of industrial districts exemplifies 'clustering', which entails "similar economic activities" co-locating in the same geographic space. As a number of researchers have recognized (e.g., Maskell, 2001), clusters are a common feature of economic activity in developed economies (e.g., shopping malls in the US) and in developing societies (e.g., artisanal gold mining in

Ivory Coast).[5] However, critics charge that academic interest in industrial districts "far exceeds their empirical significance" (Amin, 2000: 150). There is concern that few successful industrial districts have been documented, especially outside Italy, and to some extent, France (Vernus, 2016), Japan (Hashino, 2016), Denmark (Kristensen, 1989), and Spain (Domenech & Rosés, 2016).[6] This is not to say that small artisan enterprises may not be found elsewhere, particularly in developing countries with low prevalence of mass-production efficiency-based manufacturing. For example, there is the 'sports manufacturing' sector in Jalandhar (Punjab, India) and the 'machine-tool manufacturing' sector in Rajkot (Gujrat, India), but it is unclear if they provide the shared economic and social benefits that characterize Marshallian districts, largely because of dearth of systematic academic attention to them.[7] Even within the existing scholarly literature on industrial districts, there is an "overabundance of valuable case studies" and a surprising "lack of solid empirical evidence across cases, sectors, and countries" (Maskell, 2001: 923), which is a problematic for researchers interested in building a robust body of knowledge.

While the diversity of firms in industrial districts is recognized and appreciated in the academic literature (Hashino & Otsuka, 2016), researchers have generally ignored heterogeneity within the Marshallian 'industrial districts'. Bellandi (1989) identified three major forms of industrial districts in the Marshallian tradition: (a) resident firms engage in different stages of a process, as happens when the final product is assembled from the output of various sub-processes; (b) resident firms operate at the same stage in the manufacturing process, as is the case for diamond cutting cluster in Surat (Gujarat, India); and (c) resident firms are linked diagonally as each specializes in different service processes. In all three cases, the district—at a broad level—focuses on a particular industry

[5] Geographic co-location is believed to produce two types of agglomeration economies (Maskell, 2001): (a) those that arise from the spatial propinquity of industries and services in general ('urbanization economies') and (b) those that accrue from the spatial proximity of related economic activities ('locational economies'). The latter is the focus of the Marshallian 'industrial district'.

[6] The clusters in Jutland (Denmark) have received some attention in the industrial districts literature (Schmitz & Musyck, 2016), but others question their existence and performance (Engelstoft, Jensen-Butler, Smith, & Winther, 2006).

[7] There are other examples too, such as the export-oriented garment industry cluster in Bangladesh (Sonobe, 2016).

(e.g., shoes or textiles), but may encompass different 'sub-industries'. This intriguing aspect of industrial districts has not received the academic consideration it deserves. Much of the academic literature on industrial districts, however, ignores possible variations in the economic activity occurring within these districts. Consequently, industrial districts may be a popular area of inquiry, but a fine-grained nuanced understanding of the Marshallian district remains missing from the literature.

Taking exception with the Marshallian 'industrial district' itself, Markusen (2002) argues that present-day industrial districts, especially those outside Italy, do not fit Marshall's model: a region comprised of small firms with local ownership trading with each other and generally lacking the size for scale economies. Markusen's (2002) research identifies three other types of industrial districts: (a) a hub-and-spoke model centered around one or more large dominant firms (e.g., Boeing in Seattle), (b) a satellite platform model with smaller facilities of externally located large firms (e.g., Research Triangle Park in North Carolina), and (c) the state-anchored model focused around a major public or nonprofit entity (e.g., Madison, home to the flagship campus of University of Wisconsin). This identification of alternative archetypes, remarkably different from Marshall's original conception or the subsequent works of Sabel and Becattini, raise new questions about industrial districts that have not been considered before, such as the role of small firms, the possibility of transformation from one form to another, the influence of the state and the government, and so on. Clearly, the concept of industrial districts is interesting and can benefit from additional scholarship.

MARYANN FELDMAN: GEOGRAPHY AND INNOVATION

Maryann Feldman was the 2013 GAER recipient, recognized for "her contributions to the study of the geography of innovation and the role of entrepreneurial activity in the formation of regional industry clusters." Lorenzen and Carlsson (2014) categorize Feldman's research into four groups: (a) firm location, knowledge spillovers across firms, cluster formation, and local development, (b) academic entrepreneurship, including academia-industry relations, (c) public policy, and (d) miscellaneous, which comprises of multiple topics within entrepreneurship research. Notably, scholars (e.g., Sternberg, 2009) recognize Feldman (2001) as being the first to formally characterize entrepreneurial activities as predominantly 'regional events', which then opened the doors for researchers interested in spatial, or specifically regional, perspectives in entrepreneurship research.

Audretsch and Feldman (1996: 630) examined "the extent to which industrial activity clusters spatially and to link this geographic concentration to the existence of knowledge externalities." To cast light on whether there is an underlying propensity for industrial activity to cluster spatially, they relied on a database of more than 8000 commercial innovations introduced in the US in 1982.[8] The level of analysis was US states, revealing that some states (e.g., California) are home to the bulk of innovative activity, while other states (e.g., Wyoming and Montana) see no innovative activity. Feldman (1993) had also shown that product innovations tend to cluster in states with prior concentrations of innovative input, with particular states developing a comparative advantage for innovative industries that is not due to the presence of natural resources or availability of low-cost labor. Audretsch and Feldman (1996) show that industries in which knowledge externalities are more prevalent (i.e., high R&D, university research, and skilled labor) have a greater propensity for innovative activity to cluster spatially than industries in which such knowledge spillovers are not as salient, and these results are robust to controlling for the geographic concentration of production.

Based on their research, Audretsch and Feldman (1996) are able to speak to the controversial question of whether spatial clustering of innovation is due to inter-firm knowledge spillovers or to production economies of scale. Feldman and Florida (1994: 211) show that "not only do innovations cluster geographically in areas that contain concentrations of specialized resources" that reflect sound technological infrastructure (proxied by four variables: firms in related manufacturing industries, industry R&D, university R&D, and business services), but also that the geographical concentrations of specialized resources mutually, and positively, reinforce the region's innovative capacity. Interestingly, Feldman and Audretsch (1999) report that small firm innovation is positively associated with regional diversity as opposed to specialization (where diversity-specialization is assessed as the share of total employment in the

[8] The database was compiled, and quality-checked by, a private firm, The Futures Group, for the United States Small Business Administration. It was based on new product announcement sections in over 100 technology, engineering, and trade journals across every conceivable industry, and categorized innovations at the four-digit SIC level.

city accounted for by industry employment in the city, divided by the share of US employment accounted by that particular industry).

A key issue that entrepreneurship researchers have sought to understand is what makes small firms more innovative than larger firms in some industries. Feldman and her colleagues examine how small, and often new, firms are able to be innovative without the necessary investments in R&D, finding that the answer lay in knowledge spillovers from universities and academic institutions (Acs, Audretsch, & Feldman, 1994a), and sometimes even from large corporations (Acs, Audretsch, & Feldman, 1994b). As Acs et al. (1994a: 137) note, geographical "proximity between the university and corporate laboratories within a state serves as a catalyst to innovative activity for firms of all sizes, [but] the impact is apparently greater on small firms than on large firms." Knowledge spillovers tend to be highly localized, especially when the benefits are associated with face-to-face contact between the entrants and incumbents, even as benefits from labor market pooling and shared inputs travel over a greater distance (Aharonson, Baum, & Feldman, 2007). Although both large and small firms may benefit from knowledge spillovers from external institutions, the benefits seem especially pronounced for smaller firm (Feldman, 1994). Seen this way, innovation is an open activity, not confined to the boundaries of a particular firm. By locating themselves close to university R&D, and even industrial R&D and other related firms, small firms are able to leverage resources that large firms internalize.

Feldman and her colleagues take a case study-based approach to understanding clusters in some of their work. Specifically, Feldman and Schreuder (1996) focused on the historical circumstances leading up the clustering of the pharmaceutical manufacturing industry in the Mid-Atlantic region (the corridor between Philadelphia and New York City). Feldman and Francis (2003) examined the biotechnology cluster in the US Capitol region, identifying three primary drivers: incentives and infrastructure provided by the government, entrepreneurship, and pre-existing resources (e.g., skilled labor brought about by changes in federal employment policies). Feldman (2001: 887) also discussed the biotechnology cluster in the US Capitol region, calling on researchers to consider "entrepreneurs as economic agents who actively interact with their local environments, adapt to new situations, crises or opportunities using place-specific assets, and finally, build and augment local institutions." Feldman and Lowe (2008) attributed the genesis of the biotechnology sector in Cambridge (Massachusetts, USA) to the adoption of a highly restrictive ordinance that unexpectedly created a business-friendly environment for the subsequent emergence of the industry.

Over the years, a large body of literature has accumulated around the topic of 'geography of innovation' (Feldman & Kogler, 2010), discussing the role of location and proximity to innovative activity. This area of study, which came to the attention of mainstream economists with Krugman's (1991) seminal insight linking geography and trade, is also called 'new economic geography' (Clark, Feldman, & Gertler, 2000). The importance of this new area of inquiry can be described thus:

> Students in introductory classes are told that economics consists of three major questions: what to produce, how to produce, and for whom to produce. A fourth question that is increasingly important in the global economy is where to produce—where to locate the factors of production so that they are most efficient and productive. The study of the location of innovation is a subset of the question of where to locate. (Feldman & Kogler, 2010: 404)

The key question here is 'Why?', as in, why do firms chose to locate where they do. Take, for example, the much-publicized effort that recently went into deciding where the Internet retail giant Amazon should locate its second corporate headquarters. Whether or not managers make the location decision consciously, they do choose a location for their endeavors. Plummer and Pe'er (2010: 520) argued that the "choice of region, neighborhood, or street corner is not trivial, since any location serves as a market 'beachhead' for entering the competitive fray and, thus, has long-term implications for the ultimate success of new enterprises." Several national publications (e.g., Forbes and Business Week) publish competing ranks of 'best places to start or locate a business.' Governments too are not insulated from the location mania, as many countries closely monitor their rankings on the World Bank's Doing Business index, which influences corporate decisions about which countries (and selected cities) are appropriate for locating their next project.

A central contribution of Feldman's research to entrepreneurship inquiry is the idea that "industries in which knowledge spillovers are prevalent — that is, where industry R&D, university research, and skilled labor are particularly important — have a greater propensity for innovative activity to cluster than industries where knowledge externalities are less important" (Lorenzen & Carlsson, 2014: 2). The idea that there is a spatial aspect to knowledge flows is not novel in itself as several researchers who studied the Italian industrial districts have also argued that geographical concentration of innovative activities may be attributed to the better flow of information within the cluster than outside of it (Brusco, 1990; Russo, 1985). The notion of knowledge flows as a key driver of innovation within geographical agglomerations has remained generally uncontested in the academic literature (Dahl & Pedersen, 2004). Krugman (1991: 53–54) famously argued that knowledge flows "are invisible; they leave no paper trail by which they may be measured and tracked, and there is nothing to prevent the theorist from assuming anything about them that she likes." Breschi and Lissoni (2001: 976) views localized knowledge spillovers as "no more than a 'black box', whose contents remain ambiguous." Feldman and Kogler (2010: 395) acknowledge that knowledge transfer tends to be largely tacit, which makes spillovers difficult "to identify and to measure." Consequently, and perhaps unfortunately, few researchers have so far sought to peer inside the proverbial black box, so that the black-box problem has gone largely unresolved in the knowledge spillover literature. Some researchers have argued that patent citation analysis, which refers to the examination of citations to prior patents, may help gain new insights into the process underlying knowledge flows (Jaffe, Trajtenberg, & Henderson, 1993). Because patents contain geographical information about their inventors, Feldman and Kogler (2010) believe patent citations can be used to track knowledge spillovers across space. Others (e.g., Alcacer & Gittelman, 2006), however, question the patent citation methodology, arguing that patent citations data do not accurately capture knowledge flows because of the presence of examiner citations that adds measurement error.

Much of Feldman's research uses states as the unit of analysis for geographic agglomeration (e.g., Audretsch & Feldman, 1996; Feldman, 1993). Krugman (1991: 57) contends that "states aren't really the right geographical units," primarily because of a lack of correspondence between political entities and economic markets. Geographic regions where economic activity tends to be concentrated rarely align neatly with state boundaries. Further, states are of unequal population and physical area, which then biases industry comparisons. Audretsch and Feldman (1996) acknowledge the concerns about the state as the unit of analysis in geographical agglomeration research, but no progress seems to have been made to identify alternative, more appropriate, analytical units.

OLAV SORENSON: SOCIAL AND SPATIAL RELATIONSHIPS

The 2018 GAER recipient was Olav Sorenson, recognized for his contribution to showing "how entrepreneurial activity and innovation are strongly embedded in socially and spatially bounded relationships." Rickne, Ruef, and Wennberg (2018) identify three main themes in Sorenson's body of research work: (a) geography of entrepreneurial activity, (b) linking social capital with entrepreneurial activity, and (c) organizational learning and technological innovation. Notably, Sorenson has also written on other topics, such as the non-distinctive domain of entrepreneurship research (Sorenson & Stuart, 2008a), role of theory testing and replication in management science (Shi, Sorenson, & Waguespack, 2017), and formal theorizing to strengthen knowledge development in management research (Adner, Polos, Ryall, & Sorenson, 2009).

Sorenson (2018) credits his interest in economic geography as the starting point of his journey into entrepreneurship research.[9] Krugman (1991: 1) defines economic geography, based on the idea of "the location of production in space," as the "branch of economics that worries about where things happen in relation to one another." Economic geography can also be defined as the study of "the spatial distribution of economic activity, in why regions grow at different rates, and in the fundamental principles underlying cities and the structure of urban systems" (Rodríguez-Pose, 2001: 178). Because economic activities are unevenly distributed in space, the field of economic geography is concerned with explaining spatial variations in economic activities that can be accounted for by the natural differences between places (e.g., variations in climates, accessibility, and natural endowments; Ottaviano & Thisse, 2005). Many industries in the US, and elsewhere, show geographical concentration (e.g., high-tech industry and motion-picture industry), which has generally been explained as organizations benefiting economically from locating efficiently.

---

[9] For Clark, Feldman, Gertler, and Wójcik (2018: 1), geography is about the "why and so what of where," so that economic geography relates to the "where, why, and so what questions are focused on understanding economy." The word 'economy' is used in a broad sense to refer to the "totality of processes through which individuals, households, and societies make a living and sustain themselves." From their perspective, economic geography is limited not just to the formal economy, but also includes "informal economy, both 'grey', such as household production, and 'black', such as illegal drug trade."

Do decision-makers really make carefully thought-out economic decisions about the efficiency of their location choices? Based on a historical analysis of show manufacturing plants in the US from 1940 to 1989, Sorenson and Audia (2000) find that states with high geographical concentration of shoe manufacturing see both high founding and failure rates. They explain these intriguing results as suggesting that it is not the variation in economic factors (e.g., production and distribution costs) per se, but rather the structural of entrepreneurial opportunities (e.g., ties to existing entrepreneurs) that maintains geographic concentration in the shoe industry. Co-location, or geographical concentration, therefore has both benefits (in the form of knowledge about the business and access to scarce resources) and costs (in the form of intense competition).

Sorenson's most cited work to date is on venture capital investments in the US from 1986 to 1998 (Sorenson & Stuart, 2001), showing that the likelihood of a VC investing in a new venture declines sharply with distance between the VC and the target venture. Interestingly, both physical distance and industry distance between the VC and the target were significant in predicting the likelihood of investment. The spatial reach of the VCs tended to increase with experience and centrality in funding syndicates. Stuart and Sorenson (2003a) examine location-specific founding rates among dedicated biotechnology firms (DBFs), which are organizations founded to research, develop, and commercialize biotechnologies, and the impact of location on the early-life performance of these firms. They theorize and show that founding rates are higher in certain areas because resource mobilization for new ventures involves leveraging relationships (e.g., with, VCs, established firms, and key technology suppliers) that are geographically concentrated. Stuart and Sorenson (2003b) found that liquidity events (specifically, initial public offerings (IPOs) and acquisitions) impact DBF founding rates in proximate geographic areas, which they attributed to renewal of financial resources in the local vicinity, disruption of ties that bound employees to their firm firms, and availability of evidence about wealth-generating potential of new ventures in the area.

Sorenson (2003) divides the entrepreneurial process into two stages: (1) opportunity identification, which refers to coming up with an idea for a new venture, and (2) organization building, which involves constructing a company to pursue the business idea. Social networks can plan an important role in both stages (Stuart & Sorenson, 2007). Potential entrepreneurs tend to be most aware of nascent business opportunities in the industry in which she/he works, particularly if she works for a firm situated in a geographical cluster of similar firms. For new entrants to start operations and compete effectively in incumbent firms and emerging organizations, they require access to tacit knowledge, human resources, and financial capital, acquisition of all of which is facilitated by social networks. Because of the importance of social networks to accessing new opportunity and much-needed resources, entrepreneurs tend to locate their businesses in places they have been living (and industries where they have worked previously). Consequently, staying in the places where they have already lived and worked maximizes the odds of success for entrepreneurs (Dahl & Sorenson, 2012), so that those who want their business to succeed should locate in places most familiar to them.

Using a comprehensive municipality-level database of Danish entrepreneurs from 1994 to 2004, Dahl and Sorenson (2009) find that entrepreneurs place much more emphasis on being close to family and friends than on the economic characteristics of the region. Notably, the preference on locating close to 'nears and dears' is economically efficient as new ventures seem to perform better—that is, survive longer and generate greater annual profits and cash flows—when they are located in regions where founders have lived longer (Dahl & Sorenson, 2012). Prior research has argued that when entrepreneurs are motivated by 'psychic' considerations (e.g., family time), they may need to accept lower economic returns for their enterprising efforts (Gimeno, Folta, Cooper, & Woo, 1997). Dahl and Sorenson (2012) show no evidence of a financial penalty for entrepreneurs trying to gain personal satisfaction from the venture, but instead provides robust support for 'psychic premium' to those who locate close to family and friends. However, Dahl and Sorenson (2010a) document a similar preference to remain close to family and friends among Danish scientists and engineers, raising the possibility that their results may simply be an artifact of the emphasis on personal relationships in the Danish society (see also Dahl & Sorenson 2010b).

Reitzig and Sorenson (2013) looked at innovation proposals inside a multinational consumer goods firm (with more than 50,000 employees at 318 facilities across 66 countries), finding that proposal evaluators are biased in favor of idea submitted by individuals who work in the same division and facility. However, business decisions driven by social ties may not always yield positive performance benefits. Using a 20-year dataset of films released theatrically in the US between 1982 and 2001, Sorenson and Waguespack (2006) find that distributors prefer films with key personnel with whom they had prior exchange relations, and favor these films in allocating scarce resources (in the form of opening dates and promotion effort), even as films with deeper prior relations to the distributor perform worse at the box office. In a similar vein, Rogan and Sorenson (2014) analyzed data from the global advertising agency from 1995 to 2003 to find that the likelihood of two agencies merging increases when they have common clients (i.e., indirect ties), but the joint performance of the merged companies decreased (in form of lost clients and loss of sales to retained clients). Close ties are most useful for exchange of knowledge of moderate complexity, but simple information transfers well over long distance, whereas highly complex information does not transfer well within even close relationships (Sorenson, Rivkin, & Fleming, 2006).

Rickne et al. (2018) praise Sorenson and Stuart (2008b) for making a case for careful empirical examination of specific entrepreneurial phenomena using methods and tools developed in other disciplines (such as economics and sociology). At first glance, this is an uncontroversial position. As Chiles, Bluedorn, and Gupta (2007) noted, entrepreneurship researchers, following the advice to 'borrow boldly' (Gartner, Bird, & Starr, 1992), have made tremendous strides by adapting theories and methodologies from different disciplines. Where Sorenson and Stuart (2008a) take a controversial position is to explicitly criticize the popular wisdom of entrepreneurship as a distinct field of study (Shane & Venkataraman, 2000) that "explains and predicts phenomena neither explained nor predicted by other fields" (Shane, 2012: 11). Instead, Sorenson and Stuart (2008a: 519) believe entrepreneurship research is better off as a "multi-disciplinary 'invisible college' of discipline-based scholars" examining entrepreneurial phenomena with whatever theoretical and methodological tools they prefer. From their perspective, advances in knowledge about entrepreneurship will come from scholars with deep training in their respective disciplines (e.g., psychology, sociology, and economics; Alvarez, Agarwal, & Sorenson, 2006; Gupta & Gupta, 2015), some of who may collaborate across disciplinary boundaries and cross-pollinate ideas.[10]

---

[10] Despite the popular appeal of this idea, such interdisciplinary collaboration has been rare in entrepreneurship research (Zahra, 2005). It is also notable that while researchers in entrepreneurship did—and still do—come from other academic fields, a majority of entrepreneurship researchers now consider the entrepreneurship division as their primary disciplinary home in the Academy of Management (Fried, 2003).

While Sorenson has done commendable work in exploring the role of social relationships in entrepreneurship (Rickne et al., 2018), the 'content' of one's social ties has gone largely undiscussed in the literature (Borgatti, Brass, & Halgin, 2014). The phrase 'content of ties' can mean many things, such as the type of relationship (e.g., parental tie, sibling tie, or romantic tie) and what flows through the relationship (e.g., money, information, support, counsel, etc.). The different kinds of ties and their different flows have not been theorized in research on socio-spatial aspects of entrepreneurship, a gap that needs to be addressed going forward if we are to better understand how one's relationships and their network influence entrepreneurial activity.

Furthermore, academics have largely focused on the benefits of social capital (e.g., Dahl & Sorenson, 2009), overlooking the possibility that social capital may also yield negative externalities (de Vaan, Frenken, & Boschma, 2019). As Coleman (1988: S105) observed, "social capital...not only facilitates certain actions; it constrains others" and "effective norms in an area can reduce innovativeness in an area, not only deviant actions that harm others but also deviant actions that can benefit everyone." High social capital fosters conformity bias within tight communities, with regard to both values and ideas, which poses a barrier for new venture creation in nascent industries. Sorenson's research delves into the positive role that social relationships play in business founding (Rickne et al., 2018), but it ignores the possibility that behaviors 'off the beaten track' may also be less accepted in communities with strong social capital. Ongoing research on the 'bright side' of social capital has taught us much about how relationships and networks promote entrepreneurial activity. It is now time to also look at the 'dark side' of social capital to advance our understanding of the role of relationships and networks in impeding entrepreneurial activity, especially the kind of productive entrepreneurship that researchers and policy-makers are most interested in (Minniti, 2008).

Summary

This chapter focuses on four GAER awardees, namely Giacomo Beattini, Charles Sabel, Maryann Feldman, and Olav Sorenson, all of who were recognized for their contributions to research on the socio-spatial aspects of entrepreneurship. Over the past three decades, the intersection of geography and entrepreneurship has attracted an increasing number of scholars (Thornton & Flynn, 2003; Trettin & Welter, 2011). Despite growing interest, several scholars have criticized how little we know about entrepreneurship as an economic activity embedded in the social and spatial context (Malecki, 1997; Steyaert & Katz, 2004). Alvedalen and Boschma (2017) recently noted that "the systemic nature of entrepreneurial activity is still underdeveloped," by which they mean that academic understanding of the interactions between various elements that increase the "entrepreneurial performance of a region" remains rudimentary. Yet, the question of why some places grow and prosper is a fundamental question in social science that has concerned scholars and policy-makers for decades, if not centuries. The work of the four GAER awardees discussed here has done much to develop geography-entrepreneurship as an "increasingly relevant" topic of research that attracts scholars from around the world, but ample avenues remain for future inquiry (Müller, 2016: 1134).

REFERENCES

Acs, Z. J., Audretsch, D. B., & Feldman, M. P. (1994a). R&D spillovers and innovative activity. *Managerial and Decision Economics, 15*(2), 131–138.

Acs, Z. J., Audretsch, D. B., & Feldman, M. P. (1994b). R&D spillovers and recipient firm size. *Review of Economics and Statistics, 76*(2), 336–340.

Acs, Z. J., & Varga, A. (2005). Entrepreneurship, agglomeration and technological change. *Small Business Economics, 24*(3), 323–334.

Adner, R., Polos, L., Ryall, M., & Sorenson, O. (2009). The case for formal theory. *Academy of Management Review, 34*(2), 201–208.

Aharonson, B. S., Baum, J. A., & Feldman, M. P. (2007). Desperately seeking spillovers? Increasing returns, industrial organization and the location of new entrants in geographic and technological space. *Industrial and Corporate Change, 16*(1), 89–130.

Alcacer, J., & Gittelman, M. (2006). Patent citations as a measure of knowledge flows: The influence of examiner citations. *Review of Economics and Statistics, 88*(4), 774–779.

Alvarez, S. A., Agarwal, R. R., & Sorenson, O. (2006). Introduction. In S. A. Alvarez, R. R. Agarwal, & O. Sorenson (Eds.), *Handbook of entrepreneurship research: Disciplinary perspectives* (pp. 1–10). New York: Springer.

Alvedalen, J., & Boschma, R. (2017). A critical review of entrepreneurial ecosystems research: Towards a future research agenda. *European Planning Studies, 25*(6), 887–903.

Amin, A. (2000). Industrial districts. In E. Sheppard & T. J. Barnes (Eds.), *A companion to economic geography* (pp. 149–168). Malden, MA: Blackwell.

Andersson, D. E. (2005). The spatial nature of entrepreneurship. *Quarterly Journal of Austrian Economics, 8*(2), 21–34.

Audretsch, D. B., & Feldman, M. P. (1996). R&D spillovers and the geography of innovation and production. *American Economic Review, 86*(3), 630–640.

Backman, M., & Lööf, H. (2015). The geography of innovation and entrepreneurship. *The Annals of Regional Science, 55*(1), 1–6.

Becattini, G. (1979/1989). Sectors and/or districts: Some remarks on the conceptual foundations of industrial economics. In E. Goodman, J. Bamford, & P. Saynor (Eds.), *Small firms and industrial districts in Italy* (pp. 123–135). London: Routledge.

Becattini, G. (1991). Italian industrial districts: Problems and perspectives. *International Studies of Management & Organization, 21*(1), 83–90.

Becattini, G. (2001). *The caterpillar and the butterfly: An exemplary case of development in the Italy of the industrial districts.* Florence: Felice Le Monnier.

Bellandi, M. (1989). The industrial district in Marshall. In E. Goodman, J. Bamford, & P. Saynor (Eds.), *Small firms and industrial districts in Italy* (pp. 136–152). London: Routledge.

Belussi, F., & Sedita, S. R. (2019). Innovation districts. In A. M. Orum (Ed.), *The Wiley Blackwell encyclopedia of urban and regional studies* (pp. 1–5). Chichester: Wiley.

Bianchi, G. (1996). *Double shift: Towards a convergence between spatial systems of small and large enterprises?* 36th European Congress of European Regional Science Association, Zurich, Switzerland.

Borgatti, S. P., Brass, D. J., & Halgin, D. S. (2014). Social network research: Confusions, criticisms, and controversies. *Research in the Sociology of Organizations, 40,* 1–29.

Breschi, S., & Lissoni, F. (2001). Knowledge spillovers and local innovation systems: A critical survey. *Industrial and Corporate Change, 10*(4), 975–1005.

Brody, D. (1985). Review of the book *The second industrial divide. Reviews in American History, 13*(4), 612–615.

Brusco, S. (1990). The idea of the industrial district: Its genesis. In F. Pyke, G. Becattini, & W. Sengenberger (Eds.), *Industrial districts and inter-firm co-operation in Italy* (pp. 10–19). Geneva, Switzerland: International Institute for Labor Studies.

Cicarelli, J., & Cicarelli, J. (2003). *Distinguished women economists.* Westport, CT: Greenwood.

Chiles, T. H., Bluedorn, A. C., & Gupta, V. K. (2007). Beyond creative destruction and entrepreneurial discovery: A radical Austrian approach to entrepreneurship. *Organization Studies, 28*(4), 467–493.

Clark, G. L., Feldman, M. P., & Gertler, M. S. (2000). *The Oxford handbook of economic geography.* Oxford: Oxford University Press.

Clark, G. L., Feldman, M. P., Gertler, M. S., & Wójcik, D. (2018). Introduction: Economic geography in the twenty-first century. In G. Clark, M. Feldman, M. Gertler, & D. Wójcik (Eds.), *The new Oxford handbook of economic geography*. Oxford: Oxford University Press.

Coleman, J. S. (1988). Social capital in the creation of human capital. *American Journal of Sociology, 94*, S95–S120.

Dahl, M. S., & Pedersen, C. Ø. (2004). Knowledge flows through informal contacts in industrial clusters: Myth or reality? *Research Policy, 33*(10), 1673–1686.

Dahl, M. S., & Sorenson, O. (2009). The embedded entrepreneur. *European Management Review, 6*(3), 172–181.

Dahl, M. S., & Sorenson, O. (2010a). The migration of technical workers. *Journal of Urban Economics, 67*(1), 33–45.

Dahl, M. S., & Sorenson, O. (2010b). The social attachment to place. *Social Forces, 89*(2), 633–658.

Dahl, M. S., & Sorenson, O. (2012). Home sweet home: Entrepreneurs' location choices and the performance of their ventures. *Management Science, 58*(6), 1059–1071.

de Vaan, M., Frenken, K., & Boschma, R. (2019). The downside of social capital in new industry creation. *Economic Geography, 95*(4), 315–340.

Domenech, J., & Rosés, J. R. (2016). Technology transfer and the early development of the cotton textile industry in nineteenth century Spain. In T. Hashino & K. Otsuka (Eds.), *Industrial districts in history and the developing world* (pp. 25–41). Singapore: Springer.

Engelstoft, S., Jensen-Butler, C., Smith, I., & Winther, L. (2006). Industrial clusters in Denmark: Theory and empirical evidence. *Papers in Regional Science, 85*(1), 73–98.

Feldman, M. P. (1993). An examination of the geography of innovation. *Industrial and Corporate Change, 2*(3), 451–470.

Feldman, M. P. (1994). Knowledge complementarity and innovation. *Small Business Economics, 6*(5), 363–372.

Feldman, M. P. (2001). The entrepreneurial event revisited: Firm formation in a regional context. *Industrial and Corporate Change, 10*(4), 861–891.

Feldman, M. P., & Audretsch, D. B. (1999). Innovation in cities: Science-based diversity, specialization and localized competition. *European Economic Review, 43*(2), 409–429.

Feldman, M. P., & Florida, R. (1994). The geographic sources of innovation: Technological infrastructure and product innovation in the United States. *Annals of the Association of American Geographers, 84*(2), 210–229.

Feldman, M. P., & Francis, J. L. (2003). Fortune favours the prepared region: The case of entrepreneurship and the capitol region biotechnology cluster. *European Planning Studies, 11*(7), 765–788.

Feldman, M. P., & Kogler, D. F. (2010). Stylized facts in the geography of innovation. In *Handbook of the economics of innovation* (Vol. 1, pp. 381–410). North-Holland: Elsevier.

Feldman, M., & Lowe, N. (2008). Consensus from controversy: Cambridge's biosafety ordinance and the anchoring of the biotech industry. *European Planning Studies, 16*(3), 395–410.

Feldman, M., & Schreuder, Y. (1996). Initial advantage: The origins of the geographic concentration of the pharmaceutical industry in the Mid-Atlantic region. *Industrial and Corporate Change, 5*(3), 839–862.

Fried, V. H. (2003). Defining a forum for entrepreneurship scholars. *Journal of Business Venturing, 18*(1), 1–11.

Garofoli, G. (1991). The Italian model of spatial development in the 1970s and 1980s. In G. Benko & M. Dunford (Eds.), *Industrial change and regional development* (pp. 85–101). London: Belhaven.

Gartner, W. B., Bird, B. J., & Starr, J. A. (1992). Acting as if: Differentiating entrepreneurial from organizational behavior. *Entrepreneurship Theory and Practice, 16*(3), 13–32.

Gimeno, J., Folta, T. B., Cooper, A. C., & Woo, C. Y. (1997). Survival of the fittest? Entrepreneurial human capital and the persistence of underperforming firms. *Administrative Science Quarterly, 42*(4), 750–783.

Goodman, E. (1989). Introduction: The political economy of the small firm in Italy. In E. Goodman & J. Bamford (Eds.), *Small firms and industrial districts in Italy* (pp. 1–3). London: Routledge.

Gupta, V., & Gupta, A. (2015). The concept of entrepreneurial orientation. *Foundations and Trends in Entrepreneurship, 11*(2), 55–137.

Harrison, B. (1992). Industrial districts: Old wine in new bottles? *Regional Studies, 26*(5), (S1), S107–S121.

Hashino, T. (2016). Promotion of the weaving districts in modern Japan. In T. Hashino & K. Otsuka (Eds.), *Industrial districts in history and the developing world* (pp. 153–167). Singapore: Springer.

Hashino, T., & Otsuka, K. (2016). Beyond Marshallian agglomeration economies. In T. Hashino & K. Otsuka (Eds.), *Industrial districts in history and the developing world* (pp. 3–12). Singapore: Springer.

Jaffe, A. B., Trajtenberg, M., & Henderson, R. (1993). Geographic localization of knowledge spillovers as evidenced by patent citations. *Quarterly Journal of Economics, 108*(3), 577–598.

Kirchhoff, B. A. (1997). Entrepreneurship economics. In W. B. Bygrave (Ed.), *The portable MBA in entrepreneurship* (pp. 444–474). New York: Wiley.

Kristensen, P. H. (1989). Denmark: An experimental laboratory for new industrial models. *Entrepreneurship & Regional Development, 1*(3), 245–255.

Krugman, P. R. (1991). *Geography and trade*. Cambridge: MIT Press.

Kuckertz, A., & A. Prochotta (2018). *What's hot in entrepreneurship research 2018?* (Hohenheim Entrepreneurship Research Brief, No. 4). University of Hohenheim, Germany.

Landstrom, H. (2005). *Pioneers in entrepreneurship and small business research.* Boston, MA: Springer Science & Business Media.

Lorenzen, M., & Carlsson, B. (2014). Maryann Feldman: Recipient of the 2013 Global Award for Entrepreneurship Research. *Small Business Economics, 43*(1), 1–8.

Malecki, E. J. (1997). Entrepreneurs, networks, and economic development: A review of recent research. In J. A. Katz (Ed.), *Advances in entrepreneurship, firm emergence and growth* (Vol. 3, pp. 57–118). Greenwich, CT: JAI Press.

Markusen, A. (2002). Sticky places in slippery space: A typology of industrial districts. In *The new industrial geography* (pp. 120–146). London: Routledge.

Marshall, A. (1890). *Principles of economics.* London: Macmillan.

Marshall, A. (1919). *Industry and trade.* London: Macmillan.

Maskell, P. (2001). Towards a knowledge-based theory of the geographical cluster. *Industrial and Corporate Change, 10*(4), 921–943.

Minniti, M. (2008). The role of government policy on entrepreneurial activity: Productive, unproductive, or destructive? *Entrepreneurship Theory and Practice, 32*(5), 779–790.

Müller, S. (2016). A progress review of entrepreneurship and regional development: What are the remaining gaps? *European Planning Studies, 24*(6), 1133–1158.

Ottaviano, G. I., & Thisse, J. F. (2005). New economic geography: What about the N? *Environment and Planning A, 37*(10), 1707–1725.

Piore, M. J., & Sabel, C. F. (1984). *The second industrial divide.* New York: Basic books.

Plummer, L. A., & Pe'er, A. (2010). The geography of entrepreneurship. *Handbook of entrepreneurship research* (pp. 519–556). New York: Springer.

Reitzig, M., & Sorenson, O. (2013). Biases in the selection stage of bottom-up strategy formulation. *Strategic Management Journal, 34*(7), 782–799.

Rickne, A., Ruef, M., & Wennberg, K. (2018). The socially and spatially bounded relationships of entrepreneurial activity: Olav Sorenson—Recipient of the 2018 Global Award for Entrepreneurship Research. *Small Business Economics, 51*(3), 515–525.

Rodríguez-Pose, A. (2001). Killing economic geography with a "cultural turn" overdose. *Antipode, 33*(2), 176–182.

Rogan, M., & Sorenson, O. (2014). Picking a (poor) partner: A relational perspective on acquisitions. *Administrative Science Quarterly, 59*(2), 301–329.

Rubén, L. S., Isabel, N. G., & Coro, C. Y. (2017). Entrepreneurship at regional level: Temporary and neighborhood effects. *Entrepreneurship Research Journal, 7*(4), 1–12.

Russo, M. (1985). Technical change and the industrial district: The role of inter-firm relations in the growth and transformation of ceramic tile production in Italy. *Research Policy, 14,* 329–343.

Sammarra, A., & Biggiero, L. (2001). Identity and identification in industrial districts. *Journal of Management and Governance, 5*(1), 61–82.

Schmitz, H., & Musyck, B. (2016). Industrial districts in Europe: Policy lessons for developing countries? In T. Hashino & K. Otsuka (Eds.), *Industrial districts in history and the developing world* (pp. 117–151). Singapore: Springer.

Sforzi, F. (1989). The geography of industrial districts in Italy. In E. Goodman, J. Bamford, & P. Saynor (Eds.), *Small firms and industrial districts in Italy* (pp. 153–173). London: Routledge.

Shane, S. (2012). Reflections on the 2010 AMR decade award: Delivering on the promise of entrepreneurship as a field of research. *Academy of Management Review, 37*(1), 10–20.

Shane, S., & Venkataraman, S. (2000). The promise of entrepreneurship as a field of research. *Academy of Management Review, 25*(1), 217–226.

Shi, Y., Sorenson, O., & Waguespack, D. M. (2017). Temporal issues in repli-cation: The stability of centrality-based advantage. *Sociological Science, 4,* 107–122.

Sonobe, T. (2016). Emergence and subsequent development of garment clusters in Bangladesh and Tanzania. In T. Hashino & K. Otsuka (Eds.), *Industrial districts in history and the developing world* (pp. 61–79). Singapore: Springer.

Sorenson, O. (2003). Social networks and industrial geography. *Journal of Evolutionary Economics, 13,* 513–527.

Sorenson, O. (2018). Social networks and the geography of entrepreneurship. *Small Business Economics, 51*(3), 527–537.

Sorenson, O., & Audia, P. G. (2000). The social structure of entrepreneurial activity: Geographic concentration of footwear production in the United States, 1940–1989. *American Journal of Sociology, 106*(2), 424–462.

Sorenson, O., & Stuart, T. E. (2001). Syndication networks and the spatial distri-bution of venture capital investments. *American Journal of Sociology, 106*(6), 1546–1588.

Sorenson, O., & Stuart, T. E. (2008a). Entrepreneurship: A field of dreams? *Academy of Management Annals, 2*(1), 517–543.

Sorenson, O., & Stuart, T. E. (2008b). Bringing the context back in: Settings and the search for syndicate partners in venture capital investment networks. *Administrative Science Quarterly, 53*(2), 266–294.

Sorenson, O., & Waguespack, D. M. (2006). Social structure and exchange: Self-confirming dynamics in Hollywood. *Administrative Science Quarterly, 51*(4), 560–589.

Sorenson, O., Rivkin, J. W., & Fleming, L. (2006). Complexity, networks and knowledge flow. *Research Policy, 35*(7), 994–1017.

Sternberg, R. (2009). Regional dimensions of entrepreneurship. *Foundations and Trends in Entrepreneurship, 5*(4), 211–340.

Steyaert, C., & Katz, J. (2004). Reclaiming the space of entrepreneurship in society: Geographical, discursive and social dimensions. *Entrepreneurship & Regional Development, 16*(3), 179–196.

Stuart, T. E., & Sorenson, O. (2003a). The geography of opportunity: Spatial heterogeneity in founding rates and the performance of biotechnology firms. *Research Policy, 32*(2), 229–253.

Stuart, T. E., & Sorenson, O. (2003b). Liquidity events and the geographic distribution of entrepreneurial activity. *Administrative Science Quarterly, 48*(2), 175–201.

Stuart, T. E., & Sorenson, O. (2007). Strategic networks and entrepreneurial ventures. *Strategic Entrepreneurship Journal, 1*(3–4), 211–227.

Thornton, P. H., & Flynn, K. H. (2003). Entrepreneurship, networks, and geographies. *Handbook of entrepreneurship research* (pp. 401–433). Boston, MA: Springer.

Trettin, L., & Welter, F. (2011). Challenges for spatially oriented entrepreneurship research. *Entrepreneurship & Regional Development, 23*(7–8), 575–602.

Vernus, P. (2016). Trade associations and economic regulation in the Lyons Fabrique: From the 1860s to the 1920s. In T. Hashino & K. Otsuka (Eds.), *Industrial districts in history and the developing world* (pp. 83–100). Singapore: Springer.

Zahra, S. A. (2005). Entrepreneurship and disciplinary scholarship: Return to the fountainhead. In S. A. Alvarez, R. Agarwal, & O. Sorenson (Eds.), *Handbook of entrepreneurship research* (pp. 253–268). Boston, MA: Springer.

Zahra, S. A., Wright, M., & Abdelgawad, S. G. (2014). Contextualization and the advancement of entrepreneurship research. *International Small Business Journal, 32*(5), 479–500.

CHAPTER 5

From the Disciplines

Entrepreneurship researchers have long celebrated that "scholars from diverse vantage points and fields of orientation" are interested in contributing to a better understanding of entrepreneurial activity (Hisrich, 1988: 3). The belief that "no single subject discipline has a monopoly of wisdom about what entrepreneurship is, or how entrepreneurs behave" is quite widespread (Parker, 2005: 1). It is well known that entrepreneurship inquiry, like management and organizational research in general, builds on psychological, sociological, and economic scholarship (Grégoire, Noel, Dery, & Bechard, 2006; Streb & Gupta, 2011). Contributions to entrepreneurship research go beyond these disciplines, however. Theories, principles, and research methods from a variety of disciplines, including the liberal arts and natural sciences, have frequently been used in advancing knowledge about entrepreneurship. Low (2001: 21 emphasis original) contends that "entrepreneurship is a phenomenon or a set of questions that can and *should* be investigated from multiple disciplines and perspectives," an argument that continues to resonate with entrepreneurship scholars. Some go as far as to claim that "much of the best research in entrepreneurship" appears in the good journals of other disciplines (Acs & Audretsch, 2003: 5).

Landström and Benner (2010: 38) divide the academic field of entrepreneurship research into two distinct groups of scholars: a community of 'entrepreneurship researchers' with a disciplinary anchor in

© The Author(s) 2020   99
V. K. Gupta, *Great Minds in Entrepreneurship Research*,
https://doi.org/10.1007/978-3-030-44125-8_5

management studies (let's call them Type X) and another community of researchers anchored in different disciplines who sometimes do entrepreneurship research (let's call them Type Y). There is, however, another important—albeit small—research group in entrepreneurship: researchers from other disciplines who view themselves primarily as entrepreneurship scholars. These researchers participate actively in the ongoing scholarly conversation about entrepreneurial phenomena (let's call them Type Z). Type Z scholars have strong disciplinary roots, but their contributions are targeted largely at advancing the conversation in entrepreneurship. Most likely, the Type Z camp is small and scattered across several different disciplines, which makes this group of scholars seem even smaller to those on the outside.

The citations for the GAER awardees reveal that four scholars have been recognized for advancing entrepreneurship research from a disciplinary perspective: the 2000 award to Howard Aldrich, in 2003 to William Baumol, in 2006 to Israel Kirzner, and in 2010 to Josh Lerner. All four scholars have done interesting research about entrepreneurial phenomena, as discussed below in order.

Howard Aldrich: A Sociological Perspective

The 2000 GAER awardee, Howard Aldrich, was recognized for "integrating the most central questions of the field, examining the formation and evolution of new and small firms within a broader sociological research context." Over the course of his career, Aldrich (2012: 1240) saw entrepreneurship research transform "from groups of isolated scholars doing research on small businesses to an international community of departments, institutes, and foundations promoting research on new and high-growth firms." Drawing on his sociological training, Aldrich made seminal contributions to the evolution of the academic field of entrepreneurship and remained true to his disciplinary training throughout his academic career (Landström, 2005). Sociologists have long been interested in how social structures—whether in the form of norms, expectations, interpersonal relations, or institutions—constrain and facilitate human action and choices. Not surprisingly, there is a strong recognition that "the field of sociology has much to offer….to those interested in studying entrepreneurship" (Alvarez, Agarwal, & Sorenson, 2005: 6). In applauding Aldrich's contributions to entrepreneurship research, Landström (2005: 325) noted that his "work is characterized by true scientific curiosity and a theoretical strength that is unique in entrepreneurship research."

Aldrich's interest in new business founding goes back to his doctoral days when he was studying how small business owners coped with hostile conditions around them (Landström, 2005). Aldrich is seen as a prominent example of someone whose contributions to entrepreneurship inquiry rested on his deep understanding of one central theoretical framework: evolutionary theory (Landström, 2005). For Aldrich and Martinez (2001: 42), evolutionary theory uniquely brings together "in a single coherent framework a concern for entrepreneurial outcomes and the processes and contexts making them possible, using the basic concepts of variation, adaptation, selection, and retention." Because evolutionary approaches allow to study the birth of new organizations (variation), ways in which firms adapt to survive as environments change (adaptation), when such efforts succeed in increasing organizational survival (selection), and how successful arrangements are imitated by others (retention), scholars can use evolutionary theory to better understand entrepreneurial phenomena.

To make sense of Aldrich's contributions to entrepreneurship research, one needs to start by understanding the evolutionary perspective. Given that, on the whole, evolution is considered a solid body of scientific knowledge, albeit with ample subfields worthy of continued discovery and sustained research, it would seem that evolutionary theory is well understood. Unfortunately, that is far from the case. As Hodgson (2013: 973) observed, evolution is "a widely used but ambiguous term." Evolutionary theory, as is generally known, originated with the publication of Charles Darwin's seminal work *The Origin of Species* in 1859. However, Darwin did not, as many believe, "discover or invent evolution" (Dunnell, 1980: 39). Darwin, in fact, seems to have avoided the term 'evolution' and employed the phrase 'descent with modification' instead (Ruse, 1999). And yet, even during Darwin's own lifetime, evolution was being credited to Darwin, including by his critics.

For most scholars, the goal of Darwin's work was twofold: to establish the mutability of organic species in their "descent out of the past" and to offer natural selection as "the primary mechanism" to explain these variations (Gillispie, 1958: 388). As Darwin (1871: 61) wrote, "I had two distinct objects in view; firstly to show that species had not been separately created, and secondly, that natural selection had been the chief agent of change." The Darwinian position considers the evolutionary process as

comprising of three distinct mechanisms: variation, selection, and retention. Variation deals with how variety is generated and replenished in a
population, selection pertains to the factors facilitate the survival of some
variations rather than others, forcing a reduction in variety, and retention refers to how useful information concerning solutions to adaptive
problems is transmitted across generations.

Aldrich and Pfeffer's (1976: 81) explanation of the three core mechanisms of Darwinian evolution is worth repeating here in full because it is
this framework that remained consistent throughout Aldrich's subsequent
work (Landström, 2005):

> The first stage … is the occurrence of variations for whatever reason,
> planned or unplanned. In organic evolution, variations occur through the
> genetic mutation process, while in the learning process variation occurs in
> the exploratory responses made to stimuli. Variations are the raw material
> from which the selection process culls those structures or behaviors that
> are most suitable. The second stage is the operation of consistent selection
> criteria that differentially select some variations over others or selectively
> eliminate certain variations. In organic evolution the differential survival
> of certain mutant forms that are better able to exploit the food supply
> in their environment reflects the operation of a resource-based selection
> criterion. Differential reinforcement of particular exploratory responses by
> animals, in a consistent manner, is the selection stage in the learning
> process. The third stage in the ecological process involves the operation of
> a retention mechanism for the selective retention of the positively selected
> variations. Retention occurs when certain variations are preserved, dupli-
> cated, or reproduced. In organic evolution the retention mechanism is the
> chromosome-gene system. Positively selected variations survive and repro-
> duce similar others. For the learning process the memory system is the
> means whereby positively selected responses can be recalled for future use.
> The process as described is perfectly general and can be applied to any situ-
> ation where the three stages are present. The three-stage model completely
> describes the evolutionary process.

Low and Macmillan (1988) identified two major research perspectives
in entrepreneurship research: environmental determinism (population
ecology), which considers environmental selection as the decision factor
in firm survival and strategic choice, where the individual entrepreneur
decides the trajectory of the firm. Breslin (2008) views evolutionary
theory (and Aldrich's work in this area) as incorporating both major
perspectives, providing a middle-way to understand entrepreneurship.

Evolution as the middle-path is about how entrepreneurs learn as they create new organizations, and based on feedback in the form of outcomes to their efforts, adapt their strategies through interaction with the environment (Hrebiniak & Joyce, 1985).

Aldrich (1979) focuses on organizational change, particularly the "conditions under which organizations are created, grow, establish relations with important actors in their environments, adopt tactics for survival, and quite often, fail" (page 1).[1] Taking the position that the survival and growth of organizations are an attribute of the population (Astley, 1980) and Aldrich (1979) encouraged researchers to analyze total 'populations' of organizations in their environments. Freeman (1981: 1450) praised Aldrich (1979) for attempting to construct "an extensive conceptual scaffolding" on "very little empirical literature," suggesting that, when it came to the application of evolutionary theory to organizations, there was not yet enough empirical research to support the framework and arguments that Aldrich (1979) presented. Aldrich (2008: xvi) recounted that when he sought "an overarching framework for investigating organizational change" he was attracted to evolutionary logic "because it is generic framework for understanding social change...applicable at multiple levels of analysis."

Where Aldrich (1979) introduced the potential of evolutionary approach to explain organizational change, Aldrich (1999) is considered "a major leap forward" as it achieved a "stunning synthesis of the major organizational paradigms under the umbrella of evolutionary theory" (Dobbin, 2001: 1521). Wade (2002: 390) commended the "very broad, eclectic nature" of Aldrich's (1999) writing. For others (e.g., Buenger, 2000: 1004), Aldrich (1999) provides a good coverage of populations and communities, but does not meet the needs of readers who are "looking for the Darwinian imperative as it applies to organizations." Even though both Aldrich (1979) and Aldrich (1999) focused on an evolutionary approach, much had changed in Aldrich's thinking during the two decades between the two books. In the 1970s, Aldrich (2018: 22) saw himself as "an organizational sociologist studying organizations from an evolutionary point of view," but by the end of the century, he had emerged as a prominent entrepreneurship scholar. Most

---

[1] The book was originally titled *The Organizations and its Environment*, but Aldrich came to realize that "using the definite article (the) implied a homogeneity and singularity in which [he] no longer believed" (Aldrich, 2008: xvii).

Ph.D. students interested in entrepreneurship get their first exposure to Aldrich's work from reading Aldrich and Fiol (1994). By 1999, Aldrich had come to believe that "many of the phenomena that interested" him were "much easier to study in the entrepreneurial context, where things are fresh, new, and small and constituted an instant organizational laboratory with thousands of replications every day" (Aldrich, 2018: 22). Interestingly, in a departure from strict Darwinian evolutionary logic, Aldrich and Fiol (1994: 647) emphasized the "cumulative way in which entrepreneurial activity plays a role in reshaping the larger environmental context." For Aldrich and Martinez (2001: 52), emphasizing the varied actions entrepreneurs take to successfully create and manage their firm contributed to "a more evolutionary view of entrepreneurial activities."

Aldrich and Ruef (2006: 3) sought to explain the "evolutionary processes through which new organizations, populations and communities emerge, using an approach that cuts across academic disciplines." Stoelhorst (2008: 1017) commend Aldrich and Ruef (2006) for their deep dive into "Aldrich's evolutionary perspective as it took shape in the wake of the diversity of new theoretical developments of the 1970s." Many others, however, were considerably more scathing in their analysis. Describing Aldrich and Ruef (2006) a "chore to read," Glor (2006), for example, criticized it for focusing too narrowly on business organizations and ignoring the historical context within which the organizations evolved. The criticism about ahistoricity in the study of organizations is particularly salient when one considers that the "evolutionary approach encompasses many of the best features of historical research on organizations" (Lippmann & Aldrich, 2014: 125). The strength of Aldrich and Ruef (2006) lay in its treatment of evolutionary theory at multiple levels of analysis, directing attention to the processes of variation, selection, and retention that jointly produce change in systems struggling for survival. For entrepreneurship scholars, Aldrich and Ruef's (2006) message was that those evolutionary processes are driven by the entrepreneurs and organizations striving to obtain scarce resources.

Landström (2005) described Aldrich as "an internationally recognized organizational sociologist, who has highlighted entrepreneurship," praising him for effectively demonstrating "how a researcher from a core scientific discipline can contribute important insights into the field of entrepreneurship." While evolutionary theory is at the core of Aldrich's research, his research has also delved into other important areas in entrepreneurship research. His scholarship includes areas as diverse as ethnic entrepreneurship (e.g., Aldrich & Waldinger, 1990; Waldinger, Aldrich, & Ward, 1990; Zimmer & Aldrich, 1987), gender entrepreneurship (Baker, Aldrich, & Nina, 1997; Renzulli, Aldrich, & Moody, 2000; Yang & Aldrich, 2014), social networks (Aldrich & Kim, 2007; Kim & Aldrich, 2005; Kim, Aldrich, & Keister, 2006), and even crowdfunding (Aldrich, 2014), among others (e.g., Aldrich & Cliff, 2003; Aldrich & Yang, 2012; Yang & Aldrich, 2012).

Ever since the publication of Darwin (1859)'s seminal work, there has been tremendous interest in the possibility of expanding the evolutionary approach beyond the domain of biology to fields of study as diverse as language, psychology, economics, and culture (Breslin, 2010). Darwin himself suggested generalizing core Darwinian principles to cover the evolution of social entities (Hodgson, 2007). Many scholars credit Darwin with proposing that natural selection operates upon the elements of language and that natural selection favors tribal groups with moral and other propensities that served the common good (Aldrich et al. 2008). For Universal Darwinists, at a sufficiently general level of abstraction, the principles of variation, selection, and retention can be used to describe evolution within a variety of domains (Breslin, 2008).[2] However, the generalization of core Darwinian principles to other disciplines has been passionately advocated by some and vehemently resisted by others (Dennett, 1995), an ongoing debate that has not gone unnoticed even in the popular press (Wade, 2009).

Some have argued that Darwinistic explanations of organizational change ignore the interaction of the actor with the external environment through feedback (Cordes, 2006). This seems to have been the concern of Hougland and Shepard (1980: 139) when they observed that Aldrich (1979) had "little to say about how organizations influence external actors" and "ignores the "environmental *impact* of organizations." In biological evolution, the environment cannot be affected by the entities, but instead it is the organisms that cope with the environment more or less successfully. Aldrich does seem to recognize that organizations can

---

[2] The term 'Universal Darwinism' was coined by Richard Dawkins to suggest that the core Darwinian principles of variation, replication, and selection apply not only to biological phenomena but also to other open and evolving systems, including human cultural or social evolution (cf. Dawkins, 1983). Hodgson and Knudsen (2004) initially adopted the term 'universalized' Darwinism to characterize their position, but Hodgson and Knudsen (2006) employed the term "generalized" Darwinism. Both terms are now used interchangeably in the literature (Buenstorf, 2006).

affect their environment, but only in a very limited fashion. To quote Aldrich (1979: 292–293), "the 2% of all business organizations in the US with receipts of more than $1,000,000 are in good positions to influence their environments, whereas the two-thirds with less than $25,000 in receipts are poorly placed for such attempts." Notwithstanding concerns about "two empirically untestable statements" in the above sentence (Astley, 1980: 285), the truth is that even small firms have been found to have substantive impact on organizations. The popular press is replete with stories of how, despite being unprofitable, upstart firms like Uber and WeWork were able to challenge environmental constraints and forced major stakeholders to adjust to a new reality. There seems no biological equivalent of the widespread phenomena that (some, but not all) organizations are able to bring about environmental change. Indeed, Astley (1980: 286) criticized Aldrich (1979) for taking the position that "most organizations are, in an absolute sense, small, powerless, and transfixed by their environment."

Aldrich (1999) is recognized as a prominent advocate for a meta-theoretical 'evolutionary perspective' as a way to "express the conceptual core and unite separate disciplinary approaches" in the social sciences (Hodgson & Lamberg, 2018: 168). Lippmann and Aldrich (2014) explain their position thus:

> Evolutionary theory in organizational analysis is a set of heuristic propositions about how entities develop through time (Aldrich, 1979; Langton, 1984). It uses and adapts Darwinian theories of natural selection, in combination with Probability and Complexity Theories, resulting in a meta-theoretical framework that explains how organizational emergence, change, and reproduction occur through the interaction of blind and intentional variations with environmental selection forces. Recent developments in evolutionary theory have emphasized two things. First, they have focused on the multi-level nature of evolutionary processes between groups within organizations, across organizations, and across populations and communities. Second, they have demonstrated the interdependence of selection and adaptation processes. When organizational actors adapt to their environments by actively choosing particular variations, they not only select them into their own organizations but also introduce new selection forces into organizational populations through a variety of learning and isomorphic processes. (Argote & Miron-Spektor, 2011)

Evolutionary theory, as understood by Universal Darwinists, uses v-s-r logic (variation, selection, and retention) to describe phenomena within a variety of domains, which makes it quite cross-disciplinary. Glor (2006) criticizes Aldrich and Ruef (2006) for ignoring the knowledge accumulated in other social sciences and building an understanding of organizations on a very narrow knowledge base. Clearly, the academic conversation about important evolutionary issues associated with the organizational world remains in flux. Much has been learned, yet much more work still needs to be done.

WILLIAM BAUMOL: AN ECONOMIC VIEW

The 2003 GAER recipient, William Baumol, was among the first economists to highlight the absence of the entrepreneurial element in mainstream economics, encouraging fellow economists to pay attention to the role of entrepreneurship in the economy. To repeat his now famous words, from an economics perspective, the "theoretical firm is entrepreneurless – the Prince of Denmark has been expunged from the discussion of *Hamlet*" (Baumol, 1968: 68).[3] He has been hailed as "one of the great economists of the 20th century... whose stray thought on a sleepless night could change how people see the world" (*The Economist*, 2017: 33).[4] The official GAER citation honors Baumol "for his persistent effort to give the entrepreneur a key role in mainstream economic theory, for his theoretical and empirical studies of the nature of entrepreneurship, and for his analysis of the importance of institutions and incentives for the allocation of entrepreneurship."

---

[3] Schumpeter (1942: 86) uses a similar formulation: A "theoretical construction which neglects this essential element of the case neglects all that is most typically capitalist about it... it is like Hamlet without the Danish prince."

[4] The 'stray thought on a sleepless night' referred here is the principle that later came to bear his name: Baumol's cost disease. Grappling with the question of why the cost of presenting and attending arts was going up, Baumol had an epiphany one early morning in the 1960s. As Baumol recounted in an interview with the economist Alan Krueger (2001), "One night, it was 4:00 in the morning, I suddenly woke up and said I know why those costs are going up! I got up, wrote down a few notes, and went to sleep again. That's literally how it happened." At its core, Baumol's cost disease is the idea that personally delivered services—medical care, musical performances, and education, for example—will increase in price year after year. See Baumol (1967), Baumol and Bowen (1966).

Baumol's earliest contribution to entrepreneurship research stems from his seminal observations about the virtual absence of the entrepreneur from the mainstream economics literature (Baumol, 1968), urging economists to pay serious attention to the role of entrepreneurship in economic development (Schiller & Crewson, 1997). The starting point for Baumol (1968) was neoclassical economics. Conventional interpretations of the neoclassical model posit that all individuals have perfect information and their economic objectives are clearly established and unambiguously stated. In the neoclassical world, producers and consumers reach one set of prices at which the supply of each good is equal to its demand, and all markets that are assumed to exist are cleared at equilibrium prices (Wennekers & Thurik, 1999). As van Praag (1999: 317) noted, the neoclassical model, with "its production function, the logic of rational choice and perfect information; leaves no room for an active entrepreneur...the firm runs itself...[and] the entrepreneur has vanished." By the 1960s, the surprising absence of the entrepreneur from the mainstream economics literature was already being lamented by many economists (Bosma, 2011; Hamilton, 2011). Baumol's (1968) witty comment likening the entrepreneur to the Prince of Denmark earned him the reputation of being a vocal critic of the absence of the entrepreneur from the theoretical firm (Deligonul, Hult, & Cavusgil, 2008).[5]

Baumol, perhaps more than any other modern economist before him, noted the conflicted position of the entrepreneur in economic thinking. Baumol (1968: 64) observed that the entrepreneur "has long been recognized as the apex of the hierarchy that determines the behavior of the firm and thereby bears a heavy responsibility for the vitality of the free enterprise society." Yet, and despite the apparent recognition of the crucial role entrepreneurs play (Schiller & Crewson, 1997), the entrepreneurial function had "virtually disappeared from the theoretical literature" in economics (Baumol, 1968: 64). Consequently, the entrepreneur was "at the same time one of the most intriguing and one of the most elusive characters in the cast that constitutes the subject of economic analysis" (Baumol, 1968: 64). Since then, and over the past five decades,

---

[5] Some have argued that, even though the (concept of) entrepreneur may be of critical importance for growth and innovation, the problem is that it lacks operational definition and does not lend itself to fitting in an analytical tool like the neoclassical model (Bianchi & Henrekson, 2005).

a number of commentators (e.g., Audretsch, 2014; Ferrante, 2005) have given Baumol (1968) credit for highlighting the absence of the entrepreneur from the neoclassical firm, invoking his eloquent likening of the economic firm to the Shakespeare's Hamlet without the Prince of Denmark (Hamilton, 2011). Scholars, however, remained divided over the impact Baumol (1968) had on economic thinking. Reynolds et al. (2005: 208) believe that, notwithstanding the thousands of citations to Baumol's work, the fact remains that "neoclassical economic models still do not take explicit account of the entrepreneur and entrepreneurial activity." Parker (2009: 3), on the other hand, believes that while Baumol (1968) was right in criticizing economists for not writing entrepreneurship into their models, the entrepreneur is now very much a "distinctive economic actor" in the new theories and perspectives currently prevalent in the economic literature.

Baumol's (1990) work on productive, unproductive, and destructive entrepreneurial activity has left a strong legacy (Griffiths, Kickul, Bacq, & Terjesen, 2012; Padilla, 2016), inspiring a "significant amount of research" and drawing an impressive body of citations (Minniti, 2016: 2015).[6] Baumol's (1990) original idea, subsequently expanded by him and other scholars (e.g., Baumol, 1993; Boettke & Coyne, 2003), was that entrepreneurship exists in (one form or another) every society, so that what differs across societies is not the degree of the underlying entrepreneurial talent, but how it is channeled or allocated among competing choices. In some societies, creative individuals are more likely to devote their efforts toward private sector wealth creation (productive entrepreneurship); in other societies, individual labor efforts may be more concerned with securing wealth redistribution through the political and legal processes (unproductive entrepreneurship) or criminal activities

[6] It was republished in 1996 in the *Journal of Business Venturing*, widely considered the top journal in entrepreneurship research (Stewart & Cotton, 2013). To celebrate the 25-year anniversary of the publication of Baumol (1990), a mini-symposium was organized at the 2015 annual meeting of the *Southern Economic Association* where several prominent scholars presented their research exploring specific themes from Baumol's seminal article. Selected papers from the conference symposium were published in a special issue of the *Journal of Entrepreneurship and Public Policy* (Padilla, 2016). McCaffrey (2018: 179) considered it a "landmark article" that was influential "across the social sciences and management disciplines," and it was included in a selective list of "classic articles" in entrepreneurship with "an enduring impact on the field" (Gupta, Guo, & Ozkazanc-Pan, 2018: 5).

(destructive entrepreneurship). Individuals prioritize where to target their efforts based on the rate of return to different types of activities, which is influenced by the institutional environment of their society. Thus, whether enterprising individuals will use their talents to create wealth as opposed to consuming or destroying wealth will depend largely on the incentives they face (Padilla, 2016), so that it is useful for researchers and policy-makers to focus on the 'rules of the game' within which entrepreneurs operate.

A detailed discussion of Baumol's many publications is virtually impossible within the constraints of a part-chapter in a book, but a few other notable contributions of his work are worth discussing here. First, Baumol distinguished between replicative (or 'firm-organizing') entrepreneurs and innovative (or 'Schumpeterian innovating') entrepreneurs, acknowledging that while the bulk of the entrepreneurial activity in society is associated with the former, it is the latter that drives economic growth in a modern society (Griffiths et al., 2012). Innovative entrepreneurs introduce products and production techniques not available before, and replicative (or imitative) entrepreneurs help diffuse innovative products and techniques after they have already been introduced. Second, Baumol (2010) identified four key pillars of a vibrant entrepreneurial economy: (a) starting a business should be relatively easy (i.e., ease of doing business should be high); (b) socially useful entrepreneurial activity should be respected and rewarded in society (i.e., entrepreneurship should be seen as socially desirable); (c) activities that divide the economic pie, rather than expand it, should be discouraged; and (d) successful entrepreneurs and large established companies should be incentivized to innovate and grow further. Third, Baumol (with his colleagues) distinguished among four basic forms of capitalism (Baumol, Litan, & Schramm, 2007), an intriguing distinction that has gone largely unnoticed in the entrepreneurship literature: (a) state-guided capitalism where the government steers the market and decides which industries and firms deserve support (e.g., most countries in Southeast Asia), (b) oligarchic capitalism where power and wealth are concentrated with a small group of individuals and families (e.g., countries in Latin America and the Middle East), (c) corporate capitalism where giant enterprises carry out the most substantive economic activities (e.g., Continental Europe, Japan, and Korea), and (d) entrepreneurial capitalism where small, innovative firms are front and center (e.g., US).

Endres and Woods (2006: 189) believe it was "sheer 'hyperbole' for Baumol (1968: 66–67) to claim that in the 'neoclassical model' the 'theoretical firm' is entrepreneurless." So, is it really true that the entrepreneur has been absent from traditional economic thinking? Baumol (1993) himself acknowledges that it is the innovative entrepreneur, not the replicative or imitative entrepreneur, who is really missing from conventional economic models of the firm. As Baumol (1968) observed, "one hears of no...brilliant innovations, of no charisma, or any of the other stuff of which entrepreneurs are made." However, is it fair to criticize economics for ignoring the innovative entrepreneur, when such a character "is doomed to be absent from all scientific theories, economic or otherwise" (Parker, 2009: 4)? Moreover, even though more than five decades have passed since Baumol's (1968) seminal observation regarding Hamlet without the Prince of Denmark, entrepreneurship remains missing from college-level economics texts (Johansson, 2004; Kent, 1989), so that generations of students continue to graduate with an incomplete understanding of the economics process (Kent & Rushing, 1999).[7]

Over the years, Baumol's (1990) trichotomy of productive, unproductive, and destructive entrepreneurship has come under criticism from several quarters (McCaffrey, 2018). While Baumol (1990) assumed that the institutional environment is exogenously determined, others have argued that entrepreneurs can also alter the institutional setup as enterprising individuals are not passive or helpless with regard to the 'rules of the game' (Acemoglu, 1995; Henrekson & Sanandaji, 2011). In other words, instead of assuming that entrepreneurs simply react to the institutional environment as Baumol (1990) did, many scholars seek to explain how entrepreneurs act to change the institutions they find constraining or limiting (Greenwood & Suddaby, 2006; Hardy & Maguire, 2008). Davidson and Ekelund (1994: 269–270) criticize Baumol (1990) for assuming that the "rules of the game - including a system of property rights - must be exogenous determinants of economic outcomes,"

---

[7] Phipps, Strom, and Baumol (2012: 60–61) reviewed eight introductory entrepreneurship texts and found that three of them—specifically, Baumol and Blinder (2009), McConnell and Brue (2008), and Samuelson and Nordhaus (2010)—provide "enhanced discussion of the role of entrepreneurs and innovation in the economy and offer a more robust understanding of the importance of entrepreneurship to economic growth." It is possible that the Prince of Denmark is getting increased attention by economists, but the jury is still out on this issue.

which they believe impose a "static, temporal conception of economic efficiency" at odds with historical trends. Douhan and Henrekson (2010) distinguish between business and institutional entrepreneurship to argue that in focusing on institutions as allocative mechanism, Baumol (1990) overlooks that institutions can themselves become targets of entrepreneurial innovativeness. Furthermore, researchers have also questioned Baumol's (1990) very conception of productive entrepreneurship (Lucas & Fuller, 2017) and the ambiguous demarcation between unproductive and destructive entrepreneurship (Desai & Acs, 2007).

Baumol et al. (2007) proposed a four-pronged classificatory schema for identifying a country's form of capitalism: state-guided capitalism, oligarchic capitalism, corporate capitalism (or, in their words, big-firm capitalism), and entrepreneurial capitalism. Over the years, other typologies of capitalism have also been developed (e.g., Bresser-Pereira, 2012; Rajan & Zingales, 1998), so that there exist several competing classification schemes for organizing the vast heterogeneity of capitalist systems in the world (Witt & Jackson, 2016). Baumol et al. (2007)'s typology is quite appealing, but its practical usefulness in actually classifying countries is murky at best. Consider, for example, the issue surrounding categorizing US into one of the four archetypes. Baumol et al. (2007) consider US to be a prominent (perhaps, even the solo) example of entrepreneurial capitalism, but then they also classify it as corporate capitalism (for the dominant role played by large firms) and also state-guided capitalism (particularly, the agriculture, energy, and housing sectors). One may also associate the US with oligarchic capitalism, particularly if one goes by the Gini coefficient, an important indicator of wealth and income inequality, as Baumol et al. (2007) did. The World Bank puts the Gini coefficient for US at 41.5, which is in close proximity to countries like Argentina, Uruguay, and Ecuador, generally considered examples of oligarchic capitalism. The classification of other major economies using the Baumol et al. (2007) scheme is also problematic. For example, commentators and experts alike often classify China as an example of state-guided capitalism (Page, 2019), but it also has some features of oligarchic capitalism (e.g., informality and corruption), corporate capitalism (powered "more by certain national champion firms"), and entrepreneurial capitalism. A similar case may be made for India, with its middling Gini coefficient (.35), informality and corruption, large firms (with the *maharatna* and *navratna* companies), and millions of entrepreneurs running small firms. The validity and usefulness of Baumol et al.'s (2007) schema are therefore a worthwhile area for future research.

ISRAEL KIRZNER: AN AUSTRIAN POSITION

Israel Kirzner, the 2006 GAER awardee, was recognized his outstanding role in "developing the economic theory emphasizing the importance of the entrepreneur for economic growth and the functioning of the capitalist process." Ricketts (1992: 67) noted that "no other economic theorist has devoted more attention to the role of the entrepreneur in economic life than has Israel Kirzner," an observation that resonates well with many scholars (especially those subscribing to the Austrian school).[8] His most recent work, Kirzner (2019), critiques Nobel laureate Milton Friedman's universal ethic for profit (the much-discussed idea that the only social responsibility of business is to increase profits for its shareholders).

During his Ph.D. days, Kirzner wrote *The Economic Point of View: An Essay in the History of Economic Thought* for his dissertation (see Kirzner, 1960). For many scholars (e.g., Boettke, 2017), Kirzner's work on the entrepreneurial market process theory is deserving of the Nobel Prize for it helped explain how the economic system moves from disequilibrium to equilibrium (see Kirzner, 1963, 1973, 1992). Jakee and Spong (2003: 461) believe that Kirzner "has promoted the role of the entrepreneur more than any other author in the second half of the twentieth century." Kirzner (1973) is widely considered "*the* seminal modern Austrian statement on entrepreneurship" (Foss & Klein, 2010a: 105), and Kirzner frequently returned to the ideas discussed therein (Kirzner, 1979, 1992, 2009), including applying them to other areas such as regulation (Kirzner, 1985) and ethics (1989).[9]

To grasp Kirzner's contributions, it is useful to first briefly understand Austrian economics and how it relates to entrepreneurship. The term 'Austrian economics' refers to a heterodox school of thought that

---

[8] Kirzner (1960) was critical of Robbins' (1932) view of economics as the "science which studies human behavior as a relationship between ends and scarce means which have alternative ends." Kirzner believed that Robbin's definition limited economics to mechanical means-end calculus and overlooked purposeful human action. He argued that Robbins' conception of the *homo economicus* mechanically applying given means to best satisfy, although conflicting, is not able to accommodate the discovery of new means and ends and the new alignments between means and ends. This does not, however, mean that Kirzner rejected all of Robbins' ideas as is clear from his 2010 June and Edgar Memorial Lecture (see Kirzner, 2011).

[9] Kirzner's first published work related to entrepreneurship may have been Kirzner (1971).

originated with Carl Menger in Vienna and continued over the years through his disciples, including Ludwig von Mises and Nobel laureate Friedrich Hayek (Jacobson, 1992). Vaughn (1998) identified three core Austrian tenets: (a) socioeconomic phenomena should be explained in terms of ideas and actions of individuals (i.e., methodological individualism), (b) people respond to their subjective interpretation of the environment within which they operate, and (c) humans think and act in time and always under conditions of limited knowledge of the present and uncertainty about the future. While all Austrian scholars generally agree with these propositions, there is stark disagreement on their implications. A large group of Austrians believe that Austrian insights are a vital supplement to neoclassical economics, and as often articulated in the writings of Kirzner, wants the focus of economic theorizing to be on the market processes that lead to equilibrium. A much smaller group of Austrians, and as reflected in the work of Ludwig Lachmann (who was Hayek's student), argue that taking time and ignorance seriously means abandoning the notion of equilibrium and making a clean break from neoclassical economics (Chiles, Bluedorn, & Gupta, 2007).

Kirzner believed that key concepts in the Austrian tradition—specifically, subjectivity and ignorance—are basic building blocks for a theory of entrepreneurship.[10] Kirzner's embrace of these fundamental Austrian concepts led him to deny the neoclassical notion of the economy existing in a state of equilibrium characterized by perfect information, perfect competition, and perfect coordination. For Kirzner (1997a), the main attraction is actually the dynamic competitive processes that push an economy toward equilibrium. Because entrepreneurs alter the means and ends in a given situation, they are the drivers of Kirzner's equilibrating forces. Entrepreneurship, in other words, exists in an out-of-equilibrium world and is continually driving the system toward equilibrium.

The key entrepreneurial attribute in Kirzner's theory is 'alertness,' which involves being alert to hitherto unnoticed opportunities. It is alertness that gets individuals to make discoveries that help satisfy human needs and wants. Kirzner (1979: 48) defined alertness as "the ability to notice without search opportunities that have hitherto been overlooked." At other times, Kirzner variously described alertness as "an

---

[10]Foss and Klein (2010a: 98) believe that Kirzner's work "can trace its roots back to Richard Cantillon, J. B. Clark, Frank A. Fetter, and other writers," but they do not explain the specific linkages that led them to this inference.

attitude of receptiveness to available, but hitherto overlooked, opportunities" (Kirzner, 1997a: 72) and "a sense of what might be 'around
the corner,' i.e., the sense to notice that which has hitherto not been
suspected of existing at all" (Kirzner, 2009:151). Kirzner (1973) uses
the analogy that the entrepreneur is one who, upon seeing a \$10 bill in
front of him, becomes alert to its existence and acts to grab it. The alert
person grabs the \$10 bill quickly; the less alert will take longer to see the
\$10 bill and to grab it. Thus, at a basic level, Kirzner's entrepreneur is an
arbitrageur who finds a gap or mismatch across different markets and then
moves to fill that gap (through buying low and selling high). In Kirzner's framework, alertness is not the equivalent to search, which involves
a deliberate exploration of new information. For Kirzner, alertness is
about discovering something that one had not even been considered
earlier. The discovery of a Kirznerian profit opportunity, which can range
from a ten-dollar bill on the street to a pill for curing cancer, is "necessarily accompanied by the element of surprise- one that had not hitherto
realized one's ignorance" (Kirzner, 1997a: 62).

Seemingly simple and elegant, Kirzner's view of entrepreneurship has
attracted criticism not only from the radical Austrians who take a puritan-
ical view of the Austrian concept of subjectivity (Vaughn, 1992), but also
"even from like-minded travelers" (Jakee & Spong, 2003: 461). Rothbard
(1985: 282) considered Kirzner's entrepreneur "a curious formulation,"
which is particularly notable because Murray Rothbard was another
prominent member of the Austrian school. Kirzner has been criticized for
ignoring entrepreneurs' need for capital to exploit opportunities (Chiles
et al., 2007). Like Schumpeter, Kirzner too distinguished sharply between
capitalists and entrepreneurs, arguing that pure entrepreneurship requires
no capital. Kirzner insists that the pure entrepreneur neither owns nor
invests. For Kirzner, entrepreneurs perform only the discovery function,
so that they are spontaneously alert to profit opportunities, and do not
own or invest capital. Kirzner (1973: 47) lays out this position:

> Ownership and entrepreneurship are to be viewed as completely sepa-
> rate functions. Once we have adopted the convention of concentrating all
> elements of entrepreneurship into the hands of pure entrepreneurs, we have
> automatically excluded the asset owner from an entrepreneurial role. Purely
> entrepreneurial decisions are by definition reserved to decision-makers who
> own nothing at all.

Critiquing Kirzner's position that the entrepreneur only performs the discovery function and nothing else (Foss & Klein, 2010b), Rothbard (1985: 282) writes:

> Kirzner's entrepreneur... need not, apparently, risk anything. He is a free-floating wraith, disembodied from real objects. He does not, and need not, possess any assets. All he need have to earn profits is a faculty of alertness to profit opportunities. Since he need not risk any capital assets to meet the chancy fate of uncertainty, he cannot suffer any losses. But, if the Kirznerian entrepreneur owns no assets, then how in the world does he earn profits? Profits, after all, are simply the other side of the coin of an increase in the value of one's capital; losses are the reflection of a loss in capital assets. The speculator who expects a stock to rise uses money to purchase that stock; a rise or fall in the price of stock will raise or lower the value of the stock assets. If the price rises, the profits.

Kirzner has also received considerable criticism for his understanding of the role of equilibrium. Keyhani and Levesque (2016: 67) define equilibrium as "a situation in which agents...have exploited all opportunities available to them." Of course, many other definitions of economic equilibrium exist, including the familiar idea of a balance between the forces of demand and supply (Milgate, 1991). Kirzner, like most Austrians, subscribes to the idea that the natural state of the economy is not equilibrium, but disequilibrium.[11] Yet, for Kirzner, the market is always moving toward equilibrium. In formulating his 'tendency towards equilibrium' argument, Kirzner seems to have been inspired by Adam Smith who saw equilibrium as a center of gravitation of the economic system—a particular configuration of values toward which all economic forces are "continually tending to confirm" (Milgate, 1991: 228). As Smith (1776: 65) wrote:

> The natural price...is, as it were, the central price, to which the prices of all commodities are continually gravitating. Different accidents may sometimes keep them suspended a good deal above it, and sometimes force them down even somewhat below it. But whatever may the obstacles which

---

[11] Schumpeter, on the other hand, adhered closely to the neoclassical equilibrium, so that his entrepreneurs—through the exploitation of new combination—disrupt prevailing equilibrium. In Schumpeter's telling, entrepreneurs disrupt market equilibria time and again, as the next entrepreneur comes along with a new means-end combination to wake up the market from its slumber in equilibrium.

hinder them from settling in this centre of repose and continuance, they are constantly tending towards it.

Entrepreneurial actions fix errors and remove inefficiencies, closing pockets of ignorance in the market, which then ignites and reinforces a tendency toward equilibrium. As Klein (2008: 180) observes, Kirzner's entrepreneurial discovery is "simply that which causes markets to equilibrate." Ludwig Lachmann and his Austrian disciples, often labeled as the 'radical subjectivists' (Vaughn, 1998), contend that the overall tendency of the market process cannot possibly be toward equilibrium. Their argument is based on extending the Austrian notions of subjectivity from knowledge (or information) to expectations: market activity results from the aggregation of subjectively formed expectations of numerous individuals. Because of the subjectivity inherent in individual expectations, Lachmann argues, it makes no sense to think of equilibrium either within specific markets (e.g., automobiles, personal computers) or between markets, so that the idea of a general tendency toward a general state of equilibrium is indefensible.[12] To quote Lachmann (1976: 131), "no initial set of forces delimits the boundaries of events. Any force from anywhere may at any time affect our process, and forces that impinged on it yesterday may suddenly vanish from the scene. There is no end or final point of rest in sight."

Kirzner is largely dismissive of subjectivism's application to expectations and the disequilibration it portends. He claims that a key normative requirement for entrepreneurship theory is to illuminate how unintended social outcomes like market coordination occur from individual action. To make his point, Kirzner (1960) brings up the issue of how the "great city of Paris is provided with colossal quantities of food and other articles" in the absence of any central agency managing the flows of different materials. "Paris," Kirzner (2009: 150) famously observed, "does get fed." In Kirzner's framework, the flow of all the goods that a metropolis like Paris needs to sustain its population is an example of the overall coordinative thrust of the market process (Prychitko, 1997). Radical subjectivism with its emphasis on "indeterminacy and unpredictability inherent in human

---

[12] For more on the 'radical subjectivist' strand of Austrian economics , particularly as it applies to entrepreneurship, see Chiles, Vultee, Gupta, Greening, and Tuggle (2010), Chiles, Tuggle, McMullen, Bierman, and Greening (2010), and Chiles, Elias, Zarankin, and Vultee (2013).

preferences, human expectations, and human knowledge," Kirzner (1976: 42) argues, is unable to explain market coordination.

For entrepreneurship scholars, an important critique of Kirzner centers around his argument that entrepreneurs can only discover existing opportunities and not create opportunities ex-nihilo (Vaughn, 1998). Entrepreneurial opportunities, Kirzner (2009: 150) argued, are "waiting to be grasped." Kirzner (1997b: 4) goes as far as to argue that "we have to recognize that when an innovator has discovered something new, that something was metaphorically waiting to be discovered." Scholars building on Kirzner's work have come to see entrepreneurial opportunities as existing in the environment due to changes in technology, consumer preferences, or other attributes of the market or industry context (Shane & Venkataraman, 2000), which are discovered by 'alert' entrepreneurs who then take appropriate action to exploit them based on their prior knowledge (Shane, 2000). In contrast to the Kirznerian discovery view, some researchers have advocated a creation perspective that sees opportunities as actively constructed by 'imaginative' entrepreneurs (Alvarez & Barney, 2007; Chiles et al., 2007) or 'willed into being' by creative visionaries (Sarasvathy, 2001). From a creation standpoint, opportunities are "an image in the entrepreneur's mind" (Penrose, 1959: 42) that are then actualized through the interactions between entrepreneurs, other economic actors, and their environments (Aldrich & Kenworthy, 1999). Recognizing the creationist criticism of his work, Kirzner (1985) made some efforts to incorporate imagination and vision into his theory, but it proved dissatisfying to his critics (Gloria-Palermo, 2002).

Josh Lerner: Entrepreneurship and Finance

The 2010 GAER awardee, Josh Lerner, was recognized for his "pioneering research into venture capital (VC) and VC-backed entrepreneurship" and many contributions to "the synthesis of the field of finance and entrepreneurship in the form of entrepreneurial finance." As Cumming and Groh (2018: 539) explained, entrepreneurial finance is "an interdisciplinary field that covers work in finance and entrepreneurship (including entrepreneurship and management journals)." Academics have traditionally conceived of entrepreneurial finance as a relay race, where initial funding from family, friends, and fools gives way to business angels, after which the baton is handed over to VC before the initial public offering (IPO) occurs to provide an exit opportunity for investors and allows entrepreneurs to raise more capital (Harrison & Mason, 2019).

Lerner's research can be broadly divided into three areas: (i) venture capital, private equity, and entrepreneurial finance (e.g., Gompers & Lerner, 2001)[13]; (ii) intellectual property and innovation (e.g., Brunt, Lerner, & Nicholas, 2012; Lerner, 1997); and (iii) strategic alliances or other hybrid organizational forms (e.g., Lerner & Malmendier, 2010). Over the years, Lerner has also authored several books, starting with Gompers and Lerner (1999), and perhaps most notably, the award-winning, Lerner (2009). Among the academic community, Lerner is best known for his work on VC and entrepreneurial finance, with a reputation as "one of the world's leading authorities in this area" (Brauner-hjelm & Parker, 2010: 246). Cumming, Deloof, Manigart, and Wright (2019) classified research on entrepreneurial finance into four categories: entrepreneurs or the entrepreneurial firm, organizations providing finance to entrepreneurs (e.g., venture capital firms), organizations that provide funds to financiers of entrepreneurial firms (e.g., pension funds), and the region or country within which entrepreneurial firms or their investors are embedded. Lerner's research, primarily the focus on VCs, falls squarely within the stream of research dealing with individuals and firms providing financing to entrepreneurs.[14]

Simply stated, VCs are wealthy private equity investors willing to provide capital to companies with high growth potential in exchange for equity stake. Kortum and Lerner (2000: 676) define VC as "equity or equity-linked investments in young, privately held companies, where the investor is a financial intermediary who is typically active as a director, an advisor, or even a manager of the firm." VCs raise funds from a set

---

[13] Lerner's frequent co-author on VC research is Paul Gompers, one of the three most highly cited researchers in this area of academic inquiry (Cornelius & Persson, 2006). One way to study who is publishing in a particular area such as VCs and their influence on the discipline is bibliometrics, which uses statistical models to assess research based upon keyword analysis, citations, affiliations, and other relevant information available in library databases (Cancino, Merigo, Torres, & Diaz, 2018). Bibliometric analysis of 128 published papers on VCs reveals that Lerner is "quite central" to academic conversation in this area (Cornelius & Persson, 2006: 145), with only William Sahlman, Paul Gompers, and William Bygrave cited more often.

[14] The journal *Venture Capital*, launched in 1999, focuses on research related to VCs in particular, and entrepreneurial finance in general (Harrison & Mason, 1999).

of limited partners, with the goal of providing a return through selective investments into a portfolio of young, innovative companies (Yahoo, EBay, Amazon, are prominent examples of VC success stories). VC firms tend to be small and geographically clustered, often participating in deals mid-stage to late stage (Drover et al. 2017), continuing to larger and later-stage investments (Hellmann & Thiele, 2015). Because limited partners expect to get returns on their VC investments within 10 or so years, there is often a focus on realizing timely exits via an acquisition (i.e., accepting a buyout from another company) or initial public offering (IPO, where the company issues shares to the public).

Gompers and Lerner (2001) identify Boston-based American Research and Development (ARD) as the first true venture capital firm in the country. The firm, set up as a publicly traded closed-end fund, made high-risk investments in emerging companies that employed technology developed for the Second World War. After the Soviet launch of the Sputnik satellite, and spurred by fears of lagging American technical competitiveness, the Eisenhower administration introduced the Small Business Investment Act in 1958 to encourage the development of the VC industry. The act allowed for applicants who had secured a small amount of private capital to received generous marching funds from the government (see Noone & Rubel, 1970 for a detailed discussion). Corruption followed, as unscrupulous operators invested either in firms with poor prospects or in fraudulent endeavors, typically with friends or relatives running the show.

Around the same time, in 1958, the first venture capital limited partnership, Draper, Gaither, and Anderson, was formed, raising capital from a small set of investors compared to more loosely regulated closed-end funds. A few other venture funds were established in subsequent decades, but until the late 1970s the flow of money into new venture funds never exceeded a few hundred million dollars annually in the best years (Kortum & Lerner, 2000). During this period, institutional investors generally shied away from investing in VC funds. However, the 1979 amendment to the 'prudent man' rule governing pension fund investment drastically changed the landscape, as pension managers were explicitly allowed to invest in high-risk assets, including venture capital, under the new regulatory regime. VC investments increased to more than $4 billion in the mid-1908s, with upward of half of all contributions coming from pension funds. The second half of the 1990s saw another leap in VC activity, which now emerged as the dominant form of equity financing in the

US for privately held high-technology businesses, more than half of it going to information technology industries, especially communications and networking, software, and information services (Gompers & Lerner, 2001).

Lerner (1995) contends that VCs acquire in-depth knowledge of the firms they finance, in part because they have greater—and more proximal—access to the internal dynamics of the firm. Consequently, VCs serve an important oversight function in private firms. This was not an original insight into VC activities. In response to the question "What do venture capitalists do?" Gorman and Sahlman (1989) noted that VCs spend about half of their time monitoring portfolio firms. Using the VC financing database assembled by Venture Economics (cf. Lerner, 1994),[15] Lerner (1995) examines changes in board membership around CEO turnover in 271 biotechnology firms receiving VC funding between 1978 and 1989. Two interesting findings emerge: (a) as expected, VC board representation increases significantly between financing rounds when the firm's CEO is replaced in the interval than between other rounds (on average, 1.75 VC directors are added around CEO replacement versus 0.24 VC directors without CEO replacement); and (b) VC directors are twice more likely to come from funds with offices within 5 miles of the firm's headquarters than from 500 miles distance, which is attributed to transaction costs associated with frequent visits and intensive involvement required to provide effective oversight.

Does VC funding enhance technological innovation? Innovative activities are difficult to finance in competitive markets because of challenges associated with preventing knowledge from diffusing in the industry (Hall & Lerner, 2010). Kortum and Lerner (2000) examined the role of VC in encouraging innovation in twenty manufacturing industries between 1965 and 1992. Innovation is captured using information on US patents issued to inventors. Data on VC funding came from Venture Economics database (cf. Lerner, 1994) and industrial R&D expenditure from the Natural Science Foundation (NSF). Accounting for industry- and time-fixed effects, Kortum and Lerner (2000) find that R&D and VC funding together explain over one-fourth of the variation in log of the number of

---

[15] Much of the early academic literature on VC funding was based on either primary field research or archival data from Venture Economics (Drover et al., 2017). In 1991, Securities Data Company acquired Venture Economics, reintroducing it as SDC Venture Intelligence Database.

(ultimately successful) patent applications filed by US inventors in each industry and each year.[16] The potency of VC funding was estimated to anywhere from seven to 40 times that of corporate R&D investment in stimulating patenting. Large established firms prefer internal funds for financing R&D, while small and new firms benefit from the presence of VCs. However, VCs are not always a good solution to the funding gap, especially when public equity markets for VC exist are underdeveloped in a country (Hall & Lerner, 2010).

The problem with linking VC funding with innovation is endogeneity, which is the possibility that a predictor is correlated with the error term (also known as "disturbance" or "residual") in an ordinary least squares (OLS) regression model (Semadeni, Withers, & Trevis Certo, 2014). If causality runs from innovation to VCs (as Geronikolaou & Papachristou (2012) found in Europe), then the variable capturing VC investment is endogenous and correlated with the contemporaneous error term. Another concern is the possibility of autocorrelation in modeling the impact of VC investment on innovation outcomes (Faria & Barbosa, 2014). One way to establish causal inference about the association between VC funding and the innovativeness is to use an 'exogenous shock' that affects all firms (Gupta, Mortal, Chakraborty, Guo, & Turban, 2020). An exogenous shock is akin to an experimental treatment, which enables a before-and-after analysis, with each firm acting as its own control for characteristics consistent across time (Ketokivi & McIntosh, 2017). Because there is no random assignment, the design may be considered a quasi-experiment (Cook & Campbell, 1979). Such models can be very effective in making causal claims (Antonakis, Bendahan, Jacquart, & Lalive, 2010) if there are meaningful exogenous shocks that have an impact of theoretical interest (Ketokivi & McIntosh, 2017). Kortum and Lerner (2000) exploited, as an exogenous shock, the 1979 'prudent man' policy shift that freed pensions to invest in VCs. The underlying logic was that such an exogenous change should help causally identify the role of venture capital, because it is unlikely to be related to the arrival of entrepreneurial opportunities in the industry.

Does the government play a role in financing new ventures? Despite considerable academic interest in the interactions between government and business, the direct public subsidization of new ventures has received

---

[16] Successful patent applications capture patents granted, which Faria and Barbosa (2014) consider proxy for innovative output.

scarce research over the years (Malmström, Johansson, & Wincent, 2017). There is also a widespread misconception that private businesses do not receive public funds in the US. Contrary to popular belief, public funding for small and new ventures has a long history in the US. Indeed, many marquee American firms, like Apple and FedEx, received financial support through federal programs for private companies. One such program was the Small Business Innovation Development Act, enacted by Congress in July 1982, which established the Small Business Innovation Research (SBIR) program. In its original form, SBIR mandated all federal agencies with more than $100 million annual spending on external research to set aside 1.25% of their funds for small businesses. Later, Congress increased the set-aside to 2.5% (in 1992), which now stands at 3.2% (since 2017). Using a dataset of SBIR award recipients generated by US Government Accountability Office (GAO), and matching it with similar firms that did not receive the award,[17] Lerner (1999) found that awardees grew significantly faster than matched firms, though this difference was driven primarily by firms in the top one-third of the distribution. The awardees were also more likely to attract private venture financing (if the firm was in a region with high VC activity), and that the effect was strongest in technology-intensive industries (defined as high ratio of (a) intangible assets to total assets and (b) R&D spending to total sales. SBIR awards, however, may dampen R&D spending by the firm itself and not increase employment (Wallsten, 2000).

Gompers and Lerner (2001) sought to synthesize the existing empirical VC research, which had emerged as an "important area" for systematic research in the last two decades of the last century, but where academic inquiry lagged behind the actual development of the industry in the real world (Wright & Robbie, 1998: 521). At the time, total VC investments in the US were about $67 billion (in 2018, it was about $120 billion),[18] with a little more than one-third of VC funds concentrated in California. Annual inflows into venture funds had expanded from virtually zero in the mid-1970s to $105 billion in 2000 (Gompers & Lerner, 2004). Academic work on VCs during the 1980s and 1990s tended to be descriptive of how

[17] Two matching samples were created: one was matched on industry and firm size, and another on geographic location and firm size.

[18] Globally, VC investments were about $250 billion in 2018.

the investment process worked and the role of key players (Drover et al., 2017).

Tyebjee and Bruno (1984) identified five sequential steps in VC investment activity: deal origination, deal screening, deal evaluation, deal structuring, and post-investment activities. Accordingly, Gompers and Lerner (2001) advocated a 'venture cycle' view, starting with raising a venture fund, proceeding through investing in, monitoring of, and adding value to firms, continuing as the venture capital firm exits successful deals and returns capital to its investors, and finally strategic renewal with the raising of additional funds for future investments.[19] Researchers generally focused on issues raised within individual stages of VC cycle, ignoring the dynamic inter-linkages between the various stages, such as the possibility that sometimes VCs may seek to reinvest in enterprising actors who have exited from their existing portfolios (Wright & Robbie, 1998). Gompers and Lerner (2001) highlight three key gaps in academic understanding of what was then a 'young' industry. First, it is commonly believed that the returns to institutional investors from VC funds are largely uncorrelated with the public markets, but the validity of this belief is an empirical issue that should not simply be assumed. Second, much of VC activity is concentrated in the US, which raises questions as to why this is the case and what (if anything) can be done about it. Finally, after endogeneity concerns have been considered, does VC funding still have a real effect on corporate and economic outcomes after accounting?

Lerner's most cited work so far is Lerner and Tirole (2002), which is unrelated to VC research. Lerner and Tirole (2002) are interested in an altogether different question: Why do programmers, including top-notch coders, contribute freely to the development of open-source software, a public good? Notably, and as suggested by Pareto's law, the top two deciles of contributors account for about 80% of code contributed to open-source projects. Using four 'mini-cases'—Apache, Linux, Perl, and Sendmail—and drawing on economic logic, Lerner and Tirole (2002) explain that people participate in open source because of ego-gratification or career concern incentives. A major attraction of open-source projects for developers is its modularity (which allows tasks to be divided into small blocks) and its perceived enjoyment (challenges are fun to pursue). Having a leader someone who in the beginning tends to contribute

---

[19] Gompers and Lerner (1999) provided a book-length discussion of the VC cycle, subsequently expanded in Gompers and Lerner (2004).

heavily, but gradually transitions to 'holding things together'—helps attract other programmers to the project.

There is no doubt that VCs have had a transformative impact on the modern entrepreneurial landscape. Consider that more than half of IPO firms in any given year now are VC-backed. Gornall and Stre- bulaev (2015) observe that public firms that previously received VC backing account for one-fifth of the market capitalization and 44% of R&D spending of US public companies.[20] Not surprisingly, VCs have drawn more research attention than any other form of financing for entrepreneurs. Despite funding only a small fraction of start-ups, VC tends to be the most widely recognized form of financing (Drovers et al., 2017). Estimates suggest that, in the US, less than one-quarter of 1% of companies receive VC financing. As a financial intermediary, the VC industry is "modestly sized" and much smaller than other intermediaries such as mutual funds (Gompers & Lerner, 2004: 5). A large proportion of start-up financing in the US is through external debt, including debt financed through the personal balance sheets of the entrepreneur (Robb & Robinson, 2014). Although the proportion of firms that benefit from VC funding is quite small, VC financing was the most popular research area in entrepreneurial finance from 2000 to 2016 (Cumming & Groh, 2018).

In 1996, the pool of VC funds in the US was about three times larger than 21 other high-income nations put together (Jeng & Wells, 2000). Moreover, at the time, 70 percent of the VC funds in the rest of the world were in three countries with especially strong ties to the US: Israel, Canada, and Netherlands (Gompers & Lerner, 2001). Over the next two decades, VCs became globally popular, so that by 2018, the VC industry in the US was about half the global market. Interna- tional institutions such as the World Bank played a prominent role in the globalization of the VC industry, facilitating the sharing of experience and knowledge from the US to other countries seeking to develop their own VC community (Harrison & Mason, 2019). VCs are now a well- established financial intermediary in Singapore, Taiwan, and Hong Kong. VC investments are growing in popularity in former centrally planned

---

[20] Cumming (2014: 251) observes that "VC investment returns in the past decade have been on average negative in the US," with the Great Financial Crisis making matters worse for VCs trying to raise funds and entrepreneurs vying to raise capital. The COVID-19 pandemic is likely to also have a negative impact on VC investments.

economies of Central and Eastern Europe, including Hungary and Poland as well as rapidly emerging major economies like China and India (Wright, Pruthi, & Lockett, 2005). Academic research (partly) reflects the growing global popularity of VCs. By one estimate, more than half of VC research now takes place outside North America (Cornelius & Persson, 2006). However, even internationally, VC research is concentrated largely in the EU countries, with much less consideration to VCs in other parts of the world.

SUMMARY

Entrepreneurship is widely viewed as an important stimulus for positive outcomes from the micro (individual)-level to the macro (society)-level. Researchers from a variety of scholarly disciplines—economic, sociology, and psychology, for sure, but also anthropology, marketing, and finance, among others—are interested in exploring research questions that speak to the "eclectic and pervasive benefits" of entrepreneurship (Ireland & Webb, 2007: 891). This chapter discusses the work of four GAER awardees—namely, Howard Aldrich, William Baumol, Israel Kirzner, and Josh Lerner—all of who drew upon the rich literatures in their discipline to study entrepreneurship questions. They used the theoretical frameworks and methodological toolkits from their disciplinary training to study important questions of interest to entrepreneurship scholars. In doing so, they advanced the knowledge frontier of their discipline and enriched research in entrepreneurship.

REFERENCES

Acemoglu, D. (1995). Reward structures and the allocation of talent. *European Economic Review, 39*(1), 17–33.
Acs, Z. J., & Audretsch, D. B. (2003). Introduction. *Handbook of entrepreneurship research* (pp. 3–20). Boston, MA: Springer.
Aldrich, H. E. (1979). *Organizations and environments.* New Jersey: Prentice-Hall.
Aldrich, H. E. (1999). *Organizations evolving.* Thousand Oaks, CA: Sage.
Aldrich, H. E. (2008). *Organizations and environments.* Redwood City, CA: Stanford University Press.
Aldrich, H. E. (2012). The emergence of entrepreneurship as an academic field: A personal essay on institutional entrepreneurship. *Research Policy, 41*(7), 1240–1248.

Aldrich, H. E. (2014). *The democratization of entrepreneurship? Hackers, makerspaces, and crowdfunding.* Presented at the Annual Meeting of the Academy of Management, Philadelphia, PA.

Aldrich, H. E. (2018). Fifty years in the making: My career as a scholar of organizations and entrepreneurship. In *The Routledge companion to the makers of modern entrepreneurship* (pp. 26–43). London: Routledge.

Aldrich, H. E., & Cliff, J. E. (2003). The pervasive effects of family on entrepreneurship: Toward a family embeddedness perspective. *Journal of Business Venturing, 18*(5), 573–596.

Aldrich, H. E., & Fiol, C. M. (1994). Fools rush in? The institutional context of industry creation. *Academy of Management Review, 19*(4), 645–670.

Aldrich, H. E., Hodgson, G. M., Hull, D. L., Knudsen, T., Mokyr, J., & Vanberg, V. J. (2008). In defense of generalized Darwinism. *Journal of Evolutionary Economics, 18*(5), 577–596.

Aldrich, H. E., & Kenworthy, A. (1999). The accidental entrepreneur: Campbellian antinomies and organizational foundings. In J. A. C. Baum & B. McKelvey (Eds.), *Variations in organization science: In honor of Donald T. Campbell* (pp. 19–33). Newbury Park, CA: Sage.

Aldrich, H. E., & Kim, P. H. (2007). Small worlds, infinite possibilities? How social networks affect entrepreneurial team formation and search. *Strategic Entrepreneurship Journal, 1*(1–2), 147–165.

Aldrich, H. E., & Martínez, M. A. (2001). Many are called, but few are chosen: An evolutionary perspective for the study of entrepreneurship. *Entrepreneurship Theory and Practice, 25*(4), 41–56.

Aldrich, H. E., & Pfeffer, J. (1976). Environments of organizations. *Annual Review of Sociology, 2*(1), 79–105.

Aldrich, H. E., & Ruef, M. (2006). *Organizations evolving* (2nd ed.). London: Sage.

Aldrich, H. E., & Waldinger, R. (1990). Ethnicity and entrepreneurship. *Annual Review of Sociology, 16*(1), 111–135.

Aldrich, H. E., & Yang, T. (2012). Lost in translation: Cultural codes are not blueprints. *Strategic Entrepreneurship Journal, 6*(1), 1–17.

Alvarez, S. A., Agarwal, R., & Sorenson, O. (2005). Introduction. In *Handbook of entrepreneurship research* (pp. 1–10). New York: Springer.

Alvarez, S. A., & Barney, J. B. (2007). Discovery and creation: Alternative theories of entrepreneurial action. *Strategic Entrepreneurship Journal, 1*(1–2), 11–26.

Antonakis, J., Bendahan, S., Jacquart, P., & Lalive, R. (2010). On making causal claims: A review and recommendations. *Leadership Quarterly, 21*(6), 1086–1120.

Argote, L., & Miron-Spektor, E. (2011). Organizational learning: From experience to knowledge. *Organization Science, 22*(5), 1123–1137.

Astley, W. G. (1980). Review of the book *Organizations and environments*. *Organization Studies, 1*(3), 285–288.

Audretsch, D. B. (2014). From the entrepreneurial university to the university for the entrepreneurial society. *Journal of Technology Transfer, 39*(3), 313–321.

Baker, T., Aldrich, H., & Nina, L. (1997). Invisible entrepreneurs: The neglect of women business owners by mass media and scholarly journals in the USA. *Entrepreneurship & Regional Development, 9*(3), 221–238.

Baumol, W. J. (1967). Calculation of optimal product and retailer characteristics: The abstract product approach. *Journal of Political Economy, 75*(5), 674–685.

Baumol, W. J. (1968). Entrepreneurship in economic theory. *The American Economic Review, 58*(2), 64–71.

Baumol, W. J. (1990). Entrepreneurship: Productive, unproductive, and destructive. *Journal of Political Economy, 98*(5), 893–921.

Baumol, W. J. (1993). Formal entrepreneurship theory in economics: Existence and bounds. *Journal of Business Venturing, 8*(3), 197–210.

Baumol, W. J. (2010). *The microtheory of the innovative entrepreneur*. Princeton, NJ: Princeton University Press.

Baumol, W. J., & Blinder, A. S. (2009). *Economics: Principles and policy* (11th ed.). Mason, OH: Cengage Learning.

Baumol, W. J., & Bowen, W. G. (1966). *Performing arts: The economic dilemma*. New York: Twentieth Century Fund.

Baumol, W. J., Litan, R. E., & Schramm, C. J. (2007). *Good capitalism, bad capitalism, and the economics of growth and prosperity*. New Haven, CT: Yale University Press.

Bianchi, M., & Henrekson, M. (2005). Is neoclassical economics still entrepreneurless? *Kyklos, 58*(3), 353–377.

Boettke, P. J. (2017, March 14). Why Israel Kirzner deserves a Nobel prize? *Foundation for economic Education*.

Boettke, P. J., & Coyne, C. J. (2003). Entrepreneurship and development: Cause or consequence? *Advances in Austrian Economics, 6*(1), 67–87.

Bosma, N. (2011). Entrepreneurship, urbanization economies, and productivity of European regions. In Michael Fritsch (Ed.), *Handbook of research on entrepreneurship and regional development: National and regional perspectives* (pp. 107–132). Cheltenham, UK: Edward Elgar.

Braunerhjelm, P., & Parker, S. C. (2010). Josh Lerner: Recipient of the 2010 Global Award for Entrepreneurship Research. *Small Business Economics, 35*(3), 245–254.

Breslin, D. (2008). A review of the evolutionary approach to the study of entrepreneurship. *International Journal of Management Reviews, 10*(4), 399–423.

Breslin, D. (2010). Generalising Darwinism to study socio-cultural change. *International Journal of Sociology and Social Policy, 30*(7/8), 427–439.

Bresser-Pereira, L. C. (2012). The exchange rate at the center of development theory. *Advanced Studies, 26*(75), 7–28.

Brunt, L., Lerner, J., & Nicholas, T. (2012). Inducement prizes and innovation. *Journal of Industrial Economics, 60*(4), 657–696.

Buenger, V. (2000). Review of the book *Organizations evolving. Personnel Psychology, 53*(4), 1002–1005.

Buenstorf, G. (2006). How useful is generalized Darwinism as a framework to study competition and industrial evolution? *Journal of Evolutionary Economics, 16*(5), 511–527.

Cancino, C. A., Merigo, J. M., Torres, J. P., & Diaz, D. (2018). A bibliometric analysis of venture capital research. *Journal of Economics, Finance and Administrative Science, 23*(45), 182–195.

Chiles, T. H., Bluedorn, A. C., & Gupta, V. K. (2007). Beyond creative destruction and entrepreneurial discovery: A radical Austrian approach to entrepreneurship. *Organization Studies, 28*(4), 467–493.

Chiles, T. H., Elias, S. R., Zarankin, T. G., & Vultee, D. M. (2013). The kaleidic world of entrepreneurs: Developing and grounding a metaphor for creative imagination. *Qualitative Research in Organizations and Management: An International Journal, 8*(3), 276–307.

Chiles, T. H., Tuggle, C. S., McMullen, J. S., Bierman, L., & Greening, D. W. (2010a). Dynamic creation: Extending the radical Austrian approach to entrepreneurship. *Organization Studies, 31*(1), 7–46.

Chiles, T. H., Vultee, D. M., Gupta, V. K., Greening, D. W., & Tuggle, C. S. (2010b). The philosophical foundations of a radical Austrian approach to entrepreneurship. *Journal of Management Inquiry, 19*(2), 138–164.

Cook, T. D., & Campbell, D. T. (1979). The design and conduct of true experiments and quasi-experiments in field settings. In R. T. Mowday & R. M. Steers (Eds.), *Reproduced in part in research in organizations: Issues and controversies*. Santa Monica, CA: Goodyear.

Cordes, C. (2006). Darwinism in economics: From analogy to continuity. *Journal of Evolutionary Economics, 16*(5), 529–541.

Cornelius, B., & Persson, O. (2006). Who's who in venture capital research. *Technovation, 26*(2), 142–150.

Cumming, D., Deloof, M., Manigart, S., & Wright, M. (2019). New directions in entrepreneurial finance. *Journal of Banking & Finance, 100*, 252–260.

Cumming, D., & Groh, A. P. (2018). Entrepreneurial finance: Unifying themes and future directions. *Journal of Corporate Finance, 50*, 538–555.

Cumming, G. (2014). The new statistics: Why and how. *Psychological Science, 25*(1), 7–29.

Darwin, C. (1859). *The origin of species and the descent of man*. Modern library.

Darwin, C. (1871). *The descent of man, and selection in relation to sex*. London: John Murray.

Davidson, A. B., & Ekelund, R. B., Jr. (1994). Can entrepreneurship be "unproductive?" Towards an evolutionary interpretation. *Review of Social Economy, 52*(4), 266–279.

Dawkins, R. (1983). Universal Darwinism. In D. S. Bendall (Ed.), *Evolution from molecules to man*. Cambridge, UK: Cambridge University Press.

Deligonul, Z. S., Hult, G. T. M., & Cavusgil, S. T. (2008). Entrepreneuring as a puzzle: An attempt to its explanation with truncation of subjective probability distribution of prospects. *Strategic Entrepreneurship Journal, 2*(2), 155–167.

Dennett, D. C. (1995). *Darwin's dangerous idea: Evolution and the meanings of life*. New York: Simon & Schuster.

Desai, S., & Acs, Z. J. (2007). *A theory of destructive entrepreneurship*. JENA Economic Research Paper No. 2007-085.

Dobbin, F. (2001). Review of the book *Organizations evolving*. *Social Forces, 79*(4), 1521–1523.

Douhan, R., & Henrekson, M. (2010). Entrepreneurship and second-best institutions: Going beyond Baumol's typology. *Journal of Evolutionary Economics, 20*(4), 629–643.

Drover, W., Busenitz, L., Matusik, S., Townsend, D., Anglin, A., & Dushnitsky, G. (2017). A review and road map of entrepreneurial equity financing research: Venture capital, corporate venture capital, angel investment, crowdfunding, and accelerators. *Journal of Management, 43*(6), 1820–1853.

Dunnell, R. (1980). Evolutionary theory and archaeology. *Advances in Archaeological Method and Theory, 3*, 35–99.

Endres, A. M., & Woods, C. R. (2006). Modern theories of entrepreneurial behavior: A comparison and appraisal. *Small Business Economics, 26*(2), 189–202.

Faria, A. P., & Barbosa, N. (2014). Does venture capital really foster innovation? *Economics Letters, 122*(2), 129–131.

Ferrante, F. (2005). Revealing entrepreneurial talent. *Small Business Economics, 25*(2), 159–174.

Foss, N. J., & Klein, P. G. (2010a). Entrepreneurial alertness and opportunity discovery. In H. Landström & F. Lohrke (Eds.), *Historical foundations of entrepreneurship research* (pp. 98–120). Cheltenham, UK: Edward Elgar.

Foss, N. J., & Klein, P. G. (2010b). Alertness, action, and the antecedents of entrepreneurship. *Journal of Private Enterprise, 25*(2), 145–164.

Freeman, J. (1981). Review of the book *Organizations and environments*. *American Journal of Sociology, 86*(6), 1447–1450.

Geronikolaou, G., & Papachristou, G. (2012). Venture capital and innovation in Europe. *Modern Economy, 3*(4), 454–459.

Gillispie, C. C. (1958). Lamarck and Darwin in the history of science. *American Scientist, 46*(4), 388–409.

Glor, E. (2006). Review of the book *Organizations evolving. The Innovation Journal: The Public Sector Innovation Journal, 11*(2), 1–4.

Gloria-Palermo, S. (2002). Schumpeter and the old Austrian School: Interpretations and influences. In R. Arena & C. Dangel-Hagnauer (Eds.), *The contribution of Joseph A. Schumpeter to economics* (pp. 41–59). London: Routledge.

Gompers, P. A., & Lerner, J. (1999). *The venture capital cycle.* Cambridge, MA: MIT press.

Gompers, P. A., & Lerner, J. (2001). The venture capital revolution. *Journal of Economic Perspectives, 15*(2), 145–168.

Gompers, P. A., & Lerner, J. (2004). *The venture capital cycle.* Cambridge: MIT press.

Gorman, M., & Sahlman, W. A. (1989). What do venture capitalists do? *Journal of Business Venturing, 4*(4), 231–248.

Gornall, W., & Strebulaev, I. A. (2015). *The economic impact of venture capital: Evidence from public companies* (Unpublished working paper), Stanford University.

Greenwood, R., & Suddaby, R. (2006). Institutional entrepreneurship in mature fields: The big five accounting firms. *Academy of Management Journal, 49*(1), 27–48.

Grégoire, D. A., Noel, M. X., Déry, R., & Béchard, J. P. (2006). Is there conceptual convergence in entrepreneurship research? A co–citation analysis of frontiers of entrepreneurship research, 1981–2004. *Entrepreneurship Theory and Practice, 30*(3), 333–373.

Griffiths, M., Kickul, J., Bacq, S., & Terjesen, S. (2012). A dialogue with William J. Baumol: Insights on entrepreneurship theory and education. *Entrepreneurship Theory and Practice, 36*(4), 611–625.

Gupta, V. K., Guo, C. G., & Ozkazanc-Pan, B. (2018). Introduction. In G. Javadian, V. K. Gupta, D. K. Dutta, C. G. Guo, A. E. Osorio, & B. Ozkazanc-Pan (Eds.), *Foundational research in entrepreneurship studies: Insightful contributions and future pathways* (pp. 1–12). Cham, Switzerland: Palgrave Macmillan.

Gupta, V. K., Mortal, S., Chakrabarty, B., Guo, X., & Turban, D. B. (2020). CFO gender and financial statement irregularities. *Academy of Management Journal, 63*(3), 802–831.

Hall, B. H., & Lerner, J. (2010). The financing of R&D and innovation. In Bronwyn H. Hall & Nathan Rosenberg (Eds.), *Handbook of the economics of innovation* (pp. 609–639). North-Holland: Elsevier.

Hamilton, R. T. (2011). Strategy and entrepreneurship. In L. P. Dana (Eds.), *World encyclopedia of entrepreneurship* (pp. 415–425). Cheltenham: Edward Elgar.

Hardy, C., & Maguire, S. (2008). Institutional entrepreneurship. In R. Greenwood, C. Oliver, K. Sahlin-Andersson, & R. Suddaby (Eds.), *The SAGE handbook of organizational institutionalism* (pp. 198–217). London: Sage.

Harrison, R. T., & Mason, C. M. (1999). An overview of informal venture capital research. *Venture Capital, 1,* 95–100.

Harrison, R. T., & Mason, C. M. (2019). Venture capital 20 years on: Reflections on the evolution of a field. *Venture Capital, 21*(1), 1–34.

Hellmann, T., & Thiele, V. (2015). Friends or foes? The interrelationship between angel and venture capital markets. *Journal of Financial Economics, 115*(3), 639–653.

Henrekson, M., & Sanandaji, T. (2011). The interaction of entrepreneurship and institutions. *Journal of Institutional Economics, 7*(1), 47–75.

Hisrich, R. D. (1988). Entrepreneurship: Past, present, and future. *Journal of Small Business Management, 26*(4), 1–4.

Hodgson, G. M. (2007). Evolutionary and institutional economics as the new mainstream? *Evolutionary and Institutional Economics Review, 4*(1), 7–25.

Hodgson, G. M. (2013). Understanding organizational evolution: Toward a research agenda using generalized Darwinism. *Organization Studies, 34*(7), 973–992.

Hodgson, G. M., & Knudsen, T. (2004). The firm as an interactor: Firms as vehicles for habits and routines. *Journal of Evolutionary Economics, 14*(3), 281–307.

Hodgson, G. M., & Knudsen, T. (2006). Dismantling Lamarckism: Why descriptions of socio-economic evolution as Lamarckian are misleading. *Journal of Evolutionary Economics, 16*(4), 343–366.

Hodgson, G. M., & Lamberg, J. A. (2018). The past and future of evolutionary economics: Some reflections based on new bibliometric evidence. *Evolutionary and Institutional Economics Review, 15*(1), 167–187.

Hougland, J. G., Jr., & Shepard, J. M. (1980). Review of the book *Organizations and environments. Academy of Management Review, 5*(1), 139–140.

Hrebiniak, L., & Joyce, W. (1985). Organizational adaptation: Strategic choice and environmental determinism. *Administrative Science Quarterly, 30*(3), 336–349.

Ireland, D. R., & Webb, J. W. (2007). A cross-disciplinary exploration of entrepreneurship research. *Journal of Management, 33*(6), 891–927.

Jacobson, R. (1992). The "Austrian" school of strategy. *Academy of Management Review, 17*(4), 782–807.

Jakee, K., & Spong, H. (2003). Praxeology, entrepreneurship and the market process: A review of Kirzner's contribution. *Journal of the History of Economic Thought, 25*(4), 461–486.

Jeng, L. A., & Wells, P. C. (2000). The determinants of venture capital funding: Evidence across countries. *Journal of Corporate Finance, 6*(3), 241–289.

Johansson, A. W. (2004). Narrating the entrepreneur. *International Small Business Journal, 22*(3), 273–293.

Kent, C. A. (1989). The treatment of entrepreneurship in principles of economics textbooks. *The Journal of Economic Education, 20*(2), 153–164.

Kent, C. A., & Rushing, F. W. (1999). Coverage of entrepreneurship in principles of economics textbooks: An update. *The Journal of Economic Education, 30*(2), 184–188.

Ketokivi, M., & McIntosh, C. N. (2017). Addressing the endogeneity dilemma in operations management research: Theoretical, empirical, and pragmatic considerations. *Journal of Operations Management, 52*, 1–14.

Keyhani, M., & Levesque, M. (2016). The equilibrating and disequilibrating effects of entrepreneurship: Revisiting the central premises. *Strategic Entrepreneurship Journal, 10*(1), 65–88.

Kim, P. H., & Aldrich, H. E. (2005). Social capital and entrepreneurship. *Foundations and Trends in Entrepreneurship, 1*(2), 55–104.

Kim, P. H., Aldrich, H. E., & Keister, L. A. (2006). Access (not) denied: The impact of financial, human, and cultural capital on entrepreneurial entry in the United States. *Small Business Economics, 27*(1), 5–22.

Kirzner, I. M. (1960). *The economic point of view: An essay in the history of economic thought*. Auburn: Ludwig von Mises Institute.

Kirzner, I. M. (1963). Rational action and economic theory: Rejoinder. *The Journal of Political Economy, 71*(1), 84–85.

Kirzner, I. M. (1971). Entrepreneurship and the market approach to development. In F. Hayek, H. Hazliit, L. R. Read, G. Velasco, & F. A. Harper (Eds.), *Toward liberty: Essays in honor of Ludwig von Mises on the occasion of his 90th birthday, September 29, 1971* (pp. 194–208). Menlo Park: Institute for Humane Studies.

Kirzner, I. M. (1973). *Competition and entrepreneurship*. Chicago: University of Chicago Press.

Kirzner, I. M. (1976). On the method of Austrian economics. In *The foundations of modern Austrian economics* (pp. 40–51). Kansas City: Sheed and Ward.

Kirzner, I. M. (1979). *Perception, opportunity, and profit*. Chicago: University of Chicago press.

Kirzner, I. M. (1985). *Discovery and the capitalist process*. Chicago: University of Chicago Press.

Kirzner, I. M. (1989). *Discovery, capitalism and distributive justice*. Oxford: Basil Blackwell.

Kirzner, I. M. (1992). Entrepreneurship, uncertainty and Austrian economics. In B. J. Caldwell & S. Boehn (Eds.), *Austrian economics: Tensions and new directions* (pp. 85–102). Boston, MA: Kluwer Academic.

Kirzner, I. M. (1997a). Entrepreneurial discovery and the competitive market process: An Austrian approach. *Journal of Economic Literature, 35*(1), 60–85.

Kirzner, I. M. (1997b). Interview with Israel M. Kirzner. *Austrian Economics Newsletter, 17*(1), 1–8.

Kirzner, I. M. (2009). The alert and creative entrepreneur: A clarification. *Small Business Economics, 32*(2), 145–152.

Kirzner, I. M. (2011). Between useful and useless innovation: The entrepreneurial role. In David B. Audretsch, O. Falck, S. Heblich, & Adam Lederer (Eds.), *Handbook of research on innovation and entrepreneurship* (pp. 12–16). Cheltenham, UK: Edward Elgar.

Kirzner, I. M. (2019). Entrepreneurial inspiration. *Review of Austrian Economics, 32*(2), 101–105.

Klein, P. G. (2008). Opportunity discovery, entrepreneurial action, and economic organization. *Strategic Entrepreneurship Journal, 2*(3), 175–190.

Kortum, S., & Lerner, J. (2000). Assessing the contribution of venture capital to innovation. *RAND Journal of Economics, 31*(4), 674–692.

Krueger, A. B. (2001). An interview with William J. Baumol. *Journal of Economic Perspectives, 15*(3), 211–231.

Lachmann, L. M. (1976). On the central concept of Austrian economics: Market process. In E. Dolan (Ed.), *The foundations of modern Austrian economics* (pp. 126–132). Kansas City, MO: Sheed and Ward.

Landström, H. (2005). *Pioneers in entrepreneurship and small business research.* Boston, MA: Springer.

Landström, H., & Benner, M. (2010). Entrepreneurship research: A history of scholarly migration. In H. Landström & F. Lohrke (Eds.), *Historical foundations of entrepreneurship research* (pp. 15–45). Cheltenham, UK and Northampton, MA: Edward Elgar.

Langton, J. (1984). The ecological theory of bureaucracy: The case of Josiah Wedgwood and the British pottery industry. *Administrative Science Quarterly, 29*, 330–354.

Lerner, J. (1994). Venture capitalists and the decision to go public. *Journal of Financial Economics, 35*(3), 293–316.

Lerner, J. (1995). Venture capitalists and the oversight of private firms. *The Journal of Finance, 50*(1), 301–318.

Lerner, J. (1997). An empirical exploration of a technology race. *RAND Journal of Economics, 28*(2), 228–247.

Lerner, J. (1999). The government as venture capitalist: An empirical analysis of the SBIR program. *Journal of Business, 72*, 285–318.

Lerner, J. (2009). *Boulevard of broken dreams: Why public efforts to boost entrepreneurship and venture capital have failed–and what to do about it.* Princeton, NJ: Princeton University Press.

Lerner, J., & Malmendier, U. (2010). Contractibility and the design of research agreements. *American Economic Review, 100*(1), 214–246.

Lerner, J., & Tirole, J. (2002). Some simple economics of open source. *Journal of Industrial Economics, 50*(2), 197–234.

Lippmann, S., & Aldrich, H. E. (2014). History and evolutionary theory. In Marcelo Bucheli & R. Daniel Wadhwani (Eds.), *Organizations in time: History, theory, methods* (pp. 192–216). Oxford, UK: Oxford University Press.

Low, M. B. (2001). The adolescence of entrepreneurship research: Specification of purpose. *Entrepreneurship Theory and Practice, 25*(4), 17–26.

Low, M. B., & MacMillan, I. C. (1988). Entrepreneurship: Past research and future challenges. *Journal of Management, 14*(2), 139–161.

Lucas, D. S., & Fuller, C. S. (2017). Entrepreneurship: Productive, unproductive, and destructive—Relative to what? *Journal of Business Venturing Insights, 7*, 45–49.

Malmström, M., Johansson, J., & Wincent, J. (2017). Gender stereotypes and venture support decisions: How governmental venture capitalists socially construct entrepreneurs' potential. *Entrepreneurship Theory and Practice, 41*(5), 833–860.

McCaffrey, M. (2018). William Baumol's entrepreneurship: Productive, unproductive, and destructive. In G. Javadian, V. K. Gupta, D. K. Dutta, G. C. Guo, A. E. Osorio, & B. Ozkazanc-Pan (Eds.), *Foundational research in entrepreneurship studies: Insightful contributions and future pathways* (pp. 179–201). Cham, Switzerland: Palgrave MacMillan.

McConnell, C. R., & Brue, S. L. (2008). *Economics: Principles, problems, and policies* (17th ed.). Columbus, OH: McGraw-Hill.

Milgate, M. (1991). Equilibrium: Development of the concept. *The world of economics* (pp. 228–236). London: Palgrave Macmillan.

Minniti, M. (2016). The foundational contribution to entrepreneurship research of William J. Baumol. *Strategic Entrepreneurship Journal, 10*(2), 214–228.

Noone, C. M., & Rubel, S. M. (1970). *SBICs: Pioneers in organized venture capital*. Chicago: Capital.

Padilla, A. (2016). Guest editorial. *Journal of Entrepreneurship and Public Policy, 5*(2), 126–130.

Page, J. (2019, March 31). 1989 and the birth of state capitalism in China. *Wall Street Journal*.

Parker, S. C. (2005). The economics of entrepreneurship: What we know and what we don't. *Foundations and Trends in Entrepreneurship, 1*(1), 1–54.

Parker, S. C. (2009). *The economics of entrepreneurship*. Cambridge, UK: Cambridge University Press.

Penrose, E. T. (1959). *The theory of the growth of the firm*. Oxford, UK: Basil Blackwell.

Phipps, B. J., Strom, R. J., & Baumol, W. J. (2012). Principles of economics without the Prince of Denmark. *The Journal of Economic Education, 43*(1), 58–71.

Prychitko, D. L. (1997). Expanding the anarchist range: A critical reappraisal of Rothbard's contribution to the contemporary theory of anarchism. *Review of Political Economy, 9*(4), 433–455.

Rajan, R. G., & Zingales, L. (1998). Which capitalism? Lessons from the East Asian crisis. *Journal of Applied Corporate Finance, 11*(3), 40–48.

Renzulli, L. A., Aldrich, H., & Moody, J. (2000). Family matters: Gender, networks, and entrepreneurial outcomes. *Social Forces, 79*(2), 523–546.

Reynolds, P., Bosma, N., Autio, E., Hunt, S., De Bono, N., Servais, I., … Chin, N. (2005). Global entrepreneurship monitor: Data collection design and implementation 1998–2003. *Small Business Economics, 24*(3), 205–231.

Ricketts, M. (1992). Kirzner's theory of entrepreneurship—A critique. In B. J. Caldwell & S. Boehm (Eds.), *Austrian economics: Tensions and new directions* (pp. 67–102). Dordrecht, The Netherlands: Springer.

Robb, A. M., & Robinson, D. T. (2014). The capital structure decisions of new firms. *The Review of Financial Studies, 27*(1), 153–179.

Robbins, L. (1932). The nature and significance of economic science. In Daniel M. Hausman (Ed.), *The philosophy of economics: An anthology* (pp. 73–99). Cambridge: Cambridge University Press.

Rothbard, M. N. (1985). Professor Hébert on entrepreneurship. *Journal of Libertarian Studies, 7*(2), 281–286.

Ruse, M. (1999). *The Darwinian revolution: Science red in tooth and claw.* Chicago and London: University of Chicago Press.

Samuelson, P. A., & Nordhaus, W. D. (2010). *Economics* (19th ed.). Columbus, OH: McGraw-Hill.

Sarasvathy, S. D. (2001). Causation and effectuation: Toward a theoretical shift from economic inevitability to entrepreneurial contingency. *Academy of Management Review, 26*(2), 243–263.

Schiller, B. R., & Crewson, P. E. (1997). Entrepreneurial origins: A longitudinal inquiry. *Economic Inquiry, 35*(3), 523–531.

Schumpeter, J. A. (1942). *Capitalism, socialism and democracy.* New York: Harper & Brothers.

Semadeni, M., Withers, M. C., & Trevis Certo, S. (2014). The perils of endogeneity and instrumental variables in strategy research: Understanding through simulations. *Strategic Management Journal, 35*(7), 1070–1079.

Shane, S. (2000). Prior knowledge and the discovery of entrepreneurial opportunities. *Organization Science, 11*(4), 448–469.

Shane, S., & Venkataraman, S. (2000). The promise of entrepreneurship as a field of research. *Academy of Management Review, 25*(1), 217–226.

Smith, A. (1776). *The wealth of nations.* New York: The Modern Library.

Stewart, A., & Cotton, J. (2013). Making sense of entrepreneurship journals. *International Journal of Entrepreneurial Behavior & Research, 19*(3), 303–323.

Stoelhorst, J. W. (2008). Why is management not an evolutionary science? Evolutionary theory in strategy and organization. *Journal of Management Studies,* 45(5), 1008–1023.

Streb, C., & Gupta, V. K. (2011). Methodology of entrepreneurship research in a radical subjectivist paradigm. In M. Raposo, D. Smallbone, K. Balaton, & L. Hortovanyi (Eds.), *Entrepreneurship, growth and economic development: Frontiers in European entrepreneurship research* (pp. 262–288). Cheltenham, UK: Edward Elgar.

The Economist. (2017). William Baumol, a great economist, died on May 4th. Available at https://www.economist.com/finance-and-economics/2017/05/11/william-baumol-a-great-economist-died-on-may-4th.

Tyebjee, T. T., & Bruno, A. V. (1984). A model of venture capitalist investment activity. *Management Science, 30*(9), 1051–1066.

van Praag, C. M. (1999). Some classic views on entrepreneurship. *De Economist, 147*(3), 311–335.

Vaughn, K. I. (1992). The problem of order in Austrian economics: Kirzner vs. Lachmann. *Review of Political Economy, 4*(3), 251–274.

Vaughn, K. I. (1998). *Austrian economics in America: The migration of a tradition.* Cambridge, UK: Cambridge University Press.

Wade, J. B. (2002). Review of the book *Organizations evolving. Administrative Science Quarterly, 47*(2), 389–393.

Wade, N. (2009, February 9). Darwin, ahead of his time, is still influential. *New York Times.* Retrieved from http://www.nytimes.com/2009/02/10/science/10evolution.html.

Waldinger, R. D., Aldrich, H., Ward, R., & Associates (1990). *Ethnic entrepreneurs: Immigrant business in industrial societies.* Newbury Park, CA: Sage.

Wallsten, S. J. (2000). The effects of government-industry R&D programs on private R&D: The case of the small business innovation research program. *RAND Journal of Economics, 31*(1), 82–100.

Wennekers, S., & Thurik, R. (1999). Linking entrepreneurship and economic growth. *Small Business Economics, 13*(1), 27–56.

Witt, M. A., & Jackson, G. (2016). Varieties of capitalism and institutional comparative advantage: A test and reinterpretation. *Journal of International Business Studies, 47*(7), 778–806.

Wright, M., Pruthi, S., & Lockett, A. (2005). International venture capital research: From cross-country comparisons to crossing borders. *International Journal of Management Reviews, 7*(3), 135–165.

Wright, M., & Robbie, K. (1998). Venture capital and private equity: A review and synthesis. *Journal of Business Finance & Accounting, 25*(5–6), 521–570.

Yang, T., & Aldrich, H. E. (2012). Out of sight but not out of mind: Why failure to account for left truncation biases research on failure rates. *Journal of Business Venturing, 27*(4), 477–492.

Yang, T., & Aldrich, H. E. (2014). Who's the boss? Explaining gender inequality in entrepreneurial teams. *American Sociological Review, 79*(2), 303–327.

Zimmer, C., & Aldrich, H. (1987). Resource mobilization through ethnic networks: Kinship and friendship ties of shopkeepers in England. *Sociological Perspectives, 30*(4), 422–445.

CHAPTER 6

Strategy

If one were to look at the membership of Academy of Management (AoM)'s entrepreneurship division, one would notice a significant overlap with the Business Policy and Strategy (BPS, now called the Strategic Management [STR]) division. AoM allows each member to select two divisions as part of their membership. For about 50% of the members of the entrepreneurship division, their other home base is the strategic management division. When entrepreneurship became an independent division of the AoM in 1987, it was originally considered a 'spin-off' of the Business Policy and Strategy Division (Kraus & Kauranen, 2009). Brush et al. (2003: 319) sampled entrepreneurship articles published over a five-year period, finding that "64 percent of the articles had a strategy focus and 51 percent studied the firm as unit of analysis." Invoking Shakespeare's Romeo and Juliet, Venkataraman and Sarasvathy (2001) argued that entrepreneurship research without a strategic perspective is like Romeo without a balcony (and strategy research without considering the entrepreneur is like the balcony without Romeo).[1] For Schendel and Hofer (1979: 6), "the entrepreneurial choice is at the heart of the concept of strategy."

---

[1] As will be discussed later in this book, one could argue that the neglect of women in the entrepreneurship and strategy literatures is then akin to omitting Juliet from the balcony in Shakespeare's memorable drama (readers may find it informative that there really was no balcony in the original drama written by Shakespeare, but today it is difficult to imagine the famous play without the balcony).

© The Author(s) 2020
V. K. Gupta, *Great Minds in Entrepreneurship Research*,
https://doi.org/10.1007/978-3-030-44125-8_6

Yet, not everyone views the relationship between entrepreneurship and strategic management favorably. Baker and Pollock (2007: 237) lament that "strategy is succeeding in its takeover of the academic field of entrepreneurship." Shane and Venkataraman (2001) are concerned about subjecting "entrepreneurship researchers to pressure to focus on the central questions" of strategic management inquiry. Others (e.g., Alvarez & Busenitz, 2001; Hitt, Ireland, Camp, & Sexton, 2001) argue that most—if not all—of the important topics that fall under the umbrella of entrepreneurship research are already examined by strategy scholars. From this perspective, a symbiotic relationship between entrepreneurship and strategic management is virtually impossible because there is not much that entrepreneurship inquiry can contribute to strategy research.

The precise nature of the relationship between strategy and entrepreneurship remains controversial. There is an ongoing debate regarding "the degree of interdependence versus the degree of independence" between entrepreneurship and strategic management (Ireland, 2007: 8). Four scholars have been honored with the GAER for their research at the interface of strategy and entrepreneurship: Arnold Cooper (in 1998), Kathleen Eisenhardt (in 2012), Shaker Zahra (in 2015), and Sidney Winter (in 2017). Each of these scholars is now discussed in turn.

Arnold Cooper: Technical Entrepreneurship

The 1997 GAER awardee, Arnold Cooper, was a pioneer in academic inquiry on strategic management and entrepreneurship (Kuratko, 2006). The official GAER citation recognized Cooper for "his pioneering work on technical entrepreneurship, new technology-based firms and incubator organizations." Landström (2005) praised him for his wide-ranging research and sustained efforts to find answers for many of the fundamental questions that define research on entrepreneurship and technology management.

Landström (2005) identifies four prominent streams in Cooper's research: (a) R&D in small manufacturing companies, technology-based firms, entrepreneurial heterogeneity, and new firm success. Cooper's work on R&D activity of small manufacturers was based on his dissertation, where he had reported a number of case studies about small manufacturing firms. At the time, the prevailing view emphasized large-firm advantage, including in R&D where they were believed to benefit from economies of scale. Cooper (1964) compared the cost of developing particular products for large and small firms. Based on interviews with key informants (specifically, men who had been section head or department head in the development organizations of one or more large companies, usually with at least several thousand employees, before starting their own firm, often in the same field), Cooper (1964) concluded that large corporations significantly outspend small firms in developing a new product. Based on an in-depth survey of five companies and interviews with 18 executives from other firms, Cooper (1966) identified three conditions that need to be met for small firms to develop new products: at least one creative technical person in the firm, an enthusiasm for product development as a major element of firm strategy, and a willingness to take risk in the firm.

Cooper (1972) defined technology-based firms as companies emphasizing research and development or otherwise placing major emphasis on exploiting novel technical knowledge. At the time, new technology-based firms (NTBFs; Storey & Tether, 1998) were emerging in various parts of the US such as Minneapolis, Boston, Los Angeles, and San Francisco. Cooper (1973) identified three major drivers of the decision to start a NTBF: (a) attributes and characteristics of the entrepreneur, (b) external forces such as social norms and attributes toward entrepreneurship, and (c) the firm for which the entrepreneur worked prior to start a new enterprise (or the 'incubator organization'). Cooper (1970: 58) summarized the average NTBF in his research thus:

> The firm is started by two founders, both of whom are in the middle thirties. One, usually can be described as the 'driving force.' He conceives the idea and enlists the other founder. They come from the same established organization, which is where they got to know each other. Either both are in engineering development or one is in engineering and the other is a product manager or in marketing. Often, they have achieved significant prior success, with titles such as section head or director of engineering being common. Their education includes BS and MS degrees, typically in electrical engineering.

Much, though not all, of Cooper's research on incubator organizations was based on information obtained about 250 high-technology firms founded on the San Francisco Peninsula during the 1960s. Data about the founding of these firms were gathered primarily through telephone interview (Cooper, 1972). Representing virtually all of the technology-based firms started on the San Francisco peninsula in the first half of 1960 (Bruno & Cooper, 1982), these 250 firms were founded by engineers or scientists, emphasized R&D, and produce a wide range of high-tech products from instruments and computer peripherals to semiconductors and microwave equipment. As such, they differed substantially from the 'typical' new venture in the US at the time, which was likely to be a retailing or service business started by people without much formal education or managerial experience (Cooper & Bruno, 1977).

Cooper (1971) reported that small firms (independent companies with less than 500 employees) or small subsidiaries of large firms had higher spin-off rates than large corporations. Spin-offs refer to new enterprises created by individuals exiting from existing companies to create companies of their own in the same product-market space (Garvin, 1983). Spin-offs, or off-springs as they are sometimes called (Eriksson & Kuhn, 2006), benefit from industry-specific knowledge (Helfat & Lieberman, 2002) and social capital (Furlan & Grandinetti, 2016), which the founders bring with them from the former employer to the new firm. Cooper (1972) found that spin-offs are usually located in the vicinity of the parent firm, presumably because in more than 90% of new firms one or more founders were already working in the area (but see Egeln, Gottschalk, & Rammer, 2004). Cooper (1998) offered several reasons for why entrepreneurs usually start their firms where they are already living and working: existing networks that provide connections to persuade others to help them, knowledge of local suppliers and markets, latitude to start part-time, and for the spouse to continue working so that there is some income for the family. Consequently, entrepreneurship in a region is encouraged by the pool of people already living there.

Cooper and Bruno (1977) found that failure (which they defined as 'discontinuance') rates were significantly lower among NTBFs than non-technology firms. An interesting finding from this research was that a majority of firms were started by two or more full-time founders, and founder departure from the business was commonplace, even from successful businesses. The risk of failure is higher when the new firm is in a line of business where the founder has little prior professional experience. Bruno and Cooper (1982) reported that—by 1980—36.8% of these firms had discontinued, 32.4% had been acquired, and only 30.8% survived as independent firms. The typical NBTF-250 was acquired in its fourth to seventh year after founding by a publicly-owned medium-sized American firm already in the same industry as the acquired firm. Cooper (1985) examined 161 new firms discussed in national magazines, including *Inc.* magazine from January 1981 through November 1984 and in *Venture* magazine from January 1980 through June 1984, classifying them as growth-oriented firms with substantive potential or actual economic impact. Findings show that industrial firms were the incubator organizations for three-fourths of the new firms, and the spin-offs were generally in the same line of business and geographic area as the incubator organization.

In 1985, Cooper and his colleagues launched a large-scale survey study to capture the views, experiences, and attitudes of members of National Federation of Independent Business (NFIB) who had reported recently becoming owners of their own business. The survey instrument had previously been pre-tested with 154 members of the NFIB to improve clarity (Gimeno, Folta, Cooper, & Woo, 1997). Of the approximately 13,000 NFIB members surveyed, 4814 completed the questionnaire, with 2845 reported having started a business in 1984 or 1985 (Cooper, Dunkelberg, Woo, & Dennis, 1990). Focusing on new entrepreneurs who had become business owners through start-up or acquisition, Cooper, Woo, and Dunkelberg (1988) examined entrepreneurs' perceived chances of success. There was evidence of over-optimism on the past of entrepreneurs (Cassar, 2010), in that the business owners Cooper et al. (1988) sampled reported that their business was very likely to be successful, even as the same owners believed that businesses similar to their own were much less likely to succeed. Prior preparedness for the business was not associated with perceived chances for success. With the goal of identifying differences in characteristics of the entrepreneurs and in their processes of starting conditional of firm size, Cooper, Woo, and Dunkelberg (1989) focused on 1903 NFIB respondents who had started their own firm rather than buying out an existing business. In May 1986, a follow-up questionnaire was administered to these 1903 firms, resulting in 742 respondents. The entrepreneurs starting larger firms were found to be more educated, more experienced, more likely to have partners, and relied on external investors and professional advisors. Cooper, Folta, and Woo (1995) examined information search tendencies among 1176 NFIB entrepreneurs who started their own firm, finding that when entering fields familiar to them, novice entrepreneurs searched more than experienced entrepreneurs, but this pattern reversed when the business was in a field unfamiliar to the entrepreneur.

In May 1987, another survey was sent to the responding firms (Cooper, Gimeno-Gascon, & Woo, 1994), resulting in a sample of 1053 firms (385 failed firms and 668 surviving and reporting firms). Results revealed that education, industry-specific know-how and financial capital, was positively related to firm survival and growth, but having parents who were entrepreneurs contributed only to survival and number of partners only to growth. Interestingly, women-owned firms were less likely to grow, but not less likely to survive, than male-owned firms. Gimeno et al. (1997) proposed the idea of performance threshold in small businesses, describing it as the level of performance below which the firm will be dissolved, to explain the persistence of underperforming firms (or 'zombie firms'; Blažková & Dvouletý, 2020). Gimeno et al. (1997) conceived organizational exit as a choice depending on owners' human capital attributes (e.g., management experience) and subjective determination of threshold performance. Based on 1547 NFIB firms participating in the three-wave data collection, Gimeno et al. (1997) found that entrepreneurs who are more intrinsically motivated and have a family history in entrepreneurship are simply more accepting of a lower level of economic performance to remain in business. Thus, the finding that discontinuance rate among new firms is lower than expected (Cooper et al., 1990) may be driven by the subjective value that entrepreneurs get from their business.

There is a long history of typologies in entrepreneurship research. Typologies are generally useful for studying complex issues as researchers can categorize entrepreneurs into discrete categories, which allows detailed analysis and comparison between groups of subjects (Tang, Tang, & Lohrke, 2008). They bring out more vividly key differences between various forms of entrepreneurial activity and help explore 'messy' phenomena like entrepreneurship (Gupta, Wieland, & Turban, 2019). The information value of typologies comes from maximizing 'meta-contrast' such that between-group differences are larger and more salient than within-group variations. Woo, Cooper, and Dunkelberg (1991) distinguished between typologies developed from 'special characteristics' (or small number of attributes) and 'general characteristics' (or comprehensive number of attributes), using data from 510 NFIB entrepreneurs in the retail and personal services sectors to examine the robustness of the craftsmen-opportunist typology (Smith & Miner, 1983). Woo et al. (1991) found that different classification criteria produced different groupings of entrepreneurs, which raises concerns about the universality and validity of entrepreneurial types. Thus, while typologies may have the benefit of revealing patterns in complex phenomena (Gupta et al., 2019), the results of studies classifying entrepreneurs into different types need to be interpreted with caution.

KATHLEEN EISENHARDT: STRATEGIC DECISION MAKING

The 2012 GAER awardee, Kathleen Eisenhardt, was recognized for "work on strategy, strategic decision making, and innovation in rapidly changing and highly competitive markets." She is among the most published scholars in strategic management (Furrer, Thomas, & Goussevskaia, 2008), with several of her papers (namely, Eisenhardt [Eisenhardt 1989a, 1989b], Eisenhardt and Tabrizi [1995], and Eisenhardt and Martin [2000]) ranked among the most influential strategy articles over the first 25 years of the field's existence. She is also ranked among the most productive entrepreneurship scholars over the 2000–2015 period (Gupta, Ibrahim, Guo, & Markin, 2016). Several of Eisenhardt's papers (specifically, Eisenhardt [1989a], Eisenhardt and Tabrizi [1995], and Brown and Eisenhardt [1995]) are among the most influential publications in innovation research (Shafique, 2013). Clearly, Eisenhardt's work is boundary-spanning, covering a wide range of topics and informing researchers across many different academic areas (Carlsson, 2013). Eisenhardt has been ranked #17 on the list of most published strategy researchers (Furrer et al., 2008) and #8 among most published entrepreneurship researchers (Gupta et al., 2016).[2]

To understand Eisenhardt's research, it is helpful to start with Bourgeois and Eisenhardt (1988), her first major scholarly journal publication in the area of entrepreneurship. Rajagopalan, Rasheed, and Datta (1993) highlighted two main findings of Bourgeois and Eisenhardt (1988)'s examination of strategic decision processes in four microcomputer firms: in high-velocity environments, (a) "comprehensiveness, decision speed, CEO power, bold strategies, and incremental implementation lead to better performance" (p. 371), and (b) "successful firms make quick decisions, have powerful CEO's & TMT's, and seek risk and innovation but execute safe, incremental implementation" (p. 361). For many scholars (e.g., Carpenter, Geletkanycz, and Sanders, 2004), a key takeaway from Bourgeois and Eisenhardt (1988) is that not only do complex decision processes characterize the interactions of many TMTs, they may also lead

---

[2] Furrer et al. (2008) rank 37 most published strategy researchers for the 1980 to 2005 period (see also Nerur, Rasheed, and Natarajan [2008]). Gupta et al. (2016) ranked 25 most published entrepreneurship researchers for the 2000–2015 time period. Eisenhardt is the only scholar who appears on both lists.

to more successful outcomes. Snow and Thomas (1994) lauded Bourgeois and Eisenhardt (1988) for combining "three different field methods - observation, interviewing, and questionnaires." Combined with two other publications (Eisenhardt, 1989a; Eisenhardt & Bourgeois, 1988), Bourgeois and Eisenhardt (1988) offered three key ideas:

1. Focus on strategic decisions and the processes underlying these decisions. Following Mintzberg, Raisinghani, and Theoret (1976: 246), strategic decisions were defined as conscious choices made by top management, which are "important, in terms of the actions taken, the resources committed, or the precedents set." Furthermore, strategic decisions were "infrequent" and "critically affect[ed] organizational health and survival" (Eisenhardt & Zbaracki, 1992: 17).

2. Spotlight on high-velocity environments. Building on prior work on 'dynamism' (Dess & Beard, 1984) and 'volatility' (Bourgeois, 1985), high-velocity environments were conceived as those dynamic and volatile industries that are also characterized by "sharp and discontinuous change" (Eisenhardt & Bourgeois, 1988: 738). Eisenhardt (1989a: 544) explained that in high-velocity environments, "changes in demand, competition, and technology are so rapid and discontinuous that information is often inaccurate, unavailable, or obsolete." Bourgeois and Eisenhardt (1988) offered microcomputers, airlines, and banking as examples of high-velocity environments,[3] and contrasted these with "cyclical industries such as forest products and machine tools" that are high on dynamism and volatility, but do not see sharp and discontinuous change.

3. Pursue embedded multiple case designs to generate theoretical insights. Drawing on Yin's (1984) work, this approach involved "several units of analysis" (i.e., embedded) and treated "a series of cases as a series of experiments" (i.e., multiple cases), with "each

---

[3] Banking was subsequently dropped as an example of high-velocity industry (Eisenhardt & Bourgeois, 1988). As Eisenhardt recounted recently, when she started her research, both industries—banking and computing—were being disrupted, and she and her advisor (Jay Bourgeois, a newly minted PhD at the time) debated which one of the two to study (Bodner, Song, & Szulanski, 2019). Because of her engineering background, Eisenhardt turned toward studying the computing industry in the late 1970s and early 1980s, just as the personal computer was taking off.

case serving to confirm or disconfirm the inferences drawn from the others" (Eisenhardt, 1989c: 545). Originally proposed in Eisenhardt (1989a), Eisenhardt and her colleagues then published "a continuous stream" of articles that elaborated "the logic of the method and the rhetoric underpinning" it (Langley & Abdallah, 2011: 204), culminating in what is generally referred to as the 'Eisenhardt style' of inquiry (Javadian, Dobratz, Gupta, Gupta, & Martin, 2020).

These three elements—either together or individually—informed much of Eisenhardt's subsequent research (e.g., Brown & Eisenhardt, 1997; Hallen & Eisenhardt, 2012; Ozcan & Eisenhardt, 2009). Her most cited work to date is Eisenhardt (1989c), which builds on Glaser and Straus (1967) to describe the process of building theory from case studies, starting from developing specific research questions all the way to reaching closure through 'theoretical saturation.' Case studies, Eisenhardt and Graebner (2007) explain, are rich, empirical descriptions of particular instances of a phenomenon typically based on a variety of data sources. Eisenhardt (1991: 620) identified two central arguments in Eisenhardt (1989c): "multiple cases are a powerful means to create theory because they permit replication and extension among individual cases … [and]…the importance of methodological rigor" (see Dyer and Wilkins [1991] for an opposing perspective). Eisenhardt (1989c: 545) argued that "between 4 and 10 cases usually works well. With fewer than 4 cases, it is often difficult to generate theory with much complexity, and its empirical grounding is likely to be unconvincing, unless the case has several mini-cases within it." With 16250+ WoS citations till the time of this writing, Eisenhardt (1989c) is widely considered a seminal methodological reference for case study research both within the field of management and beyond (Ravenswood, 2011). Langley and Abdallah (2011: 201) explain that with its "positivist epistemology" and emphasis on "nomothetic theoretical propositions," Eisenhardt (1989c) laid the foundation for a distinct mode of qualitative inquiry. Javadian et al. (2020) examined the influence of the 'Eisenhardt style' on qualitative entrepreneurship research, presenting Santos and Eisenhardt (2009) as a relatively recent exemplar of this approach.

While Eisenhardt has been a prolific and impactful scholar with significant contributions to entrepreneurship research, only a subset of her work "can be directly and explicitly labeled as 'entrepreneurship' research" (Carlsson, 2013: 798). Of these, Brown and Eisenhardt (1997) have been most influential with 1600 + WoS citations, although it does not appear as a core article in strategy or entrepreneurship research (Ferreira, Fernandes, & Ratten, 2016; Nerur et al., 2008) or entrepreneurship inquiry (Ferreira, Reis, & Miranda, 2015). Brown and Eisenhardt (1997) report an inductive study of multiple-product innovation in six firms in the high-velocity computer industry, with three that were successful and three that were not. The main finding was that managers of firms with successful multiple-product development portfolios balanced between mechanistic and organic structures by combining explicit priorities and responsibilities with clear communication and the freedom to improvise within existing projects. Another key finding is that managers of successful product portfolios carefully managed the transition between the present and the future, while the link between past and future projects was usually an afterthought for the less successful firms. Eisenhardt and Tabrizi (1995) too looked at product innovation, delving into competing theoretical models for firms that develop product quickly to adapt to environmental changes. Using data from 72 product development projects from 36 Asian, US, and European firms operating in the high volatility computer industry, Eisenhardt and Tabrizi (1995) develop an experiential model to explain fast adaptation. In their model, fast adaption requires a powerful project leader who oversees a multifunctional team with an experiential strategy of multiple design iterations, extensive testing, and frequent project milestones.

Carlsson (2013) considers Eisenhardt and Schoonhoven (1990, 1996) to be among Eisenhardt's most influential works for entrepreneurship research. Both studies rely on the same data: semiconductor firms launched in the US between 1978 and 1985. Yet, they deal with different research questions. Eisenhardt and Schoonhoven (1990), which Ferreira et al. (2015) ranked among the top 30 entrepreneurship works in the 2001–2005 time period, examined antecedents of new firm growth, an issue that is at the heart of modern entrepreneurship research. At the time, few scholars were trying to understand why some firms, but not others, manage to grow (Davidsson, Delmar, & Wiklund, 2006), and the research literature in this area was scarce (Davidsson & Wiklund, 2006). Eisenhardt and Schoonhoven (1990) found that founding management team and market stage had significant main and interaction effects on firm growth, and these effects grew stronger over time. Eisenhardt and Schoonhoven (1996) sought to understand why firms form strategic alliances. Given the rapid proliferation of strategic alliances during the

1980s and 1990s (Dyer, Kale, & Singh, 2001; Koka & Prescott, 2002), there is considerable interest in understanding the drivers of alliance formation (Dacin, Oliver, & Roy, 2007). Eisenhardt and Schoonhoven (1996) found that strategic alliances happen when firms are in vulnerable strategic positions and strong social positions. For a firm, a vulnerable strategic position is when it competes in a highly competitive or an emergent industry or when it is pioneering technological disruption. Conversely, a firm is in a strong social position when it is helmed by large, experienced, and well-connected top management teams.

Katila, Rosenberger, and Eisenhardt (2008) examine conditions under which entrepreneurial firms choose investment partners with high potential for misappropriation over less opportunistic partners. Data were obtained from a sample of 701 ventures in five technology-focused industries (communications, software, electronics, biotechnology, and medical) over a 25-year period (1979 to 2003), which was also used for Hallen, Katila, and Rosenberger's (2014) work on of equity tie formation between young firms and established corporate 'sharks.' Katila et al. (2008) find both cooperative and competitive tendencies in the alliances. Specifically, new firms enter into alliances with larger players with the expectation of substantive manufacturing and financial resources. At the same time, they are also prepared to defend themselves from potential misappropriation through the use of trade secrets and timing the relationship to coincide with later funding rounds. Hallen and Eisenhardt (2012) examine the strategies by which managers form ties in a sample of nine young Internet security ventures (see also Hallen [2008]). Hallen and Eisenhardt (2012) find that tie formation is facilitated for firms where executives engage in 'casual dating' (a phrase they use to describe a "catalyzing strategy" that involves "informal but deliberate, repeated meetings with a few potential partners prior to attempting to form a formal tie").

Drawing on eight technology collaborations between ten organizations in the global computing and communications industries between 2001 and 2006, Davis and Eisenhardt (2011) examine why only some strategic alliances yield technological innovations. Notably, all sample companies had ample prior alliance experience: many had previous alliances and dedicated alliance function, for example (Eisenhardt, 2019). Davis and Eisenhardt (2011) find that the key to successful alliances was 'rotating leadership,' where partnering firms constructively alternate decision control.[4] Ozcan and Eisenhardt (2009) were interested in high-performing alliance portfolios (defined as a firm's set of direct ties), which they studied in a sample of six rival ventures in the wireless gaming industry. The US wireless gaming industry, which is characterized by high interdependence among several types of firms in the industry, emerged with scattered attempts to create games for wireless phones (Ozcan, 2018). Ozcan and Eisenhardt (2009) find that executives who form simultaneous ties with multiple partners and keep an eye toward the industry as a whole are more likely to have the kind of high-performing alliance portfolios that yield superior performance for the focal firm.

Some other papers are also worth discussing here, albeit briefly as they do not pertain to entrepreneurship research directly. Eisenhardt (1989b) provides an in-depth review of agency theory, which seeks to explain what happens when one party (principal) delegates work to another (agent) to perform that work. Interestingly, Eisenhardt's doctoral thesis (see Eisenhardt [1985, 1988]) was among the "first empirical studies on agency theory," which was "really taking off" at the time (Bodner, Song, & Szulanski, 2019: 364). Brown and Eisenhardt (1995) organize the extant empirical literature on product development into three broad streams (namely, rational plan, communication web, and disciplined problem solving), synthesizing their findings into a research model explaining product development success. Eisenhardt and Martin (2000) discuss dynamic capabilities, which have emerged as an important stream of research in the entrepreneurship literature (Zahra, Sapienza, & Davidsson, 2006). Eisenhardt and Santos (2002) delve into the knowledge-based view, which sees firms as "entities for producing and exchanging knowledge" in the market (Gupta, Niranjan, & Markin, 2020: 2). Davis, Eisenhardt, and Bingham (2007) focus whether, when, and how simulations—which they define as methodology "for using computer software to model the operation of 'real world' processes, systems, or events" (p. 481)—can be used for theory development in organizational research. Subsequently, Davis, Eisenhardt, and Bingham (2009) used the simulation approach to explore the tension between too much and too little structure in dynamic environments. Garg and

---

[4] As Eisenhardt (2019: 19) explained, rotating leadership is where "one company leads for a while and then flips the lead over to the other [and] then the other company leads for a while and then flips it back."

Eisenhardt (2017) looked at how first-time venture CEOs involved their board in formulating strategy, collecting rich longitudinal data on CEOs, boards, and top management teams through observations, interviews, and archival access. As Eisenhardt (2019: 23) recounted, "it's very challenging to gain entry into corporate boardrooms," but her co-author "was very fortunately and skillfully able to penetrate these companies…attend many board meetings and meet with board members and executives many times…[so they had] extensive data over time… to understand the CEO-board relationship from the CEO lens."

Eisenhardt (2019: 24) describes her research as 'abductive,' which involves "generating plausible, 'first suggestions' about phenomena and their explanations on the basis of observations from one's data" (Bamberger, 2019: 104). Sarasvathy (2001: 257) defines abduction as "creating new hypotheses purely from imagination, as opposed to deducing them from first principles or axioms [deduction] or inducing them from data or empirical findings [induction]." For Heckman and Singer (2017: 298) abductive research is about "generating and revising models, hypotheses, and data analyzed in response to surprising findings." The American philosopher-logician Charles Sander Peirce formally introduced the concept of 'abduction' as follows: "The surprising fact, C, is observed. But if A were true, C would be a matter of course. Hence, there is reason to suspect that A is true" (Kapitan, 1990: 499). Leamer (1983) likened abduction to the Sherlock Holmes methodology, guided by the principle that "[i]t is a capital mistake to theorize before you have all the evidence" (Doyle, 1891). As such, abduction is a sort of formalized guesswork where the proposed supposition is plausible (Niiniluoto, 1999). While anyone can make guesses about an observed phenomenon,[5]

---

[5] Consider the knowledge claims made about possible prevention and treatment of the novel coronavirus, including by heads of states who are vested with the authority and legitimacy to consult the best scientific minds of their country. The UK's Boris Johnson, under advisement on striving for "herd immunity" from the government's chief scientific advisor, boasted about "shaking hands continuously," including "at a hospital… where there were actually a few coronavirus patients" (Colchester, 2020). Venezuelan President Nicolás Maduro shared the recipe for a traditional ginger-lemon tea with purported anticoronavirus benefits (Vyas, 2020). The leader of Belarus, Alexander Lukashenko, advocated the use of vodka and visits to the sauna for keeping the coronavirus at bay. Chinese President Xi Jinping celebrated herbal medicines like *lianhua qingwen*, traditionally used to treat the flu. American President Donald Trump called for everyone, including those without symptoms, to take a combination of antimalarial and antibacterial drugs (Ballhaus & Hopkins, 2020). Brazil's Jair Bolsonaro claimed that Brazilians were resistant to

knowledge claims in science require that the initial conjecture be "subject to further test" (Schurz, 2008: 205). Given that abductive research makes only the weakest of knowledge claims (Bamberger, 2019), replicability and generalizability may be even more salient for abduction than is the case for other forms of scientific inquiry.

Eisenhardt (1989c: 546) embraces the notion of generalizability as reflected in the contention that her scholarship "is directed toward the development of testable hypotheses and theory which are generalizable across settings." Much of Eisenhardt's research focuses on technology-oriented high-growth firms located in the Silicon Valley and its adjoining areas. Such firms attract considerable academic attention, popular interest, and government support (Gupta et al., 2019; Marlow, 2002), but comprise a very small fraction of total entrepreneurial activity in society. Eisenhardt (2019: 18) recognizes the merits of research that reflects the reality not "just for the tech companies," but also for firms "in the 'less-tech' sectors" of the economy. Yet, it is unclear if findings from technology-oriented companies are generalizable to similar firms in other parts of the world (Isaak, Isaak, & Zybura, 2016), let alone to firms in other industries. Silicon Valley has attracted considerable interest from policy-makers and communities that have tried to access its 'secret recipe' and replicate it elsewhere (Sturgeon, 2003), but none have had much success so far (Coletti, 2010). As such, it would be interesting to examine how well research conducted on managerial issues using data from Silicon Valley firms generalizes to other similar firms or even to firms in other industries. While some believe that qualitative inquiry need not be assessed on the metric of generalizability (Smith, 2018), Wolcott (1995: 132) reminded us that qualitative researchers "cannot escape the nagging question of generalization." As Hallen and Eisenhardt (2012: 39) contend, the goal of organizational research is "accurate, parsimonious, and generalizable" findings that are valid across time and space (see also Ozcan and Eisenhardt [2009]).

---

the novel coronavirus and it would not make athletes sick (Magalhaes & Forero, 2020). Tanzania's John Magufuli encouraged people to go pray in churches and mosques to quell a 'satanic' virus that can only be cured by divine intervention (Bariyo & Parkinson, 2020). Some of these claims may prove to be true, or perhaps none or maybe all. It seems the more perplexing the observed phenomena, the more variety of guesses will be generated about it.

SHAKER ZAHRA: CORPORATE ENTREPRENEURSHIP AND BEYOND

Shaker Zahra, the 2014 GAER awardee, is widely recognized for the 'diversity' of his research, whether in research topics, methodology, or the phenomena of interest (Audretsch, 2015). The official GAER citation for Zahra honored him "for his work on the role of corporate entrepreneurship in knowledge creation, absorption, and conversion." Several of Zahra's papers (e.g., Zahra & Covin, 1995; Zahra, Ireland, & Hitt, 2000; Zahra et al., 2006) are considered highly influential in the area of strategic entrepreneurship (Ferreira et al., 2016).[6] Zahra is consistently considered among the most published researchers in entrepreneurship, both in general management journals (Gupta et al., 2016) and in specialty field journals (Markin, Swab, & Marshall, 2017).

To understand Zahra's work, it is helpful to start with a brief discussion of corporate entrepreneurship.[7] At a basic level, the term corporate entrepreneurship (CE) refers to the entrepreneurial behaviors and activities of established corporations. Sharma and Chrisman (1999: 18) define it as "… the process whereby an individual or a group of individuals, in association with an existing organization, create a new organization, or instigate renewal or innovation within that organization." It involves, Phan et al. (2009) explain, exploiting new opportunities in and by large

---

[6] The literature is not clear about the interrelationships between strategic entrepreneurship and corporate entrepreneurship. For Phan, Wright, Ucbasaran, and Tan (2009: 199), strategic entrepreneurship is one part of corporate entrepreneurship, specifically the "renewal activities that enhance a corporations' ability to compete and take risks" (see also Kuratko and Audretsch [2013]). Others (e.g., Hitt, Ireland, Sirmon, & Trahms, 2011: 59) see corporate entrepreneurship as a part of the broad field of strategic entrepreneurship that brings together "entrepreneurship's opportunity-seeking behaviors and strategic management's advantage-seeking behaviors" for the benefit of all organizations, small and large.

[7] Zahra (2018) discusses that his early research was in the area of strategic management, focusing on governance of large public corporations (e.g., Pearce and Zahra, 1991; Zahra and Pearce, 1989) and technology strategy (e.g., Zahra & Covin, 1993; Zahra & Das, 1993). Even as Zahra's research gradually moved toward more mainstream entrepreneurship topics, his interest in strategy continued (e.g., George, Zahra & Wood, 2002; Haeussler, Patzelt, & Zahra, 2012; Kelley, Ali, & Zahra, 2013; Uotila, Maula, Keil, & Zahra, 2009). This is not surprising, given that Zahra has been a vocal advocate for research at the strategy-entrepreneurship nexus (Zahra, 2018; Zahra & Dess, 2001), a position that has not always gone down well with other leading entrepreneurship researchers (e.g., Shane & Venkataraman, 2001).

firms. For many scholars, CE is "a powerful antidote to large company staleness, lack of innovation, stagnated top-line growth, and the inertia that often overtakes the large, mature companies of the world" (Thornberry, 2001: 526). Formalized most prominently in Burgelman's (1983) work, CE is now an established and ever-growing area of academic inquiry (Bierwerth, Schwens, Isidor, & Kabst, 2015).

When Zahra started working in the area of CE, the "the literature consisted mostly of case studies, descriptive reports, and testimonials" (Zahra, 2015: 727). Based on the notion that entire "firms per se act in entrepreneurial manners" (Covin & Miles, 1999: 49 italics original), Zahra (1991) defined CE as "the process of creating new business within established firms to improve organizational profitability and enhance a company's competitive position ... or the strategic renewal of existing business." At the time, others had defined CE in different ways, such as firm-level efforts toward product innovation or market development (Jennings & Lumpkin, 1989), disposition toward risk-taking, proactiveness, and innovativeness (Covin & Slevin, 1989), among others (e.g., Karagozoglu and Brown; 1988; Nielsen, Peters, & Hisrich, 1985). Zahra (1991) found that as environmental dynamism and hostility increased, companies emphasized CE more. Zahra (1993) elaborated that it was the perceived—rather than objective—attributes of the environment that encouraged CE, as it is managers' perceptions that "play an important role in shaping their responses to the environment" (Sharfman & Dean, 1991: 682). Zahra (1993) also introduced an empirically grounded four-pronged typology of the perceived environment ('dynamic growth,' 'hostile and competitive but technologically rich,' 'hospitable, growth-rich,' and 'static and impoverished' environments), but it does not seem to have found traction in the literature.

Zahra (1991) used a nine-item scale to measure CE, of which Zahra and Covin (1995) picked seven—and attribute them to Miller and Friesen (1982)—to gauge CE. Zahra (1991) found that an emphasis on CE was associated with superior accounting performance, which is also how Zahra and Covin (1995) operationalized firm performance, finding that the strength of the CE-performance relationship increases over time. Andersen (2010) considers Zahra and Covin (1995) to be among the most methodologically rigorous evidence for positive performance effects associated with firm-level entrepreneurship. Gupta and Gupta (2015) highlighted Zahra and Covin (1995) as the first successful effort to capture the relationship between firm-level entrepreneurship and performance over time. A meta-analysis of 42 studies with 43 independent samples heightens confidence in Zahra and Covin's (1995) findings: Bierwerth et al. (2015) show that CE was positively associated with firm performance, such that the positive effect was stronger for subjective performance than for objective performance. Based on Guth and Ginsberg (1990), Zahra (1996) introduced a three-dimensional conceptualization of CE as a combination of strategic renewal, venturing, and innovation, which has since become popular in the literature (Bierwerth et al. 2015).

While there is broad consensus around the idea that large firms need to behave entrepreneurially to compete with nimble upstarts (Kuratko, Hornsby, & Hayton, 2015), in practice the CE concept is "confusingly used by researchers" to explain a large variety of organizational phenomena (Christensen, 2004: 301). More than twenty years back, Covin and Miles (1999: 47) lamented that when scholars "talk about corporate entrepreneurship, they are often talking about different phenomena," a concern that remains "as valid today as it was then" (Schindehutte, Morris, Kuratko, & Hoskisson, 2018: 12). Furthermore, much empirical work has been done around CE, but it has yielded little useful knowledge as the vast majority of research involves cross-sectional investigations. For example, Bierwerth et al. (2015)'s meta-analysis finds that the magnitude of the strength of the CE-performance relationship is about 0.13 to 0.24, which is lower than the mean effect size across 196 meta-analyses in management research (Aguinis, Dalton, Bosco, Pierce, & Dalton, 2011). Unfortunately, studies that comprise the canon of CE research suffer heavily from endogeneity issues, so that we do not really know if CE causes superior performance, or higher performance boosts CE, or both CE and firm performance are caused by a third factor invisible at this time. Consequently, the accumulated knowledge around CE has made little progress over time, offering scarce evidence-based value to managers interested in heeding the "the entrepreneurial imperative of the twenty-first century" (Kuratko, 2009).

Zahra, Nielsen, and Bogner (1999) focus on the knowledge-creation processes within a firm's CE activities, laying the foundation for much of Zahra's later work that considered "knowledge in the context of CE" (Zahra, 2015: 729). Within this stream of work that delves into knowledge issues within CE, Zahra and George (2002a) may be one of the most "important and path-breaking" contributions (Audrestch,

2015). Zahra and George (2002a) sought to clarify and extend the concept of absorptive capacity introduced and developed by Cohen and Levinthal (1989, 1990, 1994), three papers that together laid the foundation for much of the subsequent research in this area (Apriliyanti & Alon, 2017; Zou, Ertug, & George, 2018). Cohen and Levinthal (1989) define absorptive capacity as a firm's ability to "identify, assimilate, and exploit knowledge from the environment." Cohen and Levinthal (1990) use research on individual cognitive structures and problem solving to develop a richer explanation of the absorptive capacity construct, putting more emphasis on the underlying processes. Cohen and Levinthal (1994) expand the notion of absorptive capacity from the firm's ability to exploit new external knowledge to also encompass the capability to predict more accurately the nature of future technological advances.

Concerned that the absorptive capacity literature was plagued by definitional ambiguity and divergent conceptualization, Zahra and George (2002a) propose a reconceptualization of the construct, marking a significant turn in Zahra's subsequent scholarship (Silva, 2015). For Zahra and George (2002a), absorptive capacity is a dynamic capability comprising of knowledge acquisition and assimilation dimension (potential capacity) and a knowledge transformation and exploitation dimension (realized capacity). Thus, absorptive capacity is comprised of four distinct—but complementary—competencies: acquisition, assimilation, transformation, and exploitation (Daspit & D'Souza, 2013). Firms cannot apply external knowledge without acquiring it first, and yet, not all firms that acquire and assimilate external knowledge are able to transform and apply it (Lin, Wu, Chang, Wang, & Lee, 2012). The extent to which absorptive capacity can be used in a specific situation to assimilate and commercially apply external knowledge is the situation-specific realized absorptive capacity of a firm (Lane, Koka, & Pathak, 2006). Notably, Zahra and George's (2002a) reconceptualization did not go unchallenged as Todorova and Durisin (2007) disagreed with transformation as a distinct dimension of absorptive capacity and considered the constructs of potential and realized absorptive capacity to be ambiguous and unclear. Flatten, Engelen, Zahra, and Brettel (2011) used German data to develop a 14-item scale capturing the four aspects of absorptive capacity and finding that transformation was indeed a dimension district from acquisition, assimilation, and application. Interestingly, Zahra and George (2002a: 191) also introduce the idea of 'absorptive capacity efficiency' as the ratio of realized to potential absorptive capacity ('RACAP to PACAP,' in their terms).

There is no doubt that a large body of research now exists on the issue of absorptive capacity (Apriliyanti & Alon, 2017). However, scholars have raised concerns that a large number of papers where absorptive capacity is included in the abstract, title, or keywords actually have little to do with absorptive capacity (Lane et al., 2006; Marabelli & Newell, 2014). Furthermore, empirical research on absorptive capacity has proved to be non-cumulative as "different definitions have often led to different operationalizations" (Duchek, 2013). The multi-level nature of absorptive capacity is conceptually appealing, but difficulties associated with collecting rich individual and firm-level data within the same study means that empirical research has lagged behind theoretical development (Marabelli & Newell, 2014). Patterson and Ambrosini (2015: 79) recognize that "although absorptive capacity is highly cited, it is still nascent and lacks robust empirical evidence and measures." Clearly, much work needs to be done in the area of absorptive capacity, as despite three decades of research in this area, academic understanding of this important construct remains rudimentary and fragmented.

Audretsch (2015) observes that Zahra's research "has been recognized by and had an impact on a broad spectrum of scholars spanning a wide range of fields and disciplines throughout the social sciences." As such, Zahra has also made substantive contributions to many other research streams that are worth mentioning here, such as family business (e.g., Zahra, 2003; Zahra and Sharma, 2004), dynamic capabilities (e.g., Zahra et al. 2006), and social entrepreneurship (e.g., Zahra, Gedajlovic, Neubaum, and Shulman, 2009). Based on analyzing 291 articles published in 30 management journals between 2001 and 2007, Debicki, Matherne, Kellermanns, and Chrisman (2009) rank Zahra among the most prolific family business researchers. Mustakallio, Autio, and Zahra (2002) use survey data from 192 Finnish family firms to find that the strength of shared vision among family members is positively associated with social interaction, and strategic decision quality and commitment. Zahra (2003) reports a mail survey of 409 manufacturing firms in Georgia, Tennessee, South Carolina, North Carolina, and Virginia, finding that family ownership and involvement in the firm as well as the interaction of family ownership with their involvement are significantly and positively associated with internationalization. Abdelgawad and Zahra (2019) discuss that a collective sense of being that reflects the founders' and owner family members' espoused religious values and beliefs supports family firms' spiritual capital, which then influences strategic renewal activities such as conflict resolution and resource allocation.

Bibliometric analysis reveals that Zahra is considered among the most important authors in the dynamic capabilities literature (Albort-Morant, Leal-Rodríguez, Fernández-Rodríguez, & Ariza-Montes, 2018). While Zahra and George (2002a) is a highly cited paper within the body of work focusing on 'applications of dynamic capability' (Di Stefano, Peteraf, & Verona, 2010), Zahra et al. (2006) did much to redefine dynamic capabilities. Barreto (2010) considered Zahra et al. (2006: 918)'s conception of dynamic capabilities as "the abilities to reconfigure a firm's resources and routines in the manner envisioned and deemed appropriate by its principal decision maker(s)" among the central definitions in the area. Ambrosini and Bowman (2009) credit Zahra et al. (2006) with emphasizing the use of dynamic capabilities is intentional and deliberate (and not just plain luck). Winter (2003) distinguished between operational and dynamic capabilities, which formed the bases for Newey and Zahra's (2009) insight that it is the interactions between dynamic and operating capabilities that build the adaptive capacity of an organization. Zahra and George (2002b: 198) contend that dynamic capabilities can help "the IT field an opportunity to frame its research questions based on situational and environmental contexts within which such technologies can enable a firm to gain and sustain a competitive advantage." Arend and Bromiley (2009), however, are critical of Zahra et al. (2006)'s notion of dynamic capabilities, noting that they do not explain the causal conditions that lead firms to develop and use dynamic capabilities.

Another topic to which Zahra has contributed much is social entrepreneurship. Bibliometric analysis ranks Zahra among the most published authors in social entrepreneurship research (Rey-Martí, Ribeiro-Soriano, & Palacios-Marqués, 2016). Although the social entrepreneurship literature is replete "with an abundance of disputes, controversies, and alternative perspectives" (Morris, Santos, & Kuratko, 2020: 1), it is also a fact that it is fast "becoming recognized as a dominant discourse within entrepreneurship research" (Kraus, Filser, O'Dwyer, & Shaw, 2014). At a basic level, social entrepreneurship is about identifying and pursuing opportunities to generate social value. Building on the works of Hayek, Kirzner, and Schumpeter, a three-pronged typology of social entrepreneurs was introduced in Zahra et al. (2009): social bricoleur (focus on local social needs), social constructionist (focus on social needs not adequately addressed by existing institutions and organizations), and social engineer (bring about revolutionary change to address systemic social problems). Zahra, Rawhouser, Bhawe, Neubaum, and Hayton (2008) identify five criteria to better understand global social opportunities: prevalence (how widespread is the problem?), relevance (do I have the resources, skills, and talent to address the problem?), urgency (how much spotlight does the problem draw?), accessibility (how difficult is the problem to understand and address?), and radicalness (how much novelty is needed to solve the problem?). Zahra, Newey, and Li (2014) build on insights from social entrepreneurship to articulate a broader agenda for international entrepreneurship that goes beyond traditional economic thinking to encompass sustainable well-being globally.[8]

SIDNEY WINTER: ROUTINES AND EVOLUTION

Sidney Winter, the 2015 GAER awardee, is considered among "outstanding and highly respected scholars" in management and organizational research (Hitt & Smith, 2005: 3). The official GAER citation recognized Winter for his "deep empirical understanding of Schumpeterian processes of dynamic competition, generation of differential technological opportunities through appropriability conditions and the mechanisms driving dynamic capabilities in firms." He is widely credited with having created (with his co-author Richard Nelson) "the foundations of an evolutionary revolution" (Augier, 2005: 345). His research has had a strong positive impact on scholarship in a range of fields, including strategic management, technology and innovation management, and innovation studies. Nelson and Winter (1977) is ranked among the most cited papers on innovation in its era (Rossetto, Bernardes, Borini, & Gattaz, 2018). Winter (2000), which integrates learning and satisficing into strategic management, is considered "an important contribution" to strategy research (Augier, 2005: 352). Several of Winter's publications—Zollo and Winter (2002), Winter (2003), Jacobides and

---

[8] International entrepreneurship research is another area where Zahra has made tremendous contributions (Servantie, Cabrol, Guieu, & Boissin, 2016). Bibliometric analysis of international entrepreneurship research finds Zahra among the most cited authors in this area (Baier-Fuentes, Merigó, Amorós, & Gaviria-Marín, 2019). His influential works in this area include Zahra and George (2002c), Zahra (2005), and Zahra et al. (2000).

Winter (2005)—form the intellectual core of the dynamic capabilities literature (Di Stefano et al. 2010). Klevorick, Levin, Nelson, and Winter (1995) is considered among the most cited papers in the history of *Strategic Management Journal* (Salter & McKelvey, 2016).

Winter's contribution to entrepreneurship research can be categorized into two main areas: evolutionary theory (Nelson & Winter, 1982) and dynamic capabilities (Zollo & Winter, 2002; Winter, 2003). Nelson and Winter (1982), which began as a talk for an economics course at California Institute of Technology in the late 1960s (Augier, 2005), critiqued neoclassical economic theory (particularly, Friedman's [1953] notion of profit maximization) to offer an evolutionary theory of economic change that incorporated 'natural selection' of firms and 'organizational genetics' to explain stability (Helfat, 1994). Nelson and Winter (1982: 9) were explicit that their use of the term 'evolutionary' is "above all a signal that we have borrowed ideas from biology, thus exercising an option to which economists are entitled in perpetuity by virtue of the stimulus our predecessor Malthus provided to Darwin's thinking." Notwithstanding the "widespread dissatisfaction" with the hegemony of the neoclassical paradigm in economics in the 1970s (Ulen, 1983: 576), the word 'evolution' was still "taboo in the social sciences" (Hodgson & Lamberg, 2018: 168). Perhaps for these reasons, Nelson and Winter (1982) was welcomed as "an epoch-making departure from orthodox theory" and "one of the most significant books of the decade" (Mirowski, 1983: 757). Two decades later, Hodgson (2003: 356) declared it "a rare and historic achievement."

Nelson and Winter (1982) draw upon four key ideas already present in the extant literature of the time: (a) Friedman's (1953) argument that 'natural selection' is helpful to understand firm behavior; (b) the 'Cambridge Controversies' about the production function and the fallacy of homogenous capital stock (Cohen & Harcourt, 2003); (c) the Carnegie charge against optimization (Cyert & March, 1963); and (d) Schumpeter's position that production possibilities at a given point of time are a temporary system outcome. These disparate streams came together in the crucible of the RAND 'idea factory,' and through a "number of turns in which chance played a major role" (Winter, 2017: 729), resulted in the evolutionary theory that Nelson and Winter (1982) proposed. Although spread out over an "introduction and six parts" (Ulen, 1983: 577), the basic thesis of Nelson and Winter's (1982) evolutionary theory is clearly laid out in the first few pages:

a. Firms are motivated by profit and engage in search for ways to improve their profits; these actions are, however, not profit-maximizing conditional on well-defined choice sets.
b. More profitable firms drive out less profitable firms ('natural selection' mechanism); this, however, does not mean the industry reaches the hypothetical state of 'equilibrium' where all profitable firms are at the optimal size and the less profitable ones are pushed out of business.
c. Firm behavior is a result of having, at any given time, certain capabilities and decision rules ('organizational genetics'), which are modified over time through deliberate learning efforts and random events.

Thus, Nelson and Winter (1982) had all three key elements of Darwin's theory of evolution: different types of firms (variety), inheritance of information through 'routines as genes' (retention), and the role of the external market environment in determining the survival and growth of firms (selection). The notion of routines built on Winter's (1964: 263) earlier conception of a "pattern of behavior that is followed repeatedly, but is subject to change if conditions change" and brought a Lamarckian perspective to evolutionary theory (Helfat, 1994). Organizational theorists generally believe that Lamarckian models allow for both planned and unplanned changes in organizational routines as the environment changes around them, which is contrary to the Darwinian position that meaningful change in organizational routines is not only infrequent and rarely adaptive but also highly risky (Usher & Evans, 1996). Nelson and Winter (1982: 11) were clear that "our theory is unabashedly Lamarckian: it contemplates both the 'inheritance' of acquired characters and the timely appearance of variation under the stimulus of adversity." Mirowski (1983: 763), however, believes that Nelson and Winter (1982) "adhere neither to a Lamarckian or a Darwinian framework with any consistency," which adds to the confusion around the meaning of 'evolution.' Nelson (2007) explains that Lamarckian refers to adoption of productive practices, which Hodgson and Knudsen (2007) find to be an unprecedented usage of the term not seen elsewhere in the literature.

The discussion of 'routines' in Nelson and Winter (1982) provided a theoretical foundation for the dynamic capabilities literature that emerged in the 1990s (Teece & Pisano, 1994). Winter (2005) explained that the words 'routines' and 'capabilities' refer to the same unobservable characteristic: "pattern of behavior that is followed repeatedly" (Winter, 1964: 263) or "decision rules" (Winter, 1971: 245).[9] Winter (1995: 148) defines routines as "a web of coordinating relationships connecting specific resources." Firms retain, replace, or modify their routines inline with Simon's satisficing principle,[10] which is the basis for the genetic stability and endogenous mutation in Nelson and Winter's (1982) evolutionary theory. It is routines, or capabilities, that enable organizations to perform their characteristic 'output' actions—"particularly, the creation of a tangible product or the provision of a service, and the development of new products and services" (Dosi, Nelson, & Winter, 2000: 1). Because routines are based on things that firms have done well in the past, Nelson and Winter (1982) considered evolutionary economic theory to be path-dependent, which refers to the "dependence of the current realization of a socio-economic process on previous states, up to the very initial conditions" (Castaldi & Dosi, 2006: 99).

Zollo and Winter (2002: 340) define dynamic capabilities as "a learned and stable pattern of collective activity through which the organization systematically generates and modifies its operating routines in pursuit of improved effectiveness." Two tautology-related problems had plagued the prior efforts to define dynamic capability: (a) defining capability as a sort of ability (e.g., Teece, Pisano, & Shuen, 1997) and (b) associating capabilities with competitive advantage (e.g., Griffith & Harvey, 2001) such that "if the firm has a dynamic capability, it must perform well, and if the firm is performing well, it should have a dynamic capability" (Cepeda & vera, 2007: 427). Zollo and Winter (2002)'s definition put forth a non-tautological view of dynamic capability based on Nelson and Winter's (1982) work on routines. Winter (2000) highlighted two major differences between routines and capabilities: (a) routines can be of any size and significance, whereas capabilities are substantial in scope and importance; and (b) routines are often invisible and unknown to management, but capabilities are at least somewhat understood by

---

[9] Nelson and Winter (1973) used the term 'capabilities' in the title. Winter (2005) shares that the original title of Nelson and Winter (1982) also included 'capabilities,' but it was deleted when the title was shortened at the publisher's request.

[10] Herbert Simon, recipient of the 1975 Nobel Prize in Economics, explained that satisficing is about searching a haystack for a 'needle sharp enough to sew with' as opposed to optimization which is about searching for 'the sharpest needle in the haystack' (Winter, 2000). From a satisficing logic, the search for alternatives stops when the first reasonable solution is found.

management. Routines are learned, highly patterned, repetitious, or quasi-repetitious, and founded in part in tacit knowledge; capabilities are complex, structured, and multidimensional (Winter, 2003).

Building on Collis (1994), Zollo and Winter (2002) distinguish between operational routines (first-order, how a firm earns its living) and dynamic capabilities (second order, how a firm changes its operational capabilities). Winter (2003) differentiates between ordinary capabilities (or operational routines) and dynamic capabilities, and both are highly patterned and well established in many respects. A capability, Winter (2000: 983) conceived, is "a high-level routine (or collection of routines) that, together with its implementing input flows, confers upon an organization's management a set of decision options for producing significant outputs of a particular type." Operational capabilities, Zollo and Winter (2002) explained, focused on the present, whereas dynamic capabilities were future-oriented. Consequently, operational capabilities help firms navigate the present and dynamic capabilities prepare the firm to adapt to changing environments. Not all organizational change requires the exercise of dynamic capabilities. Organizations also change in ways that are non-repetitive and 'intendedly rational,' which Winter (2003) describes as 'ad hoc problem solving.' The absence of practice or patterned behavior involved in such change means that it does not involve capabilities (Helfat & Winter, 2011).

There is no doubt that Nelson and Winter (1982) has had a profound influence on academic thinking about organizations. Many scholars favorably cite Alfred Marshall who wrote that the "Mecca of economics [lies] in economic biology rather than economic mechanics" (Marshall, 1948: xiv) It is commonly believed that economists of various stripes explicitly draw upon evolutionary theory to varying degrees (Wilson & Gowdy, 2013). However, the impact of Nelson and Winter (1982) has most acutely been felt in business research and much less so in economic thinking (Hodgson & Lamberg, 2018). There have been several insightful critiques of evolutionary economic theory (e.g., Witt, 2008), including its ideas of path-dependence (Garud, Kumaraswamy, & Karnoe, 2010), Lamarckian evolution (Hodgson & Knudsen, 2006), and routines (Hodgson, 2003). The dynamic capability literature also has been criticized for its vagueness, unresolved measurement issues, and tenuous empirical support (Arend & Bromiley, 2009), charges that even its most ardent supporters accept (Helfat & Peteraf, 2009). There is one aspect of Nelson and Winter (1982) that has gone largely unnoticed so far: firm profitability as the selection criterion (Winter, 1995). As Friedman (1953) suggested, and Nelson and Winter (2002) affirmed, the natural selection argument is based on profit-induced growth; that is, successful firms earn profits and expand.[11] Not surprisingly, research on small firms has shown that profitability is a key to long-term survival and growth (Davidsson, Steffens, & Fitzsimmons, 2009).

However, the emphasis on profitability is not always consistent with the reality of entrepreneurship, as evidenced from the impressive growth of firms that have never seen profitability (Somerville, 2019). Thousands of growth-hungry companies across diverse industries offer consumers free trials and discounts on home cleaning, beauty makeup, car sharing, and food delivery with scant consideration for profits (Brown, 2018a). Just four companies—co-working giant We Co., ride-sharing pioneers Uber and Lyft, and meal-delivery service DoorDash—all of who became top industry players after raising billions of dollars from investors and never turning a profit together lost about $15 billion in one year (Somerville, 2019). Indeed, many unprofitable companies often get more financial support than they asked. The 22-location hostel chain Selina, which offers beds and co-working space for 'digital nomads,' was seeking $50 million to expand when it received $95 million of equity and debt to target growth to some 50-plus locations (Brown, 2018b). Firms fuel demand with heavy discounts to first-time users and generous referral bonuses for anyone who signs up a friend, and their success spawns competitors who tend to spend even heavier on marketing. Investors report impatience with the failure of some companies to turn a profit even in the face of stupendous growth and market dominance (e.g., Uber), but the allure of creative market leaders with loyal customers hooked by attractive deals delivered at the touch of a smartphone app refuses to diminish (Somerville, 2019).

It is tempting to think that "over the long term, internet companies will likely provide goods and services that can be sold at greater than the cost of production" (Shane & Venkataraman, 2001: 14). Unfortunately, neither evolutionary theorists nor other scholars have been able to provide any guidance on a reasonable duration for long term. If profit is not a

---

[11] The emphasis on profitability is also central to Shane and Venkataraman's (2000) definition of entrepreneurship (Singh, 2001), which is now considered the dominant logic in entrepreneurial studies.

reliable criterion for natural selection in economic affairs, then it is not clear what else the criterion may be.

Mirowski (1983: 764) contends that evolutionary theories in economics must provision for "bankruptcy/death" because this is what "gives selection mechanisms their bite." A common idea of economic selection is that some firms enter an industry (organizational birth) and other—inefficient—firms are eliminated from the industry (Hodgson, 1996). Simon (1993: 134), for example, discussed that the inability to cope with rapid environmental change will "cause the firm's bankruptcy and demise." Bankrupt firms exit an industry and are replaced with new firms (Knudsen, 2008). However, bankruptcy is *not* organizational death. A cursory glance at the corporate world reveals many firms that went bankrupt and then were back in business, such as General Motors, Kodak, American Apparel, Chrysler, Marvel Entertainment, and Sbarro, to name a few. There are also companies like True Religion, a California-based denim-maker, that have gone bankrupt several times. At a basic level, filing for bankruptcy gives a financially struggling company the chance to continue operating while it executes a reorganization plan. Thus, bankruptcy is not the same as organizational death, and there is no biological analog of corporate bankruptcy. Evolutionary explanations of economic change therefore need to clearly explain how the biological notion of an organism's death will work in their models in a way that corresponds to the reality of the business world we live in.

SUMMARY

The relation between strategy and entrepreneurship research has long been a contentious issue among scholars. Notwithstanding ongoing concerns about whether these two academic fields are related to each other (or not), a growing body of research has accumulated at the intersection of strategy and entrepreneurship research. Four scholars have been recognized for making valuable contributions at the intersection of strategy and entrepreneurship research. This chapter discusses the work of Arnold Cooper, Kathleen Eisenhardt, Shaker Zahra, and Sidney Winter, all of who contributed to entrepreneurship research by using insights from strategy research. In doing so, they helped advance both fields and in some ways contributed to laying the foundation for strategic entrepreneurship research.

References

Abdelgawad, S. G., & Zahra, S. A. (2019). Family firms' religious identity and strategic renewal. *Journal of Business Ethics.* https://doi.org/10.1007/s10 551-019-04385-4.

Aguinis, H., Dalton, D. R., Bosco, F. A., Pierce, C. A., & Dalton, C. M. (2011). Meta-analytic choices and judgment calls: Implications for theory building and testing, obtained effect sizes, and scholarly impact. *Journal of Management, 37*(1), 5–38.

Albort-Morant, G., Leal-Rodríguez, A. L., Fernández-Rodríguez, V., & Ariza-Montes, A. (2018). Assessing the origins, evolution and prospects of the literature on dynamic capabilities: A bibliometric analysis. *European Research on Management and Business Economics, 24*(1), 42–52.

Alvarez, S. A., & Busenitz, L. W. (2001). The entrepreneurship of resource-based theory. *Journal of Management, 27*(6), 755–775.

Ambrosini, V., & Bowman, C. (2009). What are dynamic capabilities and are they a useful construct in strategic management? *International Journal of Management Reviews, 11*(1), 29–49.

Andersen, J. A. (2010). A critical examination of the EO-performance relationship. *International Journal of Entrepreneurial Behavior and Research, 16,* 309–328.

Apriliyanti, I. D., & Alon, I. (2017). Bibliometric analysis of absorptive capacity. *International Business Review, 26*(5), 896–907.

Arend, R. J., & Bromiley, P. (2009). Assessing the dynamic capabilities view: Spare change, everyone? *Strategic Organization, 7*(1), 75–90.

Audretsch, D. B. (2015). *Everything in its place: Entrepreneurship and the strategic management of cities, regions, and states.* New York: Oxford University Press.

Augier, M. (2005). Why is management an evolutionary science? An interview with Sidney G. Winter. *Journal of Management Inquiry, 14*(4), 344–354.

Baier-Fuentes, H., Merigó, J. M., Amorós, J. E., & Gaviria-Marín, M. (2019). International entrepreneurship: A bibliometric overview. *International Entrepreneurship and Management Journal, 15*(2), 385–429.

Baker, T., & Pollock, T. G. (2007). Making the marriage work: The benefits of strategy's takeover of entrepreneurship for strategic organization. *Strategic Organization, 5*(3), 297–312.

Ballhaus, R., & Hopkins, J. S. (2020, April 6). Trump pushes broader use of hydroxychloroquine against Coronavirus. *Wall Street Journal.*

Bamberger, P. A. (2019). On the replicability of abductive research in management and organizations: Internal replication and its alternatives. *Academy of Management Discoveries, 5*(2), 103–108.

Bariyo, N., & Parkinson, J. (2020, April 8). Tanzania's leader urges people to worship in throngs against Coronavirus. *Wall Street Journal.*

Barreto, I. (2010). Dynamic capabilities: A review of past research and an agenda for the future. *Journal of Management, 36*(1), 256–280.

Bierwerth, M., Schwens, C., Isidor, R., & Kabst, R. (2015). Corporate entrepreneurship and performance: A meta-analysis. *Small Business Economics, 45*(2), 255–278.

Blažková, I., & Dvouletý, O. (2020). Zombies: Who are they and how do firms become zombies? *Journal of Small Business Management, 1–27.*

Bodner, J., Song, S. Y., & Szulanski, G. (2019). Heuristics to navigate uncertainties: Interview with Professor Kathleen M. Eisenhardt. *Journal of Management Inquiry, 28*(3), 359–365.

Bourgeois, L. J., III. (1985). Strategic goals, perceived uncertainty, and economic performance in volatile environments. *Academy of Management Journal, 28*(3), 548–573.

Bourgeois, L. J., III, & Eisenhardt, K. M. (1988). Strategic decision processes in high velocity environments: Four cases in the microcomputer industry. *Management Science, 34*(7), 816–835.

Brown, E. (2018a, April 29). How to live in San Francisco without spending any money. *Wall Street Journal.*

Brown, E. (2018b, April 15). SoftBank's billions spur global race to pour money into startups. *Wall Street Journal.*

Brown, S. L., & Eisenhardt, K. M. (1995). Product development: Past research, present findings, and future directions. *Academy of Management Review, 20*(2), 343–378.

Brown, S. L., & Eisenhardt, K. M. (1997). The art of continuous change: Linking complexity theory and time-paced evolution in relentlessly shifting organizations. *Administrative Science Quarterly, 42*(1), 1–34.

Bruno, A. V., & Cooper, A. C. (1982). Patterns of development and acquisitions for Silicon Valley startups. *Technovation, 1*(4), 275–290.

Brush, C. G., Duhaime, I. M., Gartner, W. B., Stewart, A., Katz, J. A., Hitt, M. A., … Venkataraman, S. (2003). Doctoral education in the field of entrepreneurship. *Journal of Management, 29*(3), 309–331.

Burgelman, R. A. (1983). Corporate entrepreneurship and strategic management: Insights from a process study. *Management Science, 29*(12), 1349–1364.

Carlsson, B. (2013). Kathleen Eisenhardt: Recipient of the 2012 Global Award for Entrepreneurship Research. *Small Business Economics, 40*, 797–804.

Carpenter, M. A., Geletkanycz, M. A., & Sanders, W. G. (2004). Upper echelons research revisited: Antecedents, elements, and consequences of top management team composition. *Journal of Management, 30*(6), 749–778.

Cassar, G. (2010). Are individuals entering self-employment overly optimistic? An empirical test of plans and projections on nascent entrepreneur expectations. *Strategic Management Journal, 31*(8), 822–840.

Castaldi, C., & Dosi, G. (2006). The grip of history and the scope for novelty: Some results and open questions on path dependence in economic processes. In A. Wimmer & R. Kössler (Eds.), *Understanding change* (pp. 99–128). London: Palgrave Macmillan.

Cepeda, G., & Vera, D. (2007). Dynamic capabilities and operational capabilities: A knowledge management perspective. *Journal of Business Research, 60*(5), 426–437.

Christensen, K. S. (2004). A classification of the corporate entrepreneurship umbrella: Labels and perspectives. *International Journal of Management & Enterprise Development, 1*(4), 301–315.

Cohen, A. J., & Harcourt, G. C. (2003). Retrospectives: Whatever happened to the Cambridge capital theory controversies? *Journal of Economic Perspectives, 17*(1), 199–214.

Cohen, W. M., & Levinthal, D. A. (1989). Innovation and learning: The two faces of R&D. *The Economic Journal, 99*(397), 569–596.

Cohen, W. M., & Levinthal, D. A. (1990). Absorptive capacity: A new perspective on learning and innovation. *Administrative Science Quarterly, 35*(1), 128–152.

Cohen, W. M., & Levinthal, D. A. (1994). Fortune favors the prepared firm. *Management Science, 40*(2), 227–251.

Colchester, M. (2020, April 7). U.K. Prime Minister Boris Johnson moved to intensive care. *Wall Street Journal.*

Coletti, M. (2010). Technology and industrial clusters: How different are they to manage? *Science and Public Policy, 37*(9), 679–688.

Collis, D. J. (1994). How valuable are organizational capabilities? *Strategic Management Journal, 15*(S1), 143–152.

Cooper, A. C. (1964). R&D is more efficient in small companies. *Harvard Business Review, 42*(3), 75–83.

Cooper, A. C. (1966). Small companies can pioneer new products. *Harvard Business Review, 44,* 162–179.

Cooper, A. C. (1970, May). The Palo Alto experience. *Industrial Research,* 58–60.

Cooper, A. C. (1971). Spin-offs and technical entrepreneurship. *IEEE Transactions on Engineering Management, 18*(1), 2–6.

Cooper, A. C. (1972). Incubator organizations and technical entrepreneurship. In A. C. Cooper & J. L. Komi (Eds.), *Technical entrepreneurship: A symposium* (pp. 108–125). Milwaukee: Center for Venture Management.

Cooper, A. C. (1973). Technical entrepreneurship: What do we know? *R&D Management, 3*(2), 59–64.

Cooper, A. C. (1985). The role of incubator organizations in the founding of growth-oriented firms. *Journal of Business Venturing, 1*(1), 75–86.

Cooper, A. C. (1998). Findings on predictors of performance from a large-scale research program. *Small Enterprise Research, 6*(1), 3–9.

Cooper, A. C., & Bruno, A. V. (1977). Success among high-technology firms. *Business Horizons, 20*(2), 16–22.

Cooper, A. C., Dunkelberg, W. C., Woo, C. Y., & Dennis, W. J., Jr. (1990). *New business in America: The firms and their owners.* Washington, DC: NFIB Foundation.

Cooper, A. C., Gimeno-Gascon, F. J., & Woo, C. Y. (1994). Initial human and financial capital as predictors of new venture performance. *Journal of Business Venturing, 9*(5), 371–395.

Cooper, A. C., Woo, C. Y., & Dunkelberg, W. C. (1988). Entrepreneurs' perceived chances for success. *Journal of Business Venturing, 3*(2), 97–108.

Cooper, A. C., Woo, C. Y., & Dunkelberg, W. C. (1989). Entrepreneurship and the initial size of firms. *Journal of Business Venturing, 4*(5), 317–332.

Covin, J. G., & Miles, M. P. (1999). Corporate entrepreneurship and the pursuit of competitive advantage. *Entrepreneurship Theory and Practice, 23*(3), 47–63.

Covin, J. G., & Slevin, D. P. (1989). Strategic management of small firms in hostile and benign environments. *Strategic Management Journal, 10*(1), 75–87.

Cyert, R. M., & March, J. G. (1963). *A behavioral theory of the firm.* Englewood Cliffs, NJ: Prentice Hall.

Dacin, M. T., Oliver, C., & Roy, J. P. (2007). The legitimacy of strategic alliances: An institutional perspective. *Strategic Management Journal, 28*(2), 169–187.

Daspit, J., & D'Souza, D. (2013). Understanding the multi-dimensional nature of absorptive capacity. *Journal of Managerial Issues, 25*(3), 299–316.

Davidsson, P., & Wiklund, J. (2006). Conceptual and empirical challenges in the study of firm growth. In P. Davidsson, F. Delmar, & J. Wiklund (Eds.), *Entrepreneurship and the growth of firms* (pp. 39–61). Cheltenham, UK: Edward Elgar.

Davidsson, P., Delmar, F., & Wiklund, J. (2006). Entrepreneurship as growth; growth as entrepreneurship. In P. Davidsson, F. Delmar, & J. Wiklund (Eds.), *Entrepreneurship and the growth of firms* (pp. 21–38). Cheltenham, UK: Edward Elgar.

Davidsson, P., Steffens, P., & Fitzsimmons, J. (2009). Growing profitable or growing from profits: Putting the horse in front of the cart? *Journal of Business Venturing, 24*(4), 388–406.

Davis, J. P., & Eisenhardt, K. M. (2011). Rotating leadership and collaborative innovation: Recombination processes in symbiotic relationships. *Administrative Science Quarterly, 56*(2), 159–201.

Davis, J. P., Eisenhardt, K. M., & Bingham, C. B. (2007). Developing theory through simulation methods. *Academy of Management Review, 32*(2), 480–499.

Davis, J. P., Eisenhardt, K. M., & Bingham, C. B. (2009). Optimal structure, market dynamism, and the strategy of simple rules. *Administrative Science Quarterly, 54*(3), 413–452.

Debicki, B. J., Matherne, C. F., III, Kellermanns, F. W., & Chrisman, J. J. (2009). Family business research in the new millennium: An overview of the who, the where, the what, and the why. *Family Business Review, 22*(2), 151–166.

Dess, G., & Beard, D. (1984). Dimensions of organizational task environments. *Administrative Science Quarterly, 29*(1), 52–73.

Di Stefano, G., Peteraf, M., & Verona, G. (2010). Dynamic capabilities deconstructed: A bibliographic investigation into the origins, development, and future directions of the research domain. *Industrial and Corporate Change, 19*(4), 1187–1204.

Dosi, G., Nelson, R. R., & Winter, S. G. (2000). Introduction. In G. Dosi, R. R. Nelson, & S. G. Winter (Eds.), *The nature and dynamics of organisational capabilities* (pp. 1–22). Oxford, UK: Oxford University Press.

Doyle, A. C. (1891). *Sherlock Holmes: A scandal in Bohemia*. London: G. Newnes.

Duchek, S. (2013). Capturing absorptive capacity: A critical review and future prospects. *Schmalenbach Business Review, 65*(3), 312–329.

Dyer, W. G., Jr., & Wilkins, A. L. (1991). Better stories, not better constructs, to generate better theory: A rejoinder to Eisenhardt. *Academy of Management Review, 16*(3), 613–619.

Dyer, J. H., Kale, P., & Singh, H. (2001). How to make strategic alliances work. *Sloan Management Review, 42*(4), 37–43.

Egeln, J., Gottschalk, S., & Rammer, C. (2004). Location decisions of spin-offs from public research institutions. *Industry and Innovation, 11*(3), 207–223.

Eisenhardt, K. M. (1985). Control: Organizational and economic approaches. *Management Science, 31*(2), 134–149.

Eisenhardt, K. M. (1988). Agency-and institutional-theory explanations: The case of retail sales compensation. *Academy of Management Journal, 31*(3), 488–511.

Eisenhardt, K. M. (1989a). Making fast strategic decisions in high-velocity environments. *Academy of Management Journal, 32*(3), 543–576.

Eisenhardt, K. M. (1989b). Agency theory: An assessment and review. *Academy of Management Review, 14*(1), 57–74.

Eisenhardt, K. M. (1989c). Building theories from case study research. *Academy of Management Review, 14*(4), 532–550.

Eisenhardt, K. M. (1991). Better stories and better constructs: The case for rigor and comparative logic. *Academy of Management Review, 16*(3), 620–627.

Eisenhardt, K. M. (2019). Thoughts about research, inspirations for research and future research. In B. Boyd, R. T. Crook, J. K. Le, & A. D. Smith (Eds.), *Standing on the shoulders of giants: Traditions and innovations in research* (pp. 15–26). Bingley, UK: Emerald.

Eisenhardt, K. M., & Bourgeois, L. J., III. (1988). Politics of strategic decision making in high-velocity environments: Toward a midrange theory. *Academy of Management Journal, 31*(4), 737–770.

Eisenhardt, K. M., & Graebner, M. E. (2007). Theory building from cases: Opportunities and challenges. *Academy of Management Journal, 50*(1), 25–32.

Eisenhardt, K. M., & Martin, J. A. (2000). Dynamic capabilities: What are they? *Strategic Management Journal, 21*(10–11), 1105–1121.

Eisenhardt, K. M., & Santos, F. M. (2002). Knowledge based view: A new theory of strategy? In A. Pettigrew, H. Thomas, & R. Whittington (Eds.), *Handbook of strategy and management* (pp. 139–164). London: Sage.

Eisenhardt, K. M., & Schoonhoven, C. B. (1990). Organizational growth: Linking founding team, strategy, environment, and growth among US semiconductor ventures, 1978–1988. *Administrative Science Quarterly, 35*(3), 504–529.

Eisenhardt, K. M., & Schoonhoven, C. B. (1996). Resource-based view of strategic alliance formation: Strategic and social effects in entrepreneurial firms. *Organization Science, 7*(2), 136–150.

Eisenhardt, K. M., & Tabrizi, B. (1995). Accelerating adaptive processes: Product innovation in the global computer industry. *Administrative Science Quarterly, 40*(1), 84–110.

Eisenhardt, K. M., & Zbaracki, M. J. (1992). Strategic decision making. *Strategic Management Journal, 13*(S2), 17–37.

Eriksson, T., & Kuhn, J. M. (2006). Firm spin-offs in Denmark 1981–2000: Patterns of entry and exit. *International Journal of Industrial Organization, 24*(5), 1021–1040.

Ferreira, J. J. M., Fernandes, C. I., & Ratten, V. (2016). A co-citation bibliometric analysis of strategic management research. *Scientometrics, 109*(1), 1–32.

Ferreira, M. P., Reis, N. R., & Miranda, R. (2015). Thirty years of entrepreneurship research published in top journals: Analysis of citations, co-citations and themes. *Journal of Global Entrepreneurship Research, 5*(1), 17.

Flatten, T. C., Engelen, A., Zahra, S. A., & Brettel, M. (2011). A measure of absorptive capacity: Scale development and validation. *European Management Journal, 29*(2), 98–116.

Friedman, M. (1953). *Essays in positive economics.* Chicago: University of Chicago Press.

Furlan, A., & Grandinetti, R. (2016). Spinoffs and their endowments: Beyond knowledge inheritance theory. *Journal of Intellectual Capital, 17*(3), 570–589.

Furrer, O., Thomas, H., & Goussevskaia, A. (2008). The structure and evolution of the strategic management field: A content analysis of 26 years of strategic management research. *International Journal of Management Reviews, 10*(1), 1–23.

Garg, S., & Eisenhardt, K. M. (2017). Unpacking the CEO–board relationship: How strategy making happens in entrepreneurial firms. *Academy of Management Journal, 60*(5), 1828–1858.

Garud, R., Kumaraswamy, A., & Karnøe, P. (2010). Path dependence or path creation? *Journal of Management Studies, 47*(4), 760–774.

Garvin, D. A. (1983). Spin-offs and the new firm formation process. *California Management Review, 25*(2), 3–20.

George, G., Zahra, S. A., & Wood, D. R., Jr. (2002). The effects of business–university alliances on innovative output and financial performance: A study of publicly traded biotechnology companies. *Journal of Business Venturing, 17*(6), 577–609.

Gimeno, J., Folta, T. B., Cooper, A. C., & Woo, C. Y. (1997). Survival of the fittest? Entrepreneurial human capital and the persistence of underperforming firms. *Administrative Science Quarterly, 42*(4), 750–783.

Glaser, B., & Strauss, A. (1967). *The discovery of grounded theory: Strategies of qualitative research.* Chicago: Aldine.

Griffith, D. A., & Harvey, M. G. (2001). A resource perspective of global dynamic capabilities. *Journal of International Business Studies, 32*(3), 597–606.

Gupta, V. K., Ibrahim, S., Guo, G., & Markin, E. (2016). Entrepreneurship research in management and organizational studies: A contribution-based assessment of the literature. *New England Journal of Entrepreneurship, 19*(1), 69–86.

Gupta, V. K., Niranjan, S., & Markin, E. (2020). Entrepreneurial orientation and firm performance: The mediating role of generative and acquisitive learning through customer relationships. *Review of Managerial Science, 14,* 1123–1147.

Gupta, V. K., Wieland, A. M., & Turban, D. B. (2019b). Gender characterizations in entrepreneurship: A multi-level investigation of sex-role stereotypes about high growth, commercial, and social entrepreneurs. *Journal of Small Business Management, 57*(1), 131–153.

Gupta, V., & Gupta, A. (2015). The concept of entrepreneurial orientation. *Foundations and Trends in Entrepreneurship, 11*(2), 55–137.

Guth, W., & Ginsberg, A. (1990). Guest editors' introduction: Corporate entrepreneurship. *Strategic Management Journal, 11*, 5–15.

Haeussler, C., Patzelt, H., & Zahra, S. A. (2012). Strategic alliances and product development in high technology new firms: The moderating effect of technological capabilities. *Journal of Business Venturing, 27*(2), 217–233.

Hallen, B. L. (2008). The causes and consequences of the initial network positions of new organizations: From whom do entrepreneurs receive investments? *Administrative Science Quarterly, 53*(4), 685–718.

Hallen, B. L., & Eisenhardt, K. M. (2012). Catalyzing strategies and efficient tie formation: How entrepreneurial firms obtain investment ties. *Academy of Management Journal, 55*(1), 35–70.

Hallen, B. L., Katila, R., & Rosenberger, J. D. (2014). How do social defenses work? A resource-dependence lens on technology ventures, venture capital investors, and corporate relationships. *Academy of Management Journal, 57*(4), 1078–1101.

Heckman, J. J., & Singer, B. (2017). Abducting economics. *American Economic Review, 107*(5), 298–302.

Helfat, C. E. (1994). Evolutionary trajectories in petroleum firm R&D. *Management Science, 40*(12), 1720–1747.

Helfat, C. E., & Lieberman, M. B. (2002). The birth of capabilities: Market entry and the importance of pre-history. *Industrial and Corporate Change, 11*(4), 725–760.

Helfat, C. E., & Peteraf, M. (2009). Understanding dynamic capabilities: Progress along a developmental path. *Strategic Organization, 7*(1), 91–102.

Helfat, C. E., & Winter, S. G. (2011). Untangling dynamic and operational capabilities: Strategy for the (N)ever-changing world. *Strategic Management Journal, 32*(11), 1243–1250.

Hitt, M. A., & Smith, K. G. (2005). Introduction: The process of developing management theory. In K. G. Smith & M. A. Hitt (Eds.), *Great minds in management: The process of theory development* (pp. 1–6). New York: Oxford University Press.

Hitt, M. A., Ireland, R. D., Camp, S. M., & Sexton, D. L. (2001). Strategic entrepreneurship: Entrepreneurial strategies for wealth creation. *Strategic Management Journal, 22*(6–7), 479–491.

Hitt, M. A., Ireland, R. D., Sirmon, D. G., & Trahms, C. A. (2011). Strategic entrepreneurship: Creating value for individuals, organizations, and society. *Academy of Management Perspectives, 25*(2), 57–75.

Hodgson, G. M. (1996). *Economics and evolution: Bringing life back into economics.* Ann Arbor: University of Michigan Press.

Hodgson, G. M. (2003). The hidden persuaders: Institutions and individuals in economic theory. *Cambridge Journal of Economics, 27*(2), 159–175.

Hodgson, G. M., & Knudsen, T. (2006). Dismantling Lamarckism: Why descriptions of socio-economic evolution as Lamarckian are misleading. *Journal of Evolutionary Economics, 16*(4), 343–366.

Hodgson, G. M., & Knudsen, T. (2007). Evolutionary theorizing beyond Lamarckism: A reply to Richard Nelson. *Journal of Evolutionary Economics, 17*(3), 353–359.

Hodgson, G. M., & Lamberg, J. A. (2018). The past and future of evolutionary economics: Some reflections based on new bibliometric evidence. *Evolutionary and Institutional Economics Review, 15*(1), 167–187.

Ireland, R. D. (2007). Strategy vs. entrepreneurship. *Strategic Entrepreneurship Journal, 1*(1–2), 7–10.

Isaak, R., Isaak, A., & Zybura, J. (2016). Replicating Silicon Valley: Talent and techno-management in a culture of serendipity. In H. Wang & Y. Liu (Eds.), *Entrepreneurship and talent management from a global perspective* (pp. 149–187). Cheltenham, UK: Edward Elgar.

Jacobides, M. G., & Winter, S. G. (2005). The co-evolution of capabilities and transaction costs: Explaining the institutional structure of production. *Strategic Management Journal, 26*(5), 395–413.

Javadian, G., Dobratz, C., Gupta, A., Gupta, V. K., & Martin, J. (2020). Qualitative research in entrepreneurship studies: A state-of-science. *Journal of Entrepreneurship, 29*(2), 1–36.

Jennings, D. F., & Lumpkin, J. R. (1989). Functioning modeling corporate entrepreneurship: An empirical integrative analysis. *Journal of Management, 15*(3), 485–502.

Kapitan, T. (1990). In what way is abductive inference creative? *Transactions of the Charles S. Peirce Society, 26*(4), 499–512.

Karagozoglu, N., & Brown, W. B. (1988). Adaptive responses by conservative and entrepreneurial firms. *Journal of Product Innovation Management, 5*(4), 269–281.

Katila, R., Rosenberger, J. D., & Eisenhardt, K. M. (2008). Swimming with sharks: Technology ventures, defense mechanisms and corporate relationships. *Administrative Science Quarterly, 53*(2), 295–332.

Kelley, D. J., Ali, A., & Zahra, S. A. (2013). Where do breakthroughs come from? Characteristics of high-potential inventions. *Journal of Product Innovation Management, 30*(6), 1212–1226.

Klevorick, A. K., Levin, R. C., Nelson, R. R., & Winter, S. G. (1995). On the sources and significance of interindustry differences in technological opportunities. *Research Policy, 24*(2), 185–205.

Knudsen, T. (2008). Organizational routines in evolutionary theory. In M. C. Becker (Ed.), *Handbook of organizational routines* (pp. 125–151). Cheltenham, UK: Edward Elgar.

Koka, B. R., & Prescott, J. E. (2002). Strategic alliances as social capital: A multidimensional view. *Strategic Management Journal, 23*(9), 795–816.

Kraus, S., & Kauranen, I. (2009). Strategic management and entrepreneurship: Friends or foes? *International Journal of Business Science & Applied Management, 4*(1), 37–50.

Kraus, S., Filser, M., O'Dwyer, M., & Shaw, E. (2014). Social entrepreneurship: An exploratory citation analysis. *Review of Managerial Science, 8*(2), 275–292.

Kuratko, D. F. (2006). A tribute to 50 years of excellence in entrepreneurship and small business. *Journal of Small Business Management, 44*(3), 483–492.

Kuratko, D. F. (2009). The entrepreneurial imperative of the 21st century. *Business Horizons, 52,* 421–428.

Kuratko, D. F., & Audretsch, D. B. (2013). Clarifying the domains of corporate entrepreneurship. *International Entrepreneurship and Management Journal, 9*(3), 323–335.

Kuratko, D. F., Hornsby, J. S., & Hayton, J. (2015). Corporate entrepreneurship: The innovative challenge for a new global economic reality. *Small Business Economics, 45*(2), 245–253.

Landström, H. (2005). *Pioneers in entrepreneurship and small business research.* Boston, MA: Springer.

Lane, P. J., Koka, B. R., & Pathak, S. (2006). The reification of absorptive capacity: A critical review and rejuvenation of the construct. *Academy of Management Review, 31*(4), 833–863.

Langley, A., & Abdallah, C. (2011). Templates and turns in qualitative studies of strategy and management. In D. Bergh & D. Ketchen (Eds.), *Research methodology in strategy and management: Vol. 6—Building methodological bridges* (pp. 201–235). Bingley, UK: Emerald.

Leamer, E. E. (1983). Let's take the con out of econometrics. *The American Economic Review, 73*(1), 31–43.

Lin, C., Wu, Y. J., Chang, C., Wang, W., & Lee, C. Y. (2012). The alliance innovation performance of R&D alliances: The absorptive capacity perspective. *Technovation, 32*(5), 282–292.

Magalhaes, L., & Forero, J. (2020, April 16). Brazil president Bolsonaro fires health minister amid Coronavirus crisis. *Wall Street Journal.*

Marabelli, M., & Newell, S. (2014). Knowing, power and materiality: A critical review and reconceptualization of absorptive capacity. *International Journal of Management Reviews, 16*(4), 479–499.

Markin, E., Swab, R. G., & Marshall, D. R. (2017). Who is driving the bus? An analysis of author and institution contributions to entrepreneurship research. *Journal of Innovation & Knowledge, 2*(1), 1–9.

Marlow, S. (2002). Women and self-employment: A part of or apart from theoretical construct? *The International Journal of Entrepreneurship and Innovation, 3*(2), 83–91.

Marshall, A. (1948). *Principles of economics* (8th ed.). London: Macmillan.

Miller, D., & Friesen, P. H. (1982). Innovation in conservative and entrepreneurial firms: Two models of strategic momentum. *Strategic Management Journal, 3*(1), 1–25.

Mintzberg, H., Raisinghani, D., & Theoret, A. (1976). The structure of "unstructured" decision processes. *Administrative Science Quarterly, 21*(2), 246–275.

Mirowski, P. (1983). An evolutionary theory of economics change: A review article. *Journal of Economic Issues, 17*(3), 757–768.

Morris, M. H., Santos, S. C., & Kuratko, D. F. (2020). The great divides in social entrepreneurship and where they lead us. *Small Business Economics.* https://doi.org/10.1007/s11187-020-00318-y.

Mustakallio, M., Autio, E., & Zahra, S. A. (2002). Relational and contractual governance in family firms: Effects on strategic decision making. *Family Business Review, 15*(3), 205–222.

Nelson, R. R. (2007). Comment on: Dismantling Lamarckism: Why descriptions of socio-economic evolution as Lamarckian are misleading, by Hodgson and Knudsen. *Journal of Evolutionary Economics, 17*(3), 349–352.

Nelson, R. R., & Winter, S. G. (1973). Toward an evolutionary theory of economic capabilities. *The American Economic Review, 63*(2), 440–449.

Nelson, R. R., & Winter, S. G. (1977). In search of useful theory of innovation. *Research Policy, 6*(1), 36–76.

Nelson, R. R., & Winter, S. G. (1982). *An evolutionary theory of economic change.* Cambridge: Harvard University Press.

Nelson, R. R., & Winter, S. G. (2002). Evolutionary theorizing in economics. *Journal of Economic Perspectives, 16*(2), 23–46.

Nerur, S. P., Rasheed, A. A., & Natarajan, V. (2008). The intellectual structure of the strategic management field: An author co-citation analysis. *Strategic Management Journal, 29*(3), 319–336.

Newey, L. R., & Zahra, S. A. (2009). The evolving firm: How dynamic and operating capabilities interact to enable entrepreneurship. *British Journal of Management, 20,* S81–S100.

Nielsen, R. P., Peters, M. P., & Hisrich, R. D. (1985). Intrapreneurship strategy for internal markets—corporate, non-profit and government institution cases. *Strategic Management Journal, 6*(2), 181–189.

Niiniluoto, I. (1999). Defending abduction. *Philosophy of Science, 66,* S436–S451.

Ozcan, P. (2018). Growing with the market: How changing conditions during market growth affect formation and evolution of interfirm ties. *Strategic Management Journal, 39*(2), 295–328.

Ozcan, P., & Eisenhardt, K. M. (2009). Origin of alliance portfolios: Entrepreneurs, network strategies, and firm performance. *Academy of Management Journal, 52*(2), 246–279.

Patterson, W., & Ambrosini, V. (2015). Configuring absorptive capacity as a key process for research intensive firms. *Technovation, 36*, 77–89.

Pearce, J. A., & Zahra, S. A. (1991). The relative power of CEOs and boards of directors: Associations with corporate performance. *Strategic Management Journal, 12*(2), 135–153.

Phan, P. H., Wright, M., Ucbasaran, D., & Tan, W. L. (2009). Corporate entrepreneurship: Current research and future directions. *Journal of Business Venturing, 24*(3), 197–205.

Rajagopalan, N., Rasheed, A. M., & Datta, D. K. (1993). Strategic decision processes: Critical review and future directions. *Journal of Management, 19*(2), 349–384.

Ravenswood, K. (2011). Eisenhardt's impact on theory in case study research. *Journal of Business Research, 64*(7), 680–686.

Rey-Martí, A., Ribeiro-Soriano, D., & Palacios-Marqués, D. (2016). A bibliometric analysis of social entrepreneurship. *Journal of Business Research, 69*(5), 1651–1655.

Rossetto, D. E., Bernardes, R. C., Borini, F. M., & Gattaz, C. C. (2018). Structure and evolution of innovation research in the last 60 years: Review and future trends in the field of business through the citations and co-citations analysis. *Scientometrics, 115*(3), 1329–1363.

Salter, A. J., & McKelvey, M. (2016). Evolutionary analysis of innovation and entrepreneurship: Sidney G. Winter—recipient of the 2015 Global Award for Entrepreneurship Research. *Small Business Economics, 47*(1), 1–14.

Santos, F. M., & Eisenhardt, K. M. (2009). Constructing markets and shaping boundaries: Entrepreneurial power in nascent fields. *Academy of Management Journal, 52*(4), 643–671.

Sarasvathy, S. D. (2001). Causation and effectuation: Toward a theoretical shift from economic inevitability to entrepreneurial contingency. *Academy of Management Review, 26*(2), 243–263.

Schendel, D., & Hofer, C. W. (1979). *Strategic Management*. Boston: Little, Brown.

Schindehutte, M., Morris, M. H., Kuratko, D. F., & Hoskisson, S. (2018). Unpacking corporate entrepreneurship: A critique and extension. In D. F. Kuratko & S. Hoskinson (Eds.), *The challenges of corporate entrepreneurship in the disruptive age* (Vol. 28, pp. 11–35). Emerald: Bingley.

Schurz, G. (2008). Patterns of abduction. *Synthese, 164*(2), 201–234.

Servantie, V., Cabrol, M., Guieu, G., & Boissin, J. P. (2016). Is international entrepreneurship a field? A bibliometric analysis of the literature (1989–2015). *Journal of International Entrepreneurship, 14*(2), 168–212.

Shafique, M. (2013). Thinking inside the box? Intellectual structure of the knowledge base of innovation research (1988–2008). *Strategic Management Journal, 34*(1), 62–93.

Shane, S., & Venkataraman, S. (2000). The promise of entrepreneurship as a field of research. *Academy of Management Review, 25*(1), 217–226.

Shane, S., & Venkataraman, S. (2001). Entrepreneurship as a field of research: A response to Zahra and Dess, Singh, and Erikson. *Academy of Management Review, 26*(1), 13–16.

Sharfman, M. P., & Dean, J. W., Jr. (1991). Conceptualizing and measuring the organizational environment: A multidimensional approach. *Journal of Management, 17*(4), 681–700.

Sharma, P., & Chrisman, S. J. J. (1999). Toward a reconciliation of the definitional issues in the field of corporate entrepreneurship. *Entrepreneurship Theory & Practice, 23*(3), 35–46.

Silva, A. (2015). Shaker Zahra author bibliometric study: Analysis of scientific publications from 1985 to 2014. *Revista de Negocios, 20*(4), 44–60.

Simon, H. A. (1993). Strategy and organizational evolution. *Strategic Management Journal, 14*(S2), 131–142.

Singh, R. P. (2001). A comment on developing the field of entrepreneurship through the study of opportunity recognition and exploitation. *Academy of Management Review, 26*(1), 10–12.

Smith, B. (2018). Generalizability in qualitative research: Misunderstandings, opportunities and recommendations for the sport and exercise sciences. *Qualitative Research in Sport, Exercise and Health, 10*(1), 137–149.

Smith, N. R., & Miner, J. B. (1983). Type of entrepreneur, type of firm, and managerial motivation: Implications for organizational life cycle theory. *Strategic Management Journal, 4*(4), 325–340.

Snow, C. C., & Thomas, J. B. (1994). Field research methods in strategic management: Contributions to theory building and testing. *Journal of Management Studies, 31*(4), 457–480.

Somerville, H. (2019, December 27). Tech startups face new investor mandate: Profits over discounts. *Wall Street Journal.*

Storey, D. J., & Tether, B. S. (1998). New technology-based firms in the European Union: An introduction. *Research Policy, 26*(9), 933–946.

Sturgeon, T. J. (2003). What really goes on in Silicon Valley? Spatial clustering and dispersal in modular production networks. *Journal of Economic Geography, 3*(2), 199–225.

Tang, J., Tang, Z., & Lohrke, F. T. (2008). Developing an entrepreneurial typology: The roles of entrepreneurial alertness and attributional style. *International Entrepreneurship and Management Journal, 4*(3), 273–294.

Teece, D. J., Pisano, G., & Shuen, A. (1997). Dynamic capabilities and strategic management. *Strategic Management Journal, 18*(7), 509–533.

Teece, D., & Pisano, G. (1994). The dynamic capabilities of firms: An introduction. *Industrial and Corporate Change, 3*(3), 537–556.

Thornberry, N. (2001). Corporate entrepreneurship: Antidote or oxymoron? *European Management Journal, 19*(5), 526–533.

Todorova, G., & Durisin, B. (2007). Absorptive capacity: Valuing a reconceptualization. *Academy of Management Review, 32*(3), 774–786.

Ulen, T. S. (1983). Review of the book *An evolutionary theory of economic change. Business History Review, 57*(4), 576–578.

Uotila, J., Maula, M., Keil, T., & Zahra, S. A. (2009). Exploration, exploitation, and financial performance: Analysis of S&P 500 corporations. *Strategic Management Journal, 30*(2), 221–231.

Usher, J. M., & Evans, M. G. (1996). Life and death along gasoline alley: Darwinian and Lamarckian processes in a differentiating population. *Academy of Management Journal, 39*(5), 1428–1466.

Venkataraman, S., & Sarasvathy, S. D. (2001). Strategy and entrepreneurship. In M. A. Hitt, R. E. Freeman, & J. S. Harrison (Eds.), *Handbook of strategic management* (pp. 650–668). Oxford: Blackwell.

Vyas, K. (2020, April 7). Cow dung, garlic, and a prayer: The fight against phony cures for Coronavirus. *Wall Street Journal.*

Wilson, D. S., & Gowdy, J. M. (2013). Evolution as a general theoretical framework for economics and public policy. *Journal of Economic Behavior & Organization, 90*, S3–S10.

Winter, S. G. (1964). Economic 'natural selection' and the theory of the firm. *Yale Economic Essays, 4*(1), 225–272.

Winter, S. G. (1971). Satisficing, selection, and the innovating remnant. *The Quarterly Journal of Economics, 85*(2), 237–261.

Winter, S. G. (1995). Four Rs of profitability: Rents, resources, routines, and replication. In C. A. Montgomery (Ed.), *Resource-based and evolutionary theories of the firm: Towards a synthesis* (pp. 147–178). Boston, MA: Springer.

Winter, S. G. (2000). The satisficing principle in capability learning. *Strategic Management Journal, 21*(10–11), 981–996.

Winter, S. G. (2003). Understanding dynamic capabilities. *Strategic Management Journal, 24*(10), 991–995.

Winter, S. G. (2005). Developing evolutionary theory for economics and management. In K. G. Smith & M. A. Hitt (Eds.), *Great minds in management: The process of theory development* (pp. 509–546). Oxford, U.K.: Oxford University Pres.

Winter, S. G. (2017). Pursuing the evolutionary agenda in economics and management research. *Cambridge Journal of Economics, 41*(3), 721–747.

Witt, U. (2008). What is specific about evolutionary economics? *Journal of Evolutionary Economics, 18*(5), 547–575.

Wolcott, H. (1995). *The art of fieldwork.* Walnut Creek, CA: AltaMira.

Woo, C. Y., Cooper, A. C., & Dunkelberg, W. C. (1991). The development and interpretation of entrepreneurial typologies. *Journal of Business Venturing, 6*(2), 93–114.

Yin, R. K. (1984). *Case study research: Design and methods.* Beverly Hills, CA: Sage.

Zahra, S. A. (1991). Predictors and financial outcomes of corporate entrepreneurship: An exploratory study. *Journal of Business Venturing, 6*(4), 259–285.

Zahra, S. A. (1993). A conceptual model of entrepreneurship as firm behavior: A critique and extension. *Entrepreneurship Theory and Practice, 17*(4), 5–21.

Zahra, S. A. (1996). Governance, ownership, and corporate entrepreneurship: The moderating impact of industry technological opportunities. *Academy of Management Journal, 39*(6), 1713–1735.

Zahra, S. A. (2003). International expansion of US manufacturing family businesses: The effect of ownership and involvement. *Journal of Business Venturing, 18*(4), 495–512.

Zahra, S. A. (2005). A theory of international new ventures: A decade of research. *Journal of International Business Studies, 36*(1), 20–28.

Zahra, S. A. (2015). Corporate entrepreneurship as knowledge creation and conversion: The role of entrepreneurial hubs. *Small Business Economics, 44*(4), 727–735.

Zahra, S. A. (2018). Entrepreneurial risk taking in family firms: The wellspring of the regenerative capability. *Family Business Review, 31*(2), 216–226.

Zahra, S. A., & Covin, J. G. (1993). Business strategy, technology policy and firm performance. *Strategic Management Journal, 14*(6), 451–478.

Zahra, S. A., & Covin, J. G. (1995). Contextual influences on the corporate entrepreneurship-performance relationship: A longitudinal analysis. *Journal of Business Venturing, 10*(1), 43–58.

Zahra, S. A., & Das, S. R. (1993). Innovation strategy and financial performance in manufacturing companies: An empirical study. *Production and Operations Management, 2*(1), 15–37.

Zahra, S. A., & Dess, G. G. (2001). Entrepreneurship as a field of research: Encouraging dialogue and debate. *Academy of Management Review, 26*(1), 8–10.

Zahra, S. A., & George, G. (2002a). Absorptive capacity: A review, reconceptualization, and extension. *Academy of Management Review, 27*(2), 185–203.

Zahra, S. A., & George, G. (2002b). The net-enabled business innovation cycle and the evolution of dynamic capabilities. *Information Systems Research, 13*(2), 147–150.

Zahra, S. A., & George, G. (2002c). International entrepreneurship: The current status of the field and future research agenda. In M. A. Hitt, R. D. Ireland, S. M. Camp, & D. L. Sexton (Eds.), *Strategic entrepreneurship: Creating a new mindset* (pp. 255–288). Oxford, UK: Blackwell.

Zahra, S. A., & Pearce, J. A. (1989). Boards of directors and corporate financial performance: A review and integrative model. *Journal of Management, 15*(2), 291–334.

Zahra, S. A., & Sharma, P. (2004). Family business research: A strategic reflection. *Family Business Review, 17*(4), 331–346.

Zahra, S. A., Gedajlovic, E., Neubaum, D. O., & Shulman, J. M. (2009). A typology of social entrepreneurs: Motives, search processes and ethical challenges. *Journal of Business Venturing, 24*(5), 519–532.

Zahra, S. A., Ireland, R. D., & Hitt, M. A. (2000). International expansion by new venture firms: International diversity, mode of market entry, technological learning, and performance. *Academy of Management Journal, 43*(5), 925–950.

Zahra, S. A., Newey, L. R., & Li, Y. (2014). On the frontiers: The implications of social entrepreneurship for international entrepreneurship. *Entrepreneurship Theory and Practice, 38*(1), 137–158.

Zahra, S. A., Nielsen, A. P., & Bogner, W. C. (1999). Corporate entrepreneurship, knowledge, and competence development. *Entrepreneurship Theory and Practice, 23*(3), 169–189.

Zahra, S. A., Rawhouser, H. N., Bhawe, N., Neubaum, D. O., & Hayton, J. C. (2008). Globalization of social entrepreneurship opportunities. *Strategic Entrepreneurship Journal, 2*(2), 117–131.

Zahra, S. A., Sapienza, H. J., & Davidsson, P. (2006). Entrepreneurship and dynamic capabilities: A review, model and research agenda. *Journal of Management Studies, 43*(4), 917–955.

Zollo, M., & Winter, S. G. (2002). Deliberate the evolution of dynamic capabilities. *Organization Science, 13*(3), 339–351.

Zou, T., Ertug, G., & George, G. (2018). The capacity to innovate: A meta-analysis of absorptive capacity. *Innovation, 20*(2), 87–121.

CHAPTER 7

Sub-Domains

The present time seems a golden age for entrepreneurship research. Governments, universities, private foundations, and specialized research institutions enthusiastically support entrepreneurial inquiry. Entrepreneurship research today is a "global industry... with thousands of people around the world who consider themselves entrepreneurship scholars" (Landström, 2020: 67). Schildt, Zahra, and Sillanpaa (2006) employed co-citation analysis on entrepreneurship articles published in 2000 and 2004 to identify 25 most central research streams in entrepreneurial studies. Co-citation analysis is a popular methodology for examining the structures of scientific communication in a discipline (Gmur, 2003). Based on their research, Schildt et al. (2006) concluded that entrepreneurship research is "highly fragmented" and territorial, so that most researchers operate in their own communities. The vast majority of researchers focus on particular areas within entrepreneurship (Ferreira, Fernandes, & Kraus, 2019), sharing similar interests with other researchers who work in their area (Gartner, Davidsson, & Zahra, 2006), which reinforces specialization (Teixeira, 2011).

This chapter focuses on five GAER laureates recognized for their contributions to specific sub-domains within entrepreneurship research: Ian Macmillan (1999), William Gartner (2005), The Diana Group (2007), Bengt Johannisson (2008), and Hernando de Soto Polar (2017).

© The Author(s) 2020   183
V. K. Gupta, *Great Minds in Entrepreneurship Research*,
https://Doi.org/10.1007/978-3-030-44125-8_7

Ian Macmillan: An International Perspective

The 1999 GAER recipient Ian Macmillan was on the faculty at University of South Africa where he met Larry Cummings and Andrew Van de Ven, both from University of Wisconsin-Madison at the time (Pierce, 2005). Impressed with Macmillan's research on middle management's subversion of senior manager's strategic decisions, they invited him to the US, and in 1975, Macmillan started as a visiting professor at Northwestern University. From here, Macmillan moved to Columbia in 1976, where he started doing strategic management research using the PIMS database (e.g., Hambrick & Macmillan, 1985; Hambrick, Macmillan, & Day, 1982; Macmillan, Hambrick, & Day, 1982). At Columbia, the "guy teaching a course in entrepreneurship died of a heart attack one night," and Macmillan volunteered to teach instead, gradually attracting favorable press for his teaching (Landström, 2005: 297). Macmillan (1983) examined common patterns of manipulative behavior among entrepreneurs as they tried to start their businesses, becoming his first published work on entrepreneurship. When New York University (NYU) launched a Center for Entrepreneurship, Macmillan moved there to helm the effort.

Macmillan stayed at NYU for only two years (1984–1986), but three things happened there that were key to his subsequent career. The Center for Entrepreneurial Studies at NYU's Stern School of Business was founded by Zenas Block, a native New Yorker who had already had a successful career as a food chemist, research director, senior corporate manager, and entrepreneur. In collaboration with Block, Macmillan started the *Journal of Business Venturing* (in 1985),[1] published the book *Corporate Venturing* (Block & Macmillan, 1993; see also Macmillan, Block, & Narsimha, 1986), and launched a large international comparative research project looking at entrepreneurial drivers in 13 countries (McGrath & MacMillan, 1992; McGrath, MacMillan & Scheinberg, 1992; McGrath, MacMillan, Yang & Tsai, 1992). In 1986, Macmillan moved to Wharton School of Business at the University of Pennsylvania

---

[1] The inaugural issue started with an invited article by then-President Ronald Reagan (Reagan, 1985: 2) who talked about an "entrepreneurial age" and invited readers "to think boldly, to get outside the current framework, and to imagine what our country will be like in the 2020s." It is perhaps the only instance of a sitting-President contributing to an organizational and management journal. The journal also asked authors to "preface their article with an executive summary that directly spells out the implications for practitioners" (Macmillan, Zemann, & Amoroso, 1985), a practice that continues to this day.

in Philadelphia, where part of his mandate was to build a research environment focusing on entrepreneurship. Macmillan's research output at this stage was in the areas of corporate venturing (Venkataraman, Macmillan, & McGrath, 1992) and strategic management (McGrath, Macmillan, & Tushman, 1992; McGrath, Macmillan, & Venkataraman, 1995).

The official GAER citation for Macmillan recognizes him for "being instrumental in introducing an international perspective involving comparative studies on cultural differences in entrepreneurship and small business behavior." Jones, Coviello, and Tang (2011) categorize Macmillan's work as part of cross-cultural comparative literature in international entrepreneurship research. As mentioned earlier, it was at NYU, and in collaboration with Zenas Block, that Macmillan first floated the idea of understanding cultural differences in entrepreneurship across countries. Entrepreneurship was defined as the creation of a new venture (Brockhaus, 1987; Gartner, 1985), so that the entrepreneur was a founder of a new business. Using survey responses from over 700 entrepreneurs, McGrath and Macmillan (1992: 425) found that, across different countries, entrepreneurs share a common pattern of beliefs in "which they feel that others in their society are unwilling to take charge of their own destiny, are unwilling to work hard to earn social rewards, and are less likely to enjoy what they do." Using data from Japanese and American high-tech entrepreneurs, Ohe, Honjo, Oliva, and Macmillan (1991) found that family environment was very influential in becoming an entrepreneur in Japan, but in US, family influence was rather small and education played an important role.

Cross-national researchers often rely on Hofstede's (1980) PUMI framework to capture cultural values: 'power distance' concerns inequality within society, 'uncertainty avoidance' is about lack of tolerance for ambiguity, 'masculinity' captures gender roles in society, and 'individualism' is about the emphasis on the individual over collective in a society. McGrath, MacMillan, and Scheinberg (1992) used data from 1217 entrepreneurs and 1206 non-entrepreneurs from eight countries to find that entrepreneurs scored higher on power distance, uncertainty avoidance, masculinity, and individualism. McGrath, MacMillan, Yang, and Tsai (1992) used data from entrepreneurs in the US, Taiwan, and China to find that collectivism, uncertainty avoidance, and materialism ('working to live') are highly enduring in a culture, but power distance seems to be more malleable and amenable to change. Shane, Venkataraman, and Macmillan (1995) link national cultural values (uncertainty avoidance, individualism, and power distance) with innovation championing within established firms, testing their hypotheses using survey data collected from 30 countries. They find that high uncertainty avoidance leads to a preference for champions to work through organizational norms and rules to promote innovation, high power distance to an emphasis on getting buy-in from powerful organizational actors, and high collectivism on champions working through cross-functional collaborations.

McDougall's (1989) explicit naming and conceptualizing of the term 'international entrepreneurship' launched a new stream of research. Macmillan's work (e.g., McGrath & Macmillan, 1992; McGrath, MacMillan, & Scheinberg, 1992; McGrath, MacMillan, Yang, & Tsai, 1992) assessing how entrepreneurs compare across cultures generated awareness and enthusiasm about the diversity of entrepreneurial activity in different parts of the world (Coviello, McDougall, & Oviatt, 2011). Comparative international entrepreneurship research has been criticized for its ethnocentric bias (Terjesen, Hessels, & Li, 2016). The assumptions about entrepreneurial characteristics and attributes underlying extant research in this area are based on theory and evidence primarily generated in the US. Ahl (2006: 599) described the US-derived entrepreneurial profile as that of "an unusual and extraordinary figure with levels of achievement orientation, optimism, self-efficacy, internal locus of control, cognitive skills, and tolerance of ambiguity above the ordinary." International entrepreneurship researchers assume that the "American entrepreneurial archetype" is universal, uncritically adopting it in their work (e.g., McDougall & Oviatt, 2000; Zahra, 1993).[2] More than

---

[2] There is a widespread tendency to view entrepreneurship as something quintessentially American (Hisrich, Langan-Fox, & Grant, 2007). The early contributors to entrepreneurship research described entrepreneurial individuals based on the traits and values they believed were respected and admired in US society (Thomas & Mueller, 2000). The mythologized frontiersman and cowboy (along with other historically contemporaneous icons such as the adventurer and the big game hunter) exemplified masculine ideals romanticized in American society—rugged individualism, adventurous spirit, risk-taking, and high degree of personal autonomy (Holt & Thompson, 2004)—that were then uncritically embraced by entrepreneurship researchers. American culture was considered exceptionally amenable to entrepreneurship (Lee & Peterson, 2000). However, as Edith Wharton recalls in her autobiography, the "man who 'kept a shop' was more rigorously shut out of polite society in the original thirteen states than in post-revolutionary France" (Wharton, 1998: 11). Entrepreneurs, in US and Europe, were frequently subjected to humiliation and exclusion in elite social circles. Indeed, on both sides of the Atlantic, there was a strong "social custom one did not entertain one's tradespeople" (Brickell, 2019: 218),

three decades back, Peterson (1988: 1) noted that, "the U.S. culture of individualism and achievement has dominated the world view of entrepreneurship," an observation that remain true to this day.

Grégoire, Noel, Dery, and Bechard (2006) report that Macmillan's research provides the foundation for scholarship on new venture funding provided by venture capitalists. MacMillan, Siegel, and Narasimha's (1985) examine decision criteria used by venture capitalists to evaluate new venture proposals identifying the entrepreneur's staying power (defined as 'sustained intense effort against competition') and familiarity with the target market as major considerations in funding decisions. Based on data collected from 67 VC firms evaluating 150 venture proposals, Macmillan, Zemann, and Narasimha (1987) identified four types of successful ventures and three types of unsuccessful ventures. Successful ventures fell into one of the four categories: (a) high-tech ventures with well-qualified founding team that has a high staying power, (b) products with high levels of intellectual property protection, (c) founding teams with exceptional perseverance and a product with some level of protection from imitation, and (d) products that are dependent on strong distribution skills for success. Unsuccessful ventures fell into three categories: (a) ventures where founding team has no experience or staying power, product has no prototype, and there is no obvious market demand for the product, (b) ventures where founding team has strong credentials, but are not able to persevere in the face of early competition, and (c) ventures that lose early market share to rivals because of lack of product protection.

Macmillan, Kulow, and Khoylian (1989) found that VCs serve as a 'sounding board' for the entrepreneur, but do not generally involve themselves in the operational activities of the firm they fund. Using data collected from 62 VCs, Macmillan et al. (1989) identify three types of VCs: (a) limited involvement with the funded ventures (laissez-faire), moderate involvement with the ventures, and (c) substantive involvement with the ventures (close-trackers). The surveyed VCs reported a preference for activities with low time commitment (e.g., helping formulate business strategy or marketing plans for the venture; giving feedback on ideas from the entrepreneur), and an aversion to involvement that placed

who were frequently treated as not much more than "a lowly shopkeeper," no "better than the domestic help, like 'an obviously superior servant'."

heavy demands on their time (e.g., production planning, vendor selection, or seeking customers or distributors). Low and Macmillan (1988), widely considered a landmark publication (Chiles, Bluedorn, & Gupta, 2007; Gupta & Gupta, 2015), critically reviewed ongoing developments in entrepreneurship research and identified key challenges for the future. Starr and Macmillan (1990) offered the idea that entrepreneurs rely on social assets (friendship, liking, trust, obligation, and gratitude) to co-opt legitimacy and resources for their venture at below-market prices. Gupta, Macmillan, and Surie (2004: 246–247) introduce the construct of 'entrepreneurial leadership' as involving two key activities: envisioning and generating a scenario of possible opportunities that can be exploited to "revolutionize the current transaction set, given resource constraints" (scenario enactment) and convincing potential followers and stakeholders that "transformation of this transaction set is possible by assembling resources" (cast enactment). Using data from the GLOBE survey, they validated a 23-item measure to capture entrepreneurial leadership, which has received some criticism for not measuring the construct it purports to assess (Renko, El Tarabishy, Carsrud, & Brännback, 2015). Gruber, Macmillan, and Thompson (2008) obtained data from 142 VC-backed German firms, finding that serial entrepreneurs identify multiple alternative opportunities based on their prior experience before deciding which one to pursue in the new firm they start.

WILLIAM GARTNER: NEW VENTURE CREATION

The 2005 GAER awardee, William Gartner, was recognized for his "studies on new venture creation and entrepreneurial behavior, combining the best parts of the positivist and hermeneutic tradition." Hjorth and Johannisson (2008: 342) commend Gartner for combining "an Anglo-American positivist tradition with a European hermeneutic one." Gartner helped launch the Panel Study of Entrepreneurial Dynamics, a large-scale national survey of new venture creation (Gartner, Shaver, Carter, & Reynolds, 2004), played an instrumental role in shifting the focus of entrepreneurship research from traits to behaviors (Gartner, 1988), and emphasized the interpretive study of entrepreneurial action through discursive approaches (Gartner & Birley, 2002).

Gartner (1985), based on the conceptual work in his doctoral dissertation (Gartner, 2016), is considered a classic article in entrepreneurship research (Gupta et al., 2016). Focusing on new venture creation, Gartner (1985) presented a four-pronged framework to understand how new ventures are formed: person(s) involved in starting a new venture (actor), the way the new firm is organized (organization), the situation within which the firm is formed (environment), and the actions taken to form the new firm (process). Brahma, Tripathi, and Bijlani (2018) believe the strength of Gartner's (1985) framework is that it provided "a common language and format" for researchers interested in making sense of venture creation in a world characterized by much diversity in the businesses we see around us. Gartner (1985) also proffered that that there was no one specific set of traits and attributes that would differentiate between 'entrepreneurs' and non-entrepreneurs, an argument he went on to develop in greater length in Gartner (1988), his most-cited work so far.

Entrepreneurship researchers, Gartner (1988) urged, should abandon the search for entrepreneurial traits, instead focusing on the creation of new organizations and the activities enterprising individuals undertake in their efforts to create new firms. As Gartner (2004) recounted, Gartner (1988) originally started as a critique of Carland, Hoy, Boulton and Carland (1984)'s call for research distinguishing entrepreneurs from small business owners. Gartner (1988) cast serious epistemological doubts about the plausibility of research into the widespread notion that entrepreneurs are endowed with unique personality traits, contending that non-entrepreneurs do not lack the 'entrepreneurial stuff' (whatever it is). Carland, Hoy, and Carland (1988) accepted the merits of Gartner's (1988) behavioral approach to entrepreneurship, but reiterated that trait approaches are also legitimate to better understand who becomes an entrepreneur. Ramoglou, Gartner, and Tsang (2020) recently observed that there has been a renewed interest in the 'question of the entrepreneur,' reminding researchers that there is as much variation among entrepreneurs as there is between entrepreneurs and non-entrepreneurs, so that the search for what makes entrepreneurs different from non-entrepreneurs is just as much a futile endeavor today as it was when Gartner (1988) came out.

Katz and Gartner (1988), recipient of the 2013 Foundational Paper Award from AoM's entrepreneurship division, is another highly cited work. Focusing on organizational emergence (Gartner, 2014), Katz and Gartner (1988) posit four basic properties as central to emerging organizations: intentionality or purposeful effort, resources or tangible building blocks, boundary or place for the firm, and exchange or securing inputs and providing outputs to others. Brush, Manolova, and Edelman (2008a) used data from the National Panel Study of Entrepreneurial Dynamics (PSED) to test the Katz and Gartner (1988) model, finding that all four must be present for a nascent venture to continue organizing, but ventures that proceeded more slowly were in better position to survive. Manolova, Edelman, Brush, and Rotefoss (2012) used longitudinal Global Entrepreneurship Monitor data on 203 nascent Norwegian entrepreneurs to find that three of the four properties of emerging organizations—intentionality, boundary, exchange, but not resources—were significantly associated with the likelihood of the organizing effort.

Gartner (2007) made a commendable effort to highlight the role of narrative theories and methods to the study of entrepreneurship as a phenomenon. The basic premise of Gartner (2007) was simple: have a number of scholars look at the same qualitative data to see what insights they generate. Each contributing scholar was given an article titled "A Toy Store(y)" (also called the 'Marvel Mustang Story'; Fletcher, 2007), an autobiographical retelling of the founding and operation of a toy store in Rutland (VT) in 1965 from recognizing the initial opportunity to the liquidation sale closing the store (Allen, 2007). Six scholars then look at the story from their own perspective: O'Connor (2007) questions the very usefulness of the story; Fletcher (2007) highlights what the reader brings to the story; Baker (2007) repositions the story from the vantage point of the other characters in it; Ahl (2007) contends that the story renders the female characters invisible and bereft of voice; Hjorth (2007) questions what the main protagonist leaves unspoken to the audience; and Steyaert (2007) delves into how the individual is placed in entrepreneurship research.

Gartner (1985) has long emphasized venture creation as the defining aspect of entrepreneurship research. While the focus on new venture formation resonated with many scholars (Salamzadeh, 2015), it has also drawn criticism for being too simplistic. Shane and Venkataraman (2000: 219), for example, argue that some entrepreneurial activity may involve creation of new organizations, "entrepreneurship can also occur within an existing organization … [and] can be sold to other individuals or existing organizations." Entrepreneurship, Shane and Venkataraman (2001) contend, does not have to involve the launch of a new venture. Lumpkin and Dess (1995: 136) see new entry as the essence of entrepreneurship, which they define as "entering new or established markets with new or existing goods or services." Interestingly, they equate new entry with new venture creation, but the extent to which new entry and venture creation overlap is debatable. Consider Amazon in its early years, when it added the option for customers to buy CDs on its Web site, after seeing success with selling books online. The company enters an established market with a new service, which is consistent with 'new entry,' but no new venture is launched here. Conversely, consider the common practice of doing business as two (or more) separate firms operating from the same address and serving the same product-market. There is no new entry here, even though venture creation occurs. Looking at the modern entrepreneurship research literature, it is clear that new venture creation is now just one part—perhaps, even only a small part—of an academic field that has embraced a broader conceptualization of entrepreneurship that does not require a new venture to be launched for a phenomena to be considered entrepreneurial.

Gartner has been a passionate champion of qualitative methods in entrepreneurship research (Gartner & Birley, 2002). Gartner (2007) made a commendable effort to highlight the role of narrative theories and methods to the study of entrepreneurship as a phenomenon. Wadhwani, Kirsch, Welter, Gartner, and Jones (2020) emphasize the importance of studying entrepreneurship historically, echoing Chiles et al.'s (2007) call for a 'historical turn' in entrepreneurship studies. While qualitative inquiry is becoming increasingly popular in entrepreneurship research (Javadian, Ellis, Gupta, Gupta, & Martin, 2020), qualitative entrepreneurship scholarship in elite journals has generally "taken a fairly small tent approach" (Baker, Powell, & Fultz, 2017: 254). Despite calls for use of broad array of qualitative methods (Pratt, 2009), entrepreneurship researchers have overwhelmingly preferred a small set of well-proven qualitative approaches. Consequently, narrative and historical approaches are largely missing from qualitative entrepreneurship research published in top-tier journals (outside of special issues focused on the topic; e.g., Gartner, 2007; Wadhwani et al., 2020).

THE DIANA GROUP: FEMALE ENTREPRENEURSHIP

The 2007 GAER awardee was the Diana Group (more commonly, Diana Project), comprising of a team of five women researchers—Candida Brush, Nancy Carter, Elizabeth Gatewood, Patricia Greene, and Myra Hart—who came together to understand (non-)growth of women's businesses. The main interest of the Diana Group was in answering the question of 'Why women owned firms remain smaller than those male-owned firms?' (de Bruin, Brush, & Welter, 2006). When the 2007 award was announced, it was immediately obvious that the GAER committee had broken with tradition in recognizing the Diana Group: for the first time, the award was given to a group of researchers rather than one or two scholars and to women rather than men as had been the case in the past (Holmquist & Carter, 2009).

The original GAER citation recognized the Diana Group for "for having investigated the supply- and demand-side of venture capital for women entrepreneurs. By studying women entrepreneurs who want to grow their businesses, they demonstrate the positive potential of female entrepreneurship." Starting with the first journal article on women's entrepreneurship (Schwartz, 1976), female entrepreneurship has gradually emerged as a popular and prominent topic for research (Jennings & Brush, 2013; Poggesi, Mari, & De Vita, 2016). In the early days, women-owned firms were considered small lifestyle ventures or sole proprietorships in academic and popular discourse (Yadav & Unni, 2016). Nevertheless, by the early 1990s, Brush (1992) identified 57 empirical studies on women business owners, many of them published in conference proceedings. Academic recognition for women entrepreneurship was encouraged by the first journal special issue on this topic in *Entrepreneurship and Regional Development* (Holmquist, 1997). At the time, Baker, Aldrich, and Nina (1997) found that women entrepreneurs were largely inviable in business periodicals, elite national newspapers, and academic journals. To use the well-known colorful metaphor of Shakespeare's drama *Romeo and Juliet*, there was no Juliet on the balcony.

In 1998, the five Diana founders met in New Mexico and decided to join forces to research female entrepreneurship, focusing particularly on high-growth ventures (Brush, Greene, & Welter, 2020). Taking inspiration from the (mythological) Roman goddess of hunt, and to signal their interest in women's quest for the financial and intellectual rewards that come from entrepreneurship, they decided to call themselves 'the Diana group' (Gatewood, Brush, Carter, Greene, & Hart, 2009). Holmquist and Carter (2009: 127) commend the Diana Group for bringing "legitimacy and status to a field that was largely overlooked by the mainstream research and public policy." The relative lack of attention to female entrepreneurship at the time was not commensurate with the economic contribution of women-led businesses. As the Diana Group found, "women business owners employ more people than all the Fortune

500 companies combined" (Gatewood et al., 2009: 132). Yet, fewer than 6% of all research studies in entrepreneurship at the time studied women or included women in their samples (Brush & Edelman, 2000).

An early research interest for the Diana Group was women and VC funding. Greene, Brush, Hart, and Saparito (2001) found that women-led firms receive only about 2.4% of VC funds recorded in a 30+ -year longitudinal dataset, with the proportion of deals with female-owned firms growing in the 1990s to about 4.1%. When women-led businesses received VC funding, it was more common in early-stage ventures than buy-out or acquisition financing (Brush, Carter, Greene, Hart, & Gatewood, 2002). While women were under-represented in the VC ranks, they were not completely absent, with about 9% of people in the VC industry classified as women and some VC firms were identified as female-only (Brush et al., 2002).

Carter, Gartner, Shaver, and Gatewood (2003) examined career reasons of nascent entrepreneurs, reporting that men were more likely than women to seek financial success and opportunities in creating new products or technology. Data for nascent entrepreneurs were from the PSED, a national database of individuals in the process of starting companies. Carter, Brush, Greene, Gatewood, and Hart (2003) examined the role of human, social, and financial capital in helping women entrepreneurs get equity financing. Data came from a survey of US women business owners conducted by the National Foundation for Women Business Owners (NFWBO) in 2000. Because the proportion of women entrepreneurs seeking VC funding tends to be low (Coleman & Robb, 2012), purposeful sampling was used by filtering out Dun and Bradstreet—listed businesses not in industries associated with VC financing and located outside of Top 5 states for VC funding (CA, DC, MA, PA, and TX). Carter et al. (2003) found that only specific forms of human capital (graduate education) and financial capital (bootstrapping through the use of financial resources) were associated with receiving equity funding.

Research on women and VC funding is part of a broader stream of inquiry around whether female and male differ with respect to financial resource acquisition (Jennings & Brush, 2013). Prior research has shown that women face both supply- and demand-side barriers in securing financial capital. Supply-side hurdles include gender bias in debt financing (e.g., Haines, Orser, & Riding, 1999) and angel investment (e.g., Becker-Blease & Sohl, 2007). Demand-side barriers include women's lower proclivity to seek external funding (Coleman & Robb, 2009), perhaps because of their lower growth intentions or self-efficacy (Coleman, Henry, Orser, Foss, & Welter, 2019). Recent research has shown that stereotypical beliefs position growth-oriented ventures as the opposite of women and femininity (Gupta, Wieland & Turban, 2019), which can then influence one's entrepreneurial intentions and others' willingness to allocate resources to the ventures (Yacus, Esposito, & Yang, 2019). The pioneering efforts of the Diana Group motivated a rich stream of research on acquisition of financial resources by female entrepreneurs, particularly the mobilization of VC financing (Jennings & Brush, 2013). Unfortunately, comparatively limited attention has been given to the issue of alternative resources mobilized by female entrepreneurs (Clough, Fang, Vissa, & Wu, 2019), such as human and social resources needed by a venture to survive and grow.

From the beginning, the Diana Project was conceived as a five-phase endeavor. The first phase involved surveying the full landscape of research on women's entrepreneurship through an annotated literature review (Gatewood, Carter, Brush, Greene, & Hart, 2003). The second phase entailed generating primary research on demand-side factors associated with women's experiences in seeking growth financing (Brush, Carter, Gatewood, Greene, & Hart, 2001, 2004a), and the third phase focused on supply-side factors (Brush, Carter, Gatewood, Greene, & Hart, 2004b). The fourth phase connected supply-side and demand-side factors (Brush, Carter, Gatewood, Greene, & Hart, 2006). The fifth phase involved organizing international forums and conferences, starting with the 2003 Diana conference in Stockholm (Sweden), bringing together 20 scholars from 13 countries (Brush et al., 2020). In 2009, the *International Journal of Gender and Entrepreneurship* was launched under the editorship of Colette Henry (of Dundalk Institute of Technology, Ireland).

The Diana Project has done much to attract attention toward the important issue of women's entrepreneurship, both by conducting research in important areas (e.g., why do female-led firms receive less funding than male-led firms?) and by providing a prominent platform and networking venue for interested scholars. As Brush et al. (2020: 19) noted, the "original Diana founders were promoted largely as a result of their collective work on women's entrepreneurship [and] the same is true for most of the 23 original Diana International group as well." The recent publication of several outstanding reviews of women entrepreneurship research speaks to the proliferation of scholarship in this area (Minniti, 2009; Poggesi et al., 2016; Sullivan & Meek, 2012). Yet, while the quantity of published research on women's entrepreneurship has increased over time, this growth has masked the decreasing proportion of papers about women's entrepreneurship in high-quality journals (Jennings & Brush, 2013). If one were to eliminate special issues from consideration (e.g., de Bruin et al., 2006; de Bruin, Brush, & Welter, 2007; Hughes, Jennings, Brush, Carter, & Welter, 2012), high-status outlets are publishing even less of women's entrepreneurship research than before (Jennings & Brush, 2013). In effect, more scholars doing women's entrepreneurship research are now competing for even less quality journal space than was the case two decades back. Furthermore, the "pipeline of leading-edge papers focusing upon women's entrepreneurship appears to be pretty thin" (Jennings & Brush, 2013). Notably, the vast majority of research on women's entrepreneurship is conducted in developed countries, so that we know much less about women's entrepreneurship in developing countries (Poggesi et al., 2016).

Research on women entrepreneurship appears to have a peculiar love–hate relationship with growth-oriented ventures. A number of researchers have observed that entrepreneurship research has gradually moved from small firms to high-growth ventures (Aldrich, 2012), which is consistent with the emphasis on such firms in popular media and public policy. Some researchers believe that emphasizing high-growth entrepreneurship is unfair to women entrepreneurs as they generally run firms that are smaller and have lower intentions to grow their ventures (Marlow & McAdam, 2013). Indeed, research finds that people generally associate high-growth entrepreneurship with men and low-growth or no-growth ventures with women (Gupta et al., 2019). Others contend that high-growth firms reflect entrepreneurial success, and women entrepreneurs should be encouraged to grow their ventures (Hechavarria, Bullough, Brush, & Edelman, 2019). It is well-known that much entrepreneurship in most societies is of the low-growth, lifestyle kind (Welter, Baker, Audretsch, & Gartner, 2017), so that high-growth entrepreneurship is way more uncommon than the impression we get from popular and academic discourse on this topic. Growth firms are described as 'economic engines' and national treasure,' which is why they are talked about in the entrepreneurship literature generally, and women's entrepreneurship literature more specifically, but the discussion about women's high-growth entrepreneurial activity often seems fraught with tension and reservations.

Bengt Johannisson: A European Perspective

Bengt Johannisson, the 2008 GAER awardee, was recognized for "furthering our understanding of the importance of social networks of the entrepreneur in a regional context, and for his key role in the development of the European entrepreneurship and small business research tradition." Johannisson is well-known internationally for his service as general editor of the journal *Entrepreneurship and Regional Development* (1998–2007), ranked among top-tier field journals in entrepreneurship. The first article in the first issue of the journal *Entrepreneurship and Regional Development* was Johannisson and Nilsson (1989), which introduced and defined the term 'community entrepreneurship' to describe entrepreneurial activity at the level of a community. Johannisson's early research led him to identify what he called the "Gnosjö spirit" to capture the idea that co-located local firms both compete and collaborate with each other. Steyaert and Landström (2011) contend that "if a European School of entrepreneurship exists (Hjorth, Jones, & Gartner, 2008) in which Scandinavian thinking clearly predominates along with a Swedish theoretical platform (Landström & Johannisson, 2001), then it was instigated by the pioneering, provocative, and participative work of Johannisson."

Europe is considered the birthplace of entrepreneurship research (Fayolle, Kyro, & Ulijn, 2005). Considerable interest exists in understanding the differences in scholarly approaches toward entrepreneurship research between North American and European scholars (Welter & Lasch, 2008). Brush, Manolova, and Edelman (2008b: 261), for example, note that European journals are more likely to emphasize descriptive statistics in the articles and publish research adopting a "natural selection or collective action" approach relative to American journals that prefer explicit identification of theory and publish articles "grounded in an individual /voluntaristic view." Yet, several researchers argue that there is no unitary 'North American school' or 'European School' of entrepreneurship research (Davidsson, 2013). Only when European research is compared to North American scholarship do differences between the traditions come to fore and some semblance of commonality can be seen within the research traditions (Wiklund, Dimov, Katz, & Shepherd, 2006).

The European approach to entrepreneurship research—or perhaps more accurately, approach to entrepreneurship research in Europe—is quite varied (Welter & Lasch, 2008). Wiklund et al. (2006: 1) describe it as a "panoply of diverse ways of thinking, expressed in theories, methods, or research questions." Davidsson (2013: 106) believes the European research culture—which is quite heterogeneous (Down, 2013)—is generally more accepting of "complexity, context and deep understanding of the data at hand" and encourages research to invest in rich data collection "rather than cranking out papers based on data that are easy to come by."

Within Europe, Scandinavian or Nordic traditional of research—scholarship that is "focused on microprocesses, qualitatively oriented, case-studies based, and organization studies influenced" (Hjorth, 2008: 314)—occupies a prominent place. Geographically, the Nordic tradition includes researchers in Denmark, Finland, Iceland, Norway, and Sweden (Johannisson, 2004). The core of the Scandinavian model is the commitment "to improve the ability of society to master its problems and to enrich and equalize the living conditions of individuals and families," also described as *universalism* (Greve, 2007). There is a strong belief in the powerful role of the state in providing 'equal opportunity' for everyone, which is also reflected in the view that entrepreneurship is a target for state policy (Hjorth, 2008). Entrepreneurship is seen by politicians and decision-makers as a potent solution to the challenges of a stagnating economy and growing unemployment (Landström & Johannisson, 2001). Perhaps, as a consequence of intersection of state welfare and entrepreneurship, good access to interesting, and sometimes sensitive, information about entrepreneurial activity is available in Scandinavia (Davidsson, 2013). Johannisson's early work on family business is considered a pioneering effort in Scandinavian entrepreneurship research, and his scholarship on networks and regional development is an exemplar of "passionate curiosity" that characterizes Nordic research at its best (Horth, 2008: 329). Within Swedish entrepreneurship research, qualitative inquiry dominates, mostly focusing on case studies (Davidsson, 2013; Landström & Johannisson, 2001).

For Johannisson (1983), the key entrepreneurial characteristic was self-reliance, which was action-oriented and played an instrumental role in spreading confidence in the local community. Johannisson (1986) examines the networking strategies of entrepreneurs in four local communities in Sweden. Johannisson (1987: 61) views personal networks as the vehicle through which entrepreneurs create new organizations, proffering that entrepreneurial activity is encouraged in an environment that "simultaneously supports individualism and collectivism, anarchism and order."

Johannisson and Nilsson (1989) introduced the idea of 'community entrepreneurship,' [define]. For Johannisson (1990), entrepreneurship is embedded in inter-linked market, institutional and political arenas. Johannisson (2004) believed that entrepreneurship manifests differently in the Swedish (or Scandinavian context). As Johannisson and Monstead (1997) explained, business and community are closely intertwined in Scandinavian society, which fosters informal trust and social capital, providing an appropriate breeding ground for entrepreneurship. Johannisson (1995a) believed that local norms of collaboration and consensus within, as well as across, sectoral boundaries resulted in network approaches as most relevant to understanding entrepreneurial activity in Scandinavian societies. Johannisson (1995b) recognized the methodological challenges associated with network studies in entrepreneurship, calling for researchers to employ qualitative and quantitative approaches. Based on their study of the aftermath of hurricane Gudrun, which hit southern Sweden in January 2005, Johannisson and Olaison (2007) introduce the idea of 'emergency entrepreneurship,' which they define as self-organizing entrepreneurial activity that occurs when ordinary life practices are at stake. This can happen when community is confronted with a catastrophe instigated by nature (as is the case for hurricanes) or during pandemics (as with the COVID-19 global epidemic in 2020) or unanticipated acts of war and terrorism, all of which create emergency situations that disrupt existing behavioral scripts.

Johannisson and Monstead (1997) contend that social skills and relevant experience are more important for entrepreneurship in Sweden than formal education. Johannisson, Landström, and Rosenberg (1998) develop a measure to assess 'entrepreneurial action capability,' which could be helpful in benchmarking the competencies needed for entrepreneurship and small business. Hjorth and Johannisson (2007: 56) share challenges and problems associated with teaching entrepreneurship in Sweden, favoring "an understanding of entrepreneurship as a way to approach the everyday world – interactively with alertness, curiosity and playfulness and with a sense of responsibility for one's own initiative." Johannisson (2018) suggests that entrepreneurship pedagogy should focus on providing students with situated and actionable insights about how the entrepreneurial process work.

HERNANDO DE SOTO POLAR: INFORMAL ECONOMY

The 2017 GAER awardee, Hernando de Soto Polar, was recognized for "developing a new understanding of the institutions that underpin the informal economy as well as the role of property rights and entrepreneurship in converting the informal economy into the formal sector." De Soto's contributions are published in the form of two books—*The Other Path* (1986) and *The Mystery of Capital* (2000)—and it is the ideas discussed in these books that led to the GAER recognition (Andersson & Waldenström, 2017). De Soto advocated granting property rights to three groups that had accumulated assets in the so-called informal economy: urban residents without titles to their place of residence, traders without certificates of incorporation to the enterprises they ran, and farmers without deeds to the land they cultivated. De Soto's provocative ideas about the need for a restructured legal system and reduced interference from state bureaucracy earned him the wrath of the Shining Path (*Sendero Luminoso*) guerrilla movement in Peru, and made him the target of multiple assassination attempts,[3] the only GAER laureate to be targeted in this fashion.

De Soto (1986) examines the issue of the informal economy in an original way and draws conclusions for the Peruvian society in particular, and developing countries more generally. The book covers informality in three economic sectors of the Peruvian capital of Lima: housing, trade, and transportation. Informal housing makes up about 42% of Lima and is home to 47% of the capital's population. Informal traders dominate the retail distribution of popular consumer goods in the capital, and informal transportation controls 93% of the urban transport fleet of Lima, which captures about 80% of the seats. Because the informal economy operates outside of the official legal system, violation of norms and expectations (e.g., theft, rape) are addressed through extra-legal practices that includes lynching and executions.

The cause of Peruvian informality is unplanned migration from farming communities and rural areas to the cities, aided by the construction of national highways, improved communication system, better wages and health care in urban areas, and agricultural crises. Lima and other big cities

---

[3] The insurgent group was led by a philosophy professor Abimael Guzmán, who later wrote that the uprising has been "displaced by a plan designed and implemented by de Soto and Yankee imperialism" (De Soto, 2014).

were largely unprepared—in terms of infrastructure—to host unprecedented levels of migrants. Consequently, "to live, trade, manufacture, transport, or even consume, the cities' new inhabitants" became informals, engaging in illegal activities such as "building a house, providing a service, or developing a business" (De Soto, 1986: 11). The informal sector, De Soto (1986) explains, is considerably more productive than the formal sector and the state. The prevailing economic system in Peru was described as mercantilist, which—following the UNESCO Dictionary of Social Sciences—was defined as "the belief that the economic welfare of the state can only be secured by government regulation of a nationalist character" (p. 201). The state, De Soto (1986) contends, had failed to address the needs of the migrants or accommodate them in its plans, leaving them no choice other than to become informals. De Soto (1986) sees the informals as entrepreneurs, enterprising people "who know how to seize opportunities by managing available resources, including their own labor, relatively efficiently" (p. 243).

Based on his research, De Soto (1986) concluded that the Peruvian government's administrative and legislative procedures and regulations impede rather than encourage economic growth, and offered the path mapped out by the informal sector as the only way for the advancement of the country. Critics praised *The Other Path* as "one of those rare books that combines brilliant insight, tenacious investigation, clear prose, and practical guidance" (Perry, 1990: 170). Marquez (1990: 209) supported De Soto's position that "business activity in Peru needs the activity operating in the informal economy, and those individuals working within the informal economy should be granted the formal property rights they deserve." Hirschowitz (1989) commends De Soto for emphasizing that informality is not a problem, but needs to be considered a solution to the problems that national governments worldwide create by refusing to give property rights to their impoverished communities. Many academics, however, challenged the methods and conclusions of the book (Rossini & Thomas, 1990: 132), describing as "suspect" the statistics it presents about the current size and growth potential of the informal sector in Peru.

De Soto (2000) deals with the question of why capitalism has worked in the West (by which he means North America and Western Europe (NAWE), but does not seem to work anywhere else in the world. The disparity of wealth between NAWE on the one hand and the rest of the world on the other hand, economic and political instability in many developing countries, and high levels of poverty in many parts of the world are all signs that capitalism has not been successful there. De Soto (2000) believes that most countries around the world have not benefitted from capitalism because of "their inability to produce capital" (p. 5). In De Soto's (2000) telling, the "cities of the Third World and the former communist countries" are "teeming with entrepreneurs" and "most of the poor already possess the assets they need to make" capitalism successful. Despite having the assets, the poor lack full and clear ownership. In other words, they lack legally enforceable property rights to their assets. As a result, the poor in developing countries have "dead capital," capital that is not officially recognized. De Soto's team calculates that "the total value of the real estate held but not legally owned by the poor of the third world and former communist nations is at least $9.3 trillion" (p. 35), which is significantly more (at the time) than the total direct foreign investment into all Third World and former communist countries as well as the foreign aid or assistance from developed state governments to Third World countries.

For De Soto (2000), the situation in the developing world is comparable to conditions in eighteenth-century US when "squatters and small illegal entrepreneurs" occupied lands they did not own. "In many countries," De Soto argued, "more than eighty percent of all homes and businesses are unregistered; ancient Rome was more advanced" (Albright, 2020: 95). Yet, the lack of formal property rights is not the same as the absence of all property rights. De Soto (2000) contends that "most people in the undercapitalized urban sector" of the developing countries have some documentation "to represent their property in written form according to rules that they respect and that government, at some level, is forced to accept" (p. 184). He calls these rules 'the people's law' and uses the metaphor of the barking dog to explain them in layperson terms: Even when neither the government nor the average person in a country knows where the boundaries of a farmer's land begin and finish, the dogs on the farms know "which assets their masters controlled" (p. 163). Understanding 'people's law'—the realities on the ground—is how NAWE countries built their formal property systems, and it is what the rest of the world needs to do now.

Woodruff (2001: 1216) describes De Soto (2000) as "colorfully written and entertaining," and focusing on an important issue for the world: poverty reduction via formal property rights. For many critics (e.g., Gravois, 2005; Kinsella, 2002), De Soto's (2000) unique contribution lies in pointing out the importance of legally sorting out who owns what and using that information to facilitate access to formal property. The book received much attention by serious professionals and policy-makers (Gilbert, 2012), who were attracted by its seemingly simple message that instituting a system of property rights and information on property that is applied nationally and is 'legible' to outsiders is key to transforming assets into capital (Musembi, 2007). Yet, there were also concerns that though De Soto (2000) offered a wealth of ideas (Woodruff, 2001), there was a lack of empirical rigor and no real scientific evidence (Gilbert, 2012). Musembi (2007) accuses De Soto (2000) of ignoring the world's longest experimentation with formal titling in sub-Saharan Africa and risking the same mistakes as have already been made elsewhere. Based on data gathered from legalized self-help settlements of Bogotá, Gilbert (2002) argues that providing the illegal squatters with a title deed makes little difference to the lives of the poor, perhaps because their ownership is already so secure that it cannot even be used as collateral for it is not subject to seizure by others (Woodruff, 2001). Thorp (1990: 403) believes that the "freshness of the book lies in its documentation of life in the informal sector," yet it is "not a book to be taken seriously in academic terms."

SUMMARY

The impressive growth of academic research on entrepreneurship has led to a situation where there are now several research streams, each of which is a fertile area of scientific inquiry in itself. While some may consider the proliferations of these research clusters to be detrimental for entrepreneurship, a key contribution of the distinct clusters is in highlighting topics previously overlooked in the broader literature. This chapter focuses on the work of five GAER laureates, namely Ian Macmillan, William Gartner, The Diana Group, Bengt Johannisson, and Hernando de Soto Polar, honored for their work in specific areas of inquiry within the entrepreneurship literature. The GAER recognized the pioneering role of these researchers in drawing academic attention to nascent areas of inquiry, and also enhanced their legitimacy, which should draw more scholars to research in these areas.

REFERENCES

Ahl, H. (2006). Why research on women entrepreneurs needs new directions. *Entrepreneurship Theory and Practice, 30*(5), 595–621.

Ahl, H. (2007). Sex business in the toy store: A narrative analysis of a teaching case. *Journal of Business Venturing, 22*(5), 673–693.

Albright, M. (2020). *Hell and other destinations: A 21st century memoir.* New York: Harper Collins.

Aldrich, H. E. (2012). The emergence of entrepreneurship as an academic field: A personal essay on institutional entrepreneurship. *Research Policy, 41*(7), 1240–1248.

Allen, T. (2007). A toy store (y). *Journal of Business Venturing, 22*(5), 628–636.

Andersson, M., & Waldenström, D. (2017). Hernando de Soto: Recipient of the 2017 Global Award for entrepreneurship research. *Small Business Economics, 49*(4), 721–728.

Baker, T. (2007). Resources in play: Bricolage in the toy store (y). *Journal of Business Venturing, 22*(5), 694–711.

Baker, T. E., Aldrich, H., & Nina, L. (1997). Invisible entrepreneurs: The neglect of women business owners by mass media and scholarly journals in the USA. *Entrepreneurship & Regional Development, 9*(3), 221–238.

Baker, T., Powell, E. E., & Fultz, A. E. F. (2017). Whatddya know? Qualitative methods in entrepreneurship. In S. Jain & R. Mir (Eds.), *Routledge companion to qualitative research in organization studies* (pp. 248–262). New York and London: Taylor & Francis.

Becker-Blease, J. R., & Sohl, J. E. (2007). Do women-owned businesses have equal access to angel capital? *Journal of Business Venturing, 22*(4), 503–521.

Block, Z., & MacMillan, I. C. (1993). *Corporate venturing: Creating new businesses within the firm.* Boston, MA: Harvard Business School Press.

Brahma, M., Tripathi, S. S., & Bijlani, S. (2018). New venture creation: From Gartner to the present. In G. Javadian, V. K. Gupta, D. Dutta, G. Guo, A. Osorio, & B. Ozkazanc-Pan (Eds.), *Foundational research in entrepreneurship studies* (pp. 77–102). Cham, Switzerland: Palgrave Macmillan.

Brickell, F. C. (2019). *The Cartiers: The untold story of the family behind the jewelry empire.* New York: Ballantine Books.

Brockhaus, R. H. (1987). Entrepreneurial folklore. *Journal of Small Business Management, 25*(3), 1–6.

Brush, C. G. (1992). Research on women business owners: Past trends, a new perspective and future directions. *Entrepreneurship Theory and Practice, 16,* 5–30.

Brush, C. G., Carter, N. M., Gatewood, E. J., Greene, P. G., & Hart, M. M. (2001). *An investigation of women-led firms and venture capital investment* (Report to the United States Small Business Administration, Office of Advocacy, and the National Women's Business Council). Washington, DC.

Brush, C. G., Carter, N. M., Gatewood, E. J., Greene, P. G., & Hart, M. M. (2004a). *Gatekeepers of venture growth: The role and participation of women in the venture capital industry.* Kansas City, MO: Ewing Marion Kauffman Foundation.

Brush, C. G., Carter, N. M., Gatewood, E. J., Greene, P. G., & Hart, M. M. (2004b). *Clearing the hurdles: Women building high-growth businesses.* Upper Saddle River, NJ: FT/Prentice Hall.

Brush, C. G., Carter, N. M., Gatewood, E., Greene, P. G., & Hart, M. M. (Eds.). (2006). *Women and entrepreneurship: Contemporary classics.* Cheltenham, UK: Edward Elgar.

Brush, C. G., Carter, N. M., Greene, P. G., Hart, M. M., & Gatewood, E. (2002). The role of social capital and gender in linking financial suppliers and entrepreneurial firms: A framework for future research. *Venture Capital: An International Journal of Entrepreneurial Finance, 4*(4), 305–323.

Brush, C. G., & Edelman, L. F. (2000). Women entrepreneurs' opportunities for database research. *Databases for the Study of Entrepreneurship, 4,* 445–484.

Brush, C. G., Greene, P. G., & Welter, F. (2020). The Diana project: A legacy for research on gender in entrepreneurship. *International Journal of Gender and Entrepreneurship, 12*(1), 7–25.

Brush, C. G., Manolova, T. S., & Edelman, L. F. (2008a). Properties of emerging organizations: An empirical test. *Journal of Business Venturing, 23*(5), 547–566.

Brush, C. G., Manolova, T. S., & Edelman, L. F. (2008b). Separated by a common language? Entrepreneurship research across the Atlantic. *Entrepreneurship Theory and Practice, 32*(2), 249–266.

Carland, J. W., Hoy, F., Boulton, W. R., & Carland, J. A. C. (1984). Differentiating entrepreneurs from small business owners: A conceptualization. *Academy of Management Review, 9*(2), 354–359.

Carland, J. W., Hoy, F., & Carland, J. A. C. (1988). "Who is an entrepreneur?" is a question worth asking. *American Journal of Small Business, 12*(4), 33–39.

Carter, N., Brush, C., Greene, P., Gatewood, E., & Hart, M. (2003). Women entrepreneurs who break through to equity financing: The influence of human, social and financial capital. *Venture Capital: An International Journal of Entrepreneurial Finance, 5*(1), 1–28.

Carter, N. M., Gartner, W. B., Shaver, K. G., & Gatewood, E. J. (2003). The career reasons of nascent entrepreneurs. *Journal of Business Venturing, 18*(1), 13–39.

Chiles, T. H., Bluedorn, A. C., & Gupta, V. K. (2007). Beyond creative destruction and entrepreneurial discovery: A radical Austrian approach to entrepreneurship. *Organization Studies, 28*(4), 467–493.

Clough, D. R., Fang, T. P., Vissa, B., & Wu, A. (2019). Turning lead into gold: How do entrepreneurs mobilize resources to exploit opportunities? *Academy of Management Annals, 13*(1), 240–271.

Coleman, S., & Robb, A. (2009). A comparison of new firm financing by gender: Evidence from the Kauffman firm survey data. *Small Business Economics, 33*(4), 397–411.

Coleman, S., Henry, C., Orser, B., Foss, L., & Welter, F. (2019). Policy support for women entrepreneurs' access to financial capital: Evidence from Canada, Germany, Ireland, Norway, and the United States. *Journal of Small Business Management, 57*(Suppl. 2), 296–322.

Coleman, S., & Robb, A. (2012). *A rising tide: Financing strategies for women-owned firms*. Stanford, CA: Stanford Press.

Coviello, N. E., McDougall, P. P., & Oviatt, B. M. (2011). The emergence, advance and future of international entrepreneurship research—An introduction to the special forum. *Journal of Business Venturing, 26*(6), 625–631.

Davidsson, P. (2013). Some reflection on research 'schools' and geographies. *Entrepreneurship & Regional Development, 25*(1–2), 100–110.

de Bruin, A., Brush, C. G., & Welter, F. (2006). Introduction to the special issue: Towards building cumulative knowledge on women's entrepreneurship. *Entrepreneurship Theory and Practice, 30*(5), 585–593.

de Bruin, A., Brush, C. G., & Welter, F. (2007). Advancing a framework for coherent research on women's entrepreneurship. *Entrepreneurship Theory and Practice, 31*(3), 323–339.

De Soto, H. (1986). *The other path*. Lima, Peru: Instituto Libertad y Democracia.

De Soto, H. (2000). *The mystery of capital: Why capitalism triumphs in the West and fails everywhere else*. New York: Basic Books.

De Soto, H. (2014, October 10). The capitalist cure for terrorism. *Wall Street Journal*.

Down, S. (2013). The distinctiveness of the European tradition in entrepreneurship research. *Entrepreneurship & Regional Development, 25*(1–2), 1–4.

Fayolle, A., Kyrö, P., & Ulijn, J. M. (Eds.). (2005). *Entrepreneurship research in Europe: Outcomes and perspectives*. Cheltenham, UK: Edward Elgar.

Ferreira, J. J., Fernandes, C. I., & Kraus, S. (2019). Entrepreneurship research: Mapping intellectual structures and research trends. *Review of Managerial Science, 13*(1), 181–205.

Fletcher, D. (2007). 'Toy story': The narrative world of entrepreneurship and the creation of interpretive communities. *Journal of Business Venturing, 22*(5), 649–672.

Gartner, W. B. (1985). A conceptual framework for describing the phenomenon of new venture creation. *Academy of Management Review, 10*(4), 696–706.

Gartner, W. B. (1988). "Who is an entrepreneur?" is the wrong question. *American Journal of Small Business, 12*(4), 11–32.

Gartner, W. B. (2004). The edge defines the (w) hole: Saying what entrepreneurship is (not). In D. Hjorth & C. Steyaert (Eds.), *Narrative and discursive approaches in entrepreneurship* (pp. 245–254). Cheltenham, UK: Edward Elgar.

Gartner, W. B. (2007). Entrepreneurial narrative and a science of the imagination. *Journal of Business Venturing, 22*(5), 613–627.

Gartner, W. B. (2014). Introduction. In W. B. Gartner (Eds.), *Entrepreneurship as organizing: Selected papers of William B. Gartner* (pp. ix–xi). Cheltenham, UK: Edward Elgar.

Gartner, W. B. (2016). Anecdotes of destiny. In D. B. Audretsch & E. E. Lehmann (Eds.), *The Routledge companion to the makers of modern entrepreneurship* (pp. 130–145). London: Routledge.

Gartner, W. B., & Birley, S. (2002). Introduction to the special issue on qualitative methods in entrepreneurship research. *Journal of Business Venturing, 17*(5), 387–395.

Gartner, W. B., Davidsson, P., & Zahra, S. A. (2006). Are you talking to me? The nature of community in entrepreneurship scholarship. *Entrepreneurship Theory and Practice, 30*(3), 321–331.

Gartner, W. B., Shaver, K. G., Carter, N. M., & Reynolds, P. D. (Eds.). (2004). *Handbook of entrepreneurial dynamics: The process of business creation.* Thousand Oaks, CA: Sage.

Gatewood, E. J., Brush, C. G., Carter, N. M., Greene, P. G., & Hart, M. M. (2009). Diana: A symbol of women entrepreneurs' hunt for knowledge, money, and the rewards of entrepreneurship. *Small Business Economics, 32*(2), 129–144.

Gatewood, E. R., Carter, N. M., Brush, C. G., Greene, P. G., & Hart, M. M. (Eds.). (2003). *Women entrepreneurs, their ventures, and the venture capital industry.* Stockholm: ESBRI.

Gilbert, A. (2002). On the mystery of capital and the myths of Hernando de Soto: What difference does legal title make? *International Development Planning Review, 24*(1), 1–19.

Gilbert, A. (2012). De Soto's 'the mystery of capital': Reflections on the book's public impact. *International Development Planning Review, 34*(3), v–xviii.

Gmür, M. (2003). Co-citation analysis and the search for invisible colleges: A methodological evaluation. *Scientometrics, 57*(1), 27–57.

Gravois, J. (2005, January 28). The De Soto delusion. *Slate.*

Greene, P. G., Brush, C. G., Hart, M. M., & Saparito, P. (2001). Patterns of venture capital funding: Is gender a factor? *Venture Capital, 3*(1), 63–83.

Grégoire, D. A., Noel, M. X., Déry, R., & Béchard, J. P. (2006). Is there conceptual convergence in entrepreneurship research? A co–citation analysis of frontiers of entrepreneurship research, 1981–2004. *Entrepreneurship Theory and Practice, 30*(3), 333–373.

Greve, B. (2007). What characterise the Nordic welfare state model. *Journal of Social Sciences, 3*(2), 43–51.

Gruber, M., MacMillan, I. C., & Thompson, J. D. (2008). Look before you leap: Market opportunity identification in emerging technology firms. *Management Science, 54*(9), 1652–1665.

Gupta, V. K., Dutta, D. K., Guo, G., Javadian, G., Jiang, C., Osorio, A. E., et al. (2016). Classics in entrepreneurship research: Enduring insights, future promises. *New England Journal of Entrepreneurship, 19*(1), 7–16.

Gupta, V. K., & Gupta, A. (2015). Relationship between entrepreneurial orientation and firm performance in large organizations over time. *Journal of International Entrepreneurship, 13*(1), 7–27.

Gupta, V. K., Wieland, A. M., & Turban, D. B. (2019). Gender characterizations in entrepreneurship: A multi-level investigation of sex-role stereotypes about high-growth, commercial, and social entrepreneurs. *Journal of Small Business Management, 57*(1), 131–153.

Gupta, V., MacMillan, I. C., & Surie, G. (2004). Entrepreneurial leadership: Developing and measuring a cross-cultural construct. *Journal of Business Venturing, 19*(2), 241–260.

Haines, G. H., Jr., Orser, B. J., & Riding, A. L. (1999). Myths and realities: An empirical study of banks and the gender of small business clients. *Canadian Journal of Administrative Sciences, 16*(4), 291–307.

Hambrick, D. C., & Macmillan, I. C. (1985). Efficiency of product R&D in business units: The role of strategic context. *Academy of Management Journal, 28*(3), 527–547.

Hambrick, D. C., MacMillan, I. C., & Day, D. L. (1982). Strategic attributes and performance in the BCG matrix—A PIMS-based analysis of industrial product businesses. *Academy of Management Journal, 25*(3), 510–531.

Hechavarria, D., Bullough, A., Brush, C., & Edelman, L. (2019). High-growth women's entrepreneurship: Fueling social and economic development. *Journal of Small Business Management, 57*(1), 5–13.

Hisrich, R., Langan-Fox, J., & Grant, S. (2007). Entrepreneurship research and practice. *American Psychologist, 62*(6), 575–589.

Hirschowitz, R. (1989). Book Review: The other path: The invisible revolution in the third world. *South African Journal of Economics, 57*(4), 266–272.

Hjorth, D. (2007). Lessons from Iago: Narrating the event of entrepreneurship. *Journal of Business Venturing, 22*(5), 712–732.

Hjorth, D. (2008). Nordic entrepreneurship research. *Entrepreneurship Theory and Practice, 32*(2), 313–338.

Hjorth, D., & Johannisson, B. (2007). Learning as an entrepreneurial process. In A. Fayolle (Ed.), *Handbook of research in entrepreneurship education: Vol. 1. A general perspective* (pp. 46–66). Cheltenham, UK: Edward Elgar.

Hjorth, D., & Johannisson, B. (2008). Building new roads for entrepreneurship research to travel by: On the work of William B. Gartner. *Small Business Economics, 31*(4), 341–350.

Hjorth, D., Jones, C., & Gartner, W. B. (2008). Introduction for 'recreating/recontextualising entrepreneurship'. *Scandinavian Journal of Management, 24*(2), 81–84.

Hofstede, G. (1980). Culture and organizations. *International Studies of Management & Organization, 10*(4), 15–41.

Holmquist, C. (1997). The other side of the coin or another coin? Women's entrepreneurship as a complement or an alternative? *Entrepreneurship and Regional Development, 9*, 179–182.

Holmquist, C., & Carter, S. (2009). The Diana project: Pioneering women studying pioneering women. *Small Business Economics, 32*(2), 121–128.

Holt, D. B., & Thompson, C. J. (2004). Man-of-action heroes: The pursuit of heroic masculinity in everyday consumption. *Journal of Consumer Research, 31*(2), 425–440.

Hughes, K. D., Jennings, J. E., Brush, C., Carter, S., & Welter, F. (2012). Extending women's entrepreneurship research in new directions. *Entrepreneurship Theory and Practice, 36*(3), 429–442.

Javadian, G., Dobratz, C., Gupta, A., Gupta, V. K., & Martin, J. (2020). Qualitative research in entrepreneurship studies: A state-of-science. *Journal of Entrepreneurship, 29*(2), 1–36.

Jennings, J. E., & Brush, C. G. (2013). Research on women entrepreneurs: Challenges to (and from) the broader entrepreneurship literature? *Academy of Management Annals, 7*(1), 663–715.

Johannisson, B. (1983). Swedish evidence for the potential of local entrepreneurship in regional development. *European Small Business Journal, 1*(2), 11–24.

Johannisson, B. (1986). Network strategies: Management technology for entrepreneurship and change. *International Small Business Journal, 5*(1), 19–30.

Johannisson, B. (1987). Anarchists and organizers: Entrepreneurs in a network perspective. *International Studies of Management & Organization, 17*(1), 49–63.

Johannisson, B. (1990). Community entrepreneurship-cases and conceptualization. *Entrepreneurship & Regional Development, 2*(1), 71–88.

Johannisson, B. (1995a). Entrepreneurial networking in the Scandinavian context—Theoretical and empirical positioning. *Entrepreneurship & Regional Development, 7*(3), 189–192.

Johannisson, B. (1995b). Paradigms and entrepreneurial networks—Some methodological challenges. *Entrepreneurship & Regional Development, 7*(3), 215–232.

Johannisson, B. (2004). Entrepreneurship in Scandinavia: Bridging individualism and collectivism. *Crossroads of Entrepreneurship, 3*, 225–241.

Johannisson, B. (2018). Limits to and prospects of entrepreneurship education in the academic context. In *A research agenda for entrepreneurship education.* Cheltenham, UK: Edward Elgar.

Johannisson, B., & Mønsted, M. (1997). Contextualizing entrepreneurial networking: The case of Scandinavia. *International Studies of Management & Organization, 27*(3), 109–136.

Johannisson, B., & Nilsson, A. (1989). Community entrepreneurs: Networking for local development. *Entrepreneurship & Regional Development, 1*(1), 3–19.

Johannisson, B., & Olaison, L. (2007). The moment of truth—Reconstructing entrepreneurship and social capital in the eye of the storm. *Review of Social Economy, 65*(1), 55–78.

Johannisson, B., Landström, H., & Rosenberg, J. (1998). University training for entrepreneurship—An action frame of reference. *European Journal of Engineering Education, 23*(4), 477–496.

Jones, M. V., Coviello, N., & Tang, Y. K. (2011). International entrepreneurship research (1989–2009): A domain ontology and thematic analysis. *Journal of Business Venturing, 26*(6), 632–659.

Katz, J., & Gartner, W. B. (1988). Properties of emerging organizations. *Academy of Management Review, 13*(3), 429–441.

Kinsella, S. (2002). Review of the book Hernando de Soto. The mystery of capital: Why capitalism triumphs in the west and fails everywhere else. *Journal of Libertarian Studies, 16*(1), 99.

Landström, H. (2005). *Pioneers in entrepreneurship and small business research.* New York: Springer.

Landström, H. (2020). The evolution of entrepreneurship as a scholarly field. *Foundations and Trends® in Entrepreneurship, 16*(2), 65–243.

Landström, H., & Johannisson, B. (2001). Theoretical foundations of Swedish entrepreneurship and small-business research. *Scandinavian Journal of Management, 17*(2), 225–248.

Lee, S. M., & Peterson, S. J. (2000). Culture, entrepreneurial orientation, and global competitiveness. *Journal of World Business, 35*(4), 401–416.

Low, M. B., & MacMillan, I. C. (1988). Entrepreneurship: Past research and future challenges. *Journal of Management, 14*(2), 139–161.

Lumpkin, G. T., & Dess, G. G. (1995). Simplicity as a strategy-making process: The effects of stage of organizational development and environment on performance. *Academy of Management Journal, 38*(5), 1386–1407.

MacMillan, I. C. (1983). The politics of new venture management. *Harvard Business Review*, *61*(6), 8–16.

MacMillan, I. C., Block, Z., & Narasimha, P. S. (1986). Corporate venturing: Alternatives, obstacles encountered, and experience effects. *Journal of Business Venturing*, *1*(2), 177–191.

MacMillan, I. C., Hambrick, D. C., & Day, D. L. (1982). The product portfolio and profitability—A PIMS-based analysis of industrial-product businesses. *Academy of Management Journal*, *25*(4), 733–755.

MacMillan, I. C., Kulow, D. M., & Khoylian, R. (1989). Venture capitalists' involvement in their investments: Extent and performance. *Journal of Business Venturing*, *4*(1), 27–47.

MacMillan, I. C., Siegel, R., & Narasimha, P. S. (1985). Criteria used by venture capitalists to evaluate new venture proposals. *Journal of Business Venturing*, *1*(1), 119–128.

MacMillan, I. C., Zemann, L., & Amoroso, D. (1985). Comments from the editors. *Journal of Business Venturing*, *1*(1), 5.

MacMillan, I. C., Zemann, L., & Narasimha, P. S. (1987). Criteria distinguishing successful from unsuccessful ventures in the venture screening process. *Journal of Business Venturing*, *2*(2), 123–137.

Manolova, T. S., Edelman, L. F., Brush, C. G., & Rotefoss, B. (2012). Properties of emerging organizations: Empirical evidence from Norway. *Small Business Economics*, *39*(3), 763–781.

Marlow, S., & McAdam, M. (2013). Gender and entrepreneurship: Advancing debate and challenging myths; Exploring the mystery of the under-performing female entrepreneur. *International Journal of Entrepreneurial Behaviour & Research*, *19*(1), 114–124.

Marquez, A. (1990). Review of the book 'the other path' by Hernando De Soto. *Boston College Third World Law Journal*, *10*(1), 204.

McDougall, P. P. (1989). International versus domestic entrepreneurship: New venture strategic behavior and industry structure. *Journal of Business Venturing*, *4*(6), 387–400.

McDougall, P. P., & Oviatt, B. M. (2000). International entrepreneurship: The intersection of two research paths. *Academy of Management Journal*, *43*(5), 902–906.

McGrath, R. G., & MacMillan, I. C. (1992). More like each other than anyone else? A cross-cultural study of entrepreneurial perceptions. *Journal of Business Venturing*, *7*(5), 419–429.

McGrath, R. G., MacMillan, I. C., & Scheinberg, S. (1992). Elitists, risk-takers, and rugged individualists? An exploratory analysis of cultural differences between entrepreneurs and non-entrepreneurs. *Journal of Business Venturing*, *7*(2), 115–135.

McGrath, R. G., MacMillan, I. C., & Tushman, M. L. (1992). The role of executive team actions in shaping dominant designs: Towards the strategic shaping of technological progress. *Strategic Management Journal, 13*(S2), 137–161.

McGrath, R. G., MacMillan, I. C., & Venkataraman, S. (1995). Defining and developing competence: A strategic process paradigm. *Strategic Management Journal, 16*(4), 251–275.

McGrath, R. G., MacMillan, I. C., Yang, E. A. Y., & Tsai, W. (1992). Does culture endure, or is it malleable? Issues for entrepreneurial economic development. *Journal of Business Venturing, 7*(6), 441–458.

Minniti, M. (2009). *Gender issues in entrepreneurship.* Boston: Now.

Musembi, C. N. (2007). De Soto and land relations in rural Africa: Breathing life into dead theories about property rights. *Third World Quarterly, 28*(8), 1457–1478.

O'Connor, E. S. (2007). Reader beware: Doing business with a store (y) of knowledge. *Journal of Business Venturing, 22*(5), 637–648.

Ohe, T., Honjo, S., Oliva, M., & MacMillan, I. C. (1991). Entrepreneurs in Japan and Silicon Valley: A study of perceived differences. *Journal of Business Venturing, 6*(2), 135–144.

Perry, D. L. (1990). Review of the book: Hernando de Soto 'The other path: The invisible revolution in the third world'. *Journal of Business Ethics, 9*(3), 170.

Peterson, R. (1988). Understanding and encouraging entrepreneurship internationally. *Journal of Small Business Management, 26*(2), 1–8.

Pierce, J. L. (2005). Reflections on 'my career'. Accessible at https://www.d.umn.edu/~jpierce/career.pdf.

Poggesi, S., Mari, M., & De Vita, L. (2016). What's new in female entrepreneurship research? Answers from the literature. *International Entrepreneurship and Management Journal, 12*(3), 735–764.

Pratt, M. (2009). From the editors: The lack of a boilerplate: Tips on writing up (and rewriting) qualitative research. *Academy of Management Journal, 52*(5), 856–858.

Ramoglou, S., Gartner, W. B., & Tsang, E. W. (2020). "Who is an entrepreneur?" is (still) the wrong question. *Journal of Business Venturing Insights, 13.* https://doi.org/10.1016/j.jbvi.2020.e00168.

Reagan, R. (1985). Why this is an entrepreneurial age. *Journal of Business Venturing, 1*(1), 1–4.

Renko, M., El Tarabishy, A., Carsrud, A. L., & Brännback, M. (2015). Understanding and measuring entrepreneurial leadership style. *Journal of Small Business Management, 53*(1), 54–74.

Rossini, R. G., & Thomas, J. J. (1990). The size of the informal sector in Peru: A critical comment on Hernando de Soto's El Otro Sendero. *World Development, 18*(1), 125–135.

Salamzadeh, A. (2015). New venture creation: Controversial perspectives and theories. *Economic Analysis, 48*(3–4), 101–109.

Schildt, H. A., Zahra, S. A., & Sillanpää, A. (2006). Scholarly communities in entrepreneurship research: A co–citation analysis. *Entrepreneurship Theory and Practice, 30*(3), 399–415.

Schwartz, E. B. (1976). Entrepreneurship—New female frontier. *Journal of Contemporary Business, 5*(1), 47–76.

Shane, S., & Venkataraman, S. (2000). The promise of entrepreneurship as a field of research. *Academy of Management Review, 25*(1), 217–226.

Shane, S., & Venkataraman, S. (2001). Entrepreneurship as a field of research: A response to Zahra and Dess, Singh, and Erikson. *Academy of Management Review, 26*(1), 13–16.

Shane, S., Venkataraman, S., & MacMillan, I. (1995). Cultural differences in innovation championing strategies. *Journal of Management, 21*(5), 931–952.

Starr, J., & MacMillan, I. (1990). Resource cooptation via social contracting: Resource acquisition strategies for new ventures. *Strategic Management Journal, 11,* 79–92.

Steyaert, C. (2007). Of course that is not the whole (toy) story: Entrepreneurship and the cat's cradle. *Journal of Business Venturing, 22*(5), 733–751.

Steyaert, C., & Landström, H. (2011). Enacting entrepreneurship research in a pioneering, provocative and participative way: On the work of Bengt Johannisson. *Small Business Economics, 36*(2), 123–134.

Sullivan, D. M., & Meek, W. R. (2012). Gender and entrepreneurship: A review and process model. *Journal of Managerial Psychology, 27,* 428–458.

Teixeira, A. A. (2011). Mapping the (in) visible college (s) in the field of entrepreneurship. *Scientometrics, 89*(1), 1–36.

Terjesen, S., Hessels, J., & Li, D. (2016). Comparative international entrepreneurship: A review and research agenda. *Journal of Management, 42*(1), 299–344.

Thomas, A. S., & Mueller, S. L. (2000). A case for comparative entrepreneurship: Assessing the relevance of culture. *Journal of International Business Studies, 31*(2), 287–301.

Thorp, R. (1990). Reviews: Heranando de Soto: The other path. *Journal of Latin American Studies, 22*(1–2), 403–405.

Venkataraman, S., MacMillan, I., & McGrath, R. (1992). Progress in research on corporate venturing. In D. L. Sexton, & J. D. Kasarda, (Eds.), *The state of the art of entrepreneurship* (pp. 487–519). Boston: PWS-Kent.

Wadhwani, R. D., Kirsch, D., Welter, F., Gartner, W. B., & Jones, G. G. (2020). Context, time, and change: Historical approaches to entrepreneurship research. *Strategic Entrepreneurship Journal, 14*(1), 3–19.

Welter, F., & Lasch, F. (2008). Entrepreneurship research in Europe: Taking stock and looking forward. *Entrepreneurship Theory and Practice, 32*(2), 241–248.

Welter, F., Baker, T., Audretsch, D. B., & Gartner, W. B. (2017). Everyday entrepreneurship—A call for entrepreneurship research to embrace entrepreneurial diversity. *Entrepreneurship Theory and Practice, 41*(3), 311–321.

Wharton, E. (1998). *A backward glance: An autobiography.* New York: Simon & Schuster.

Wiklund, J., Dimov, D., Katz, J. A., & Shepherd, D. A. (Eds.). (2006). Europe and entrepreneurship research. In *Advances in entrepreneurship, firm emergence and growth: Vol. 9. Entrepreneurship: Frameworks and empirical investigations from forthcoming leaders of European research* (pp. 1–8). Bingley, UK: Emerald.

Woodruff, C. (2001). Review of the book De Soto's The mystery of capital. *Journal of Economic Literature, 39*(4), 1215–1223.

Yacus, A. M., Esposito, S. E., & Yang, Y. (2019). The influence of funding approaches, growth expectations, and industry gender distribution on high-growth women entrepreneurs. *Journal of Small Business Management, 57*(1), 59–80.

Yadav, V., & Unni, J. (2016). Women entrepreneurship: Research review and future directions. *Journal of Global Entrepreneurship Research, 6*(1), 12–30.

Zahra, S. A. (1993). A conceptual model of entrepreneurship as firm behavior: A critique and extension. *Entrepreneurship Theory and Practice, 17*(4), 5–21.

CHAPTER 8

Overall Program

More than twenty years back, Shane (1997) identified twenty most productive scholars in entrepreneurship research. Focusing on 472 articles published between 1987 and 1994 in 19 journals shortlisted by Macmillan (1991, 1993)'s survey of well-regarded tenured researchers at major universities, Shane (1997)'s list included many scholars who were later recognized by GAER: Arnie Cooper (GAER 1997), Ian Macmillan (GAER 1999), Paul Reynolds (GAER 2004), and Scott Shane (GAER 2009). Since then, many efforts have been made to identify key contributors to entrepreneurship research, yielding divergent results. Teixeira (2011)'s scientometric-based approach identified 163 influential researchers in entrepreneurship, of which 18 had already been recognized by the GAER by that time, and three have since been awarded the GAER (Kathy Eisenhardt in 2012, Shaker Zahra 2014, and Boyan Jovanovic 2019). When Gupta, Ibrahim, Guo, and Markin (2016) examined researchers publishing entrepreneurship inquiry in general management journals over the 2000–2015 time period,[1] only two GAER awardees appeared in the top-20 scholars they identified: Scott Shane and Kathy Eisenhardt. Markin, Swab, and Marshall (2017) examined the most productive researchers in the six most reputed field journals

---

[1] The journals they covered were *Academy of Management Review, Academy of Management Journal, Strategic Management Journal, Administrative Science Quarterly, Journal of Management, Management Science,* and *Organization Science.*

© The Author(s) 2020   215
V. K. Gupta, *Great Minds in Entrepreneurship Research,*
https://doi.org/10.1007/978-3-030-44125-8_8

in entrepreneurship,[2] identifying three GAER awardees in the top-20 scholars: Zoltan Acs, David Audretsch, and Shaker Zahra.

Over the years, three scholars have been honored with the GAER for their overall research program: David Storey (in 1998), Paul Reynolds (in 2004), and Scott Shane (in 2009). Of these, one (Storey) is UK-based, while the other two are based in the US. Despite the many differences between them, all three scholars became involved in entrepreneurship research when the field was still struggling for legitimacy and since then have had long and productive careers focused on entrepreneurship-related inquiry (Gartner, 2014). This chapter discusses the work of these three scholars.

David Storey: Looking Differently at Job Creation

David Storey, the 1998 GAER awardee, is ranked among the most influential entrepreneurship researchers (Landstrom, Harirchi, & Astrom, 2012), one of the few European scholars to make it to the list otherwise dominated by US-based researchers. The official GAER citation recognizes Storey for his "focus on unbiased, large-scale and high-quality research, and for the initiation and coordination of extensive national and cross-national research programs on the central small business issues." He is considered the most prominent exponent of small business inquiry in the UK, with a strong policy-oriented research agenda.

Storey first attracted attention with the publication of his 1982 book *Entrepreneurship and the New Firm*, which critically reviewed the evidence for the job creation potential of small firms. Storey (1982) argued that large firms are responsible for the majority of new jobs created and lost in an economy, a provocative stance that challenged Birch's (1979) popular position at the time. Focusing on the UK manufacturing sector, Storey (1982) believed that small firms will never generate a sufficient number of jobs to replace jobs lost from the closure or relocation of large firms, especially because the majority of new firms disappear within a few years of their founding (when they are still quite small). In 1983, Storey published *The Small Firm: An International Survey*, where he recognized the shift in interest from large firms to small firms. Storey (1983) attributed this radical change in interest to two reasons: replacing

---

[2] For some reason, they excluded *Entrepreneurship & Regional Development*, widely recognized among the top field journals in entrepreneurship.

capital-intensive projects, which he believed favored large firms, with labor-intensive projects because of macroeconomic shocks (e.g., oil-crisis of the 1970s) and increasing demand for services and one-off products (customized goods) relative to mass-manufactured goods. Covering small firms in developed countries (e.g., US, Japan, Sweden) and developing countries (e.g., Malaysia, Philippines, Thailand), Storey (1983) identified that while there are several cross-national variations in the problems that small firms face some challenges such as difficulties in raising finance, dealings with government, and managing economic downturns are common across countries.

In 1987, Storey, with Steven Johnson, published *Job Generation and Labour Market Change*, which argued that it is the quality—not the quantity—of small firms which is important for economic growth and job creation. Recognizing that small firms were growing in importance in most developed countries, Storey and Johnson (1987) found that the mechanisms for why this happened varied greatly across societies. Through their study of Birmingham (UK), Boston (USA), and Bologna (Italy) regions, Storey and Johnson (1987) encouraged policy-makers to be mindful of the circumstances of their economy when developing public policy for small firms. In 1987, Storey, with Kevin Keasey, Robert Watson, and Pooran Wynarczyk, published *The Performance of Small Firms*, which emphasized that small firms are not simply 'scaled down' versions of large firms and that failure rates are more than ten times as high for new small firms as for large well-established firms. The central defining attribute of small firms, Storey, Keasey, Watson, and Wynarczyk (1987) observed, is failure. The smaller the firm, Storey et al. (1987) found, the higher the probability of failure.

Storey's most cited work, and the one that was probably most responsible for the GAER honor (Storey, 2014), is his 1994 book *Understanding the Small Business Sector* (Landström et al., 2012). The book came from a large-scale research program on small businesses funded by the ESRC in 1987, which provided rich data that led to books on three other topics: rural and urban firms (Curran & Storey, 1993), small firms and employment (Atkinson & Storey, 1994), and finance in small firms (Hughes & Storey, 1994). Storey (1994) synthesized the large amount of research on small firms, analyzing data to find that the small business share of employment and output in manufacturing in the UK had increased over the past decade-and-half, and made suggestions for addressing 'knee-jerk' policy-making that targeted small firms. Storey (1994) argued that, no matter how one defines small firms, 95% of all businesses in Europe were small firms, but the interest of the small business owner and those of society do not always overlap.

Storey has also published several influential articles (Landstrom, 2005), some of which are discussed here. A prominent stream of Storey's research centers around new firm formation (Reynolds, Storey, & Westhead, 1994a), which is considered fundamental to economic well-being of a region. Using a multi-country dataset, Reynolds, Storey, and Westhead (1994b) report that (a) average new firm birth rates are roughly similar across several developed countries and regional variations within countries are quite similar, and (b) the processes underlying new firm births at the regional level seem consistent across countries. Storey (1991) contends that to understand the creation of new ventures at the regional level, one needs to understand the important role of unemployment in people starting businesses. Storey and Jones (1987) found that the rate of new firm formation is positively associated with regional rate of unemployment, so that more new firms are created when job shedding is higher. Using longitudinal data from three British regions (England, Scotland, and Wales), van Stel and Storey (2004) find that new firm formation has either no or small positive relationship with lagged job creation, but the relationship is negative in 'low enterprise' areas, presumably because they have "comparatively low levels of entrepreneurial and human capital" (Landström, 2005: 196). Mueller, van Stel, and Storey (2008) also report that in Britain the employment impact of new firm formation is significantly positive in the high-enterprise counties, but negative in low-enterprise counties.

Another interesting stream of research in Storey's work relates to discouraged borrowers (Kon & Storey, 2003), which refers to otherwise good borrowers who do not apply for a bank loan because they feel they will be rejected (Freel, Carter, Tagg, & Mason, 2012). Using data from the 1998 US Survey of Small Business Finances, which collected information on the use of credit by small businesses with fewer than 500 employees, Han, Fraser, and Storey (2009) found that riskier borrowers are more likely to be discouraged, but this effect is contingent on the length of the relationship the firm has with the financial institution. Quality of information improves when there is a longer financial relationship, which increases the likelihood of discouragement among high-risk borrowers, but lowers it for low-risk borrowers.

Based on data obtained from the First National Baseline Survey of small businesses in Trinidad and Tobago, Storey (2004) found no evidence that entrepreneur gender has an effect on whether a small business reports having sought a bank loan at any time in the history of the business or when load was denied to a business who applied for it. Capelleras, Mole, Greene, and Storey (2008) used survey data from de novo independent firms in the Spain (a highly-regulated country) and Britain (a lightly-regulated country) to document that growth rates of firms are similar across the two regulatory regimes, although registered firms grow faster in less regulation than in more regulation. Parker, Storey, and van Witteloostuijn (2010) identified 708 UK-based gazelles ('high-growth' firms), finding that growth rate is substantially lower for gazelles in the second time period than in an earlier time period, which runs counter to the long-standing Gibrat's Law of random firm growth.

PAUL REYNOLDS: LARGE-SCALE EMPIRICAL INVESTIGATIONS

The 2004 GAER awardee, Paul Reynolds, is recognized for "organizing several exemplary innovative and large-scale empirical investigations into the nature of entrepreneurship and its role in economic development." Reynolds (2005) shares that his interest in entrepreneurship started at University of Minnesota when the Center for Urban and Regional Affairs provided funding for a survey of new firms in Minnesota to test David Birch's seminal thesis that new and small firms create jobs. The original Minnesota survey was followed by a similar effort in Pennsylvania and another one in Minnesota. Data for new firms from Minnesota were used for a comparative study of factors that explain societal contributions and survival potential of new firms (Reynolds, 1987). Since then, Reynolds has been devoted to large-scale survey data collection from entrepreneurs and small business (Davidsson, 2005). His co-authored paper, Reynolds et al., (1994b), is considered a landmark paper in the journal *Regional Studies*. Three of his works—Reynolds and White (1997); Reynolds, Hay, Bygrave, Camp, and Autio (2000); and Reynolds, Camp, Bygrave, Autio, and Hay (2001)—are ranked among the core contributors in entrepreneurship research. For Davidsson (2005: 351), Reynolds has "made a deeper and more lasting mark in entrepreneurship than almost any contemporary scholar."

Reynolds conducted a large-scale study of regional factors affecting variation in new firm births, both within the US (Reynolds, Miller, & Maki, 1995) and across six countries internationally (Reynolds et al., 1994b). These studies found that the same five factors—demand growth, urbanization, higher unemployment, local wealth, and an economy with a high proportion of small firms—predicted about 60–90% of variation in firm birth rate (Davidsson, 2005). In 1990, Reynolds moved from the sociology department at Minnesota to a chaired position in entrepreneurship at Marquette University, where he launched another large-scale study to study nascent entrepreneurship in Wisconsin (Reynolds, 2000). Nascent entrepreneurs were defined as people working to start a new business, but one that was not operational yet, and was soon to become a popular topic in entrepreneurship research (Wagner, 2006). The Wisconsin Entrepreneurial Climate Study conducted in Spring 1993 and funded by the Wisconsin Housing and Economic Development Authority replicated the efforts previously done in Minnesota and Pennsylvania to gauge the extent of nascent entrepreneurship in the state. Reynolds was also able to piggyback onto the University of Michigan Institute for Social Research Survey of Consumer Attitudes to collect pilot data on a small national sample of nascent entrepreneurs (Reynolds, Carter, Gartner, & Greene, 2004). Both studies revealed about 4% prevalence rate of nascent entrepreneurship in society (Reynolds, 2000), suggesting that it was possible to capture early-stage entrepreneurial activity (before the venture is formed) through surveys and a large population had to be surveyed to get a reasonable number of positive matches (people actually engaged in trying to start a venture). Because a very small proportion of working-age adults self-identified themselves as nascent entrepreneurs, identifying a generalizable sample of individuals trying to start a business has been likened to 'finding a needle in a haystack' (Gartner, Shaver, Carter, & Reynolds, 2004): A lot of hay (people who are not attempting to start businesses) needs to be sorted through to find the few needles (individuals engaged in business creation) that one is looking for.

   Carter, Gartner, and Reynolds (1996) analyzed new venture creation activities undertaken by 71 nascent entrepreneurs identified from the Wisconsin survey and the Michigan pilot data. As the entrepreneurship research community at the time became aware of the project and the research design, there was interest in a collaborative effort to study nascent entrepreneurship nationally. Unfortunately, no single institution was willing to fund the massive expenses of identifying individuals in the process of business creation and then track their business creation efforts over several years (Gartner et al., 2004). Two funding proposals were rejected by the US National Science Foundation (Reynolds, 2005). An open meeting was organized by Nancy Carter, Bill Gartner, and Paul Reynolds during the April 1995 Babson College Kauffman Foundation Entrepreneurship Research Conference at the London Business School, which led to a second organizational meeting at the Chicago O'Hare airport hotel in November 1995. Interested researchers convinced their institutions to contribute $10,000 each per annum for two years, launching the Entrepreneurial Research Consortium (ERC).

As a result of these efforts, the US Panel Study of Entrepreneurial Dynamics (PSED) was born. The initial screening was based on a random digit dialing telephone interview of 64,622 individuals in 1998–2000. It identified a cohort of 830 nascent entrepreneurs, individuals who self-reported as working to launch a new business, whether by themselves or for an employer (McCann, 2017). This identification assumes that when individuals begin to take some action to create a new firm, they are at the nascent entrepreneurship stage, where they are distinct from the rest of the population not engaged in any steps toward business creation. The self-identified nascent entrepreneurs were matched with a comparison group of non-entrepreneurs, so that both groups are representative of the national population of adults 18 years old and older. The efforts of these people were then tracked over a two-year period, with detailed phone surveys and mail questionnaires to obtain information about them and the opportunities they were pursuing. This was done twice, at 12 and 24 months after the first interview. This panel is referred to as the PSED I (Gartner et al., 2004).

The three-stage PSED I model—identification of a representative sample of those actively involved in firm creation (Stage 1), detailed interview with nascent entrepreneurs paid $25 (Stage 2), and annual follow-up interviews (Stage 3)—was also adopted for PSED II, which was launched in 2005 (Reynolds, 2011). The Ewing Marion Kauffman Foundation provided financial support for PSED II. A total of 31,845 households were contacted in Stage 1 by Opinion Research Corporation of Princeton (New Jersey). It identified 1214 individuals as nascent entrepreneurs to be interviewed for Stage 2. Yearly interviews were conducted between 2005 and 2011 (Thiess, Sirén, & Grichnik, 2016).

The PSED efforts resulted in two large-scale, multi-wave datasets (Reynolds & Curtin, 2012). The screening and four waves of the PSED I yielded a dataset of 1261 cases (830 nascent entrepreneurs) and over six thousand variables. The screening and six waves of the PSED II yielded a dataset of 1214 cases (all nascent entrepreneurs) and over eight thousand variables. Although there was a six-year lag between the identification of nascent entrepreneur cohorts in these two projects, the research procedures were quite similar, but not completely identical (see Reynolds and Curtin (2008) for detailed discussion of the difference between the two efforts). Over the years, PSED I and II data have formed the bases of a number of dissertations (e.g., Kim, 2006; Meeks, 2004) and journal papers (e.g., Reynolds et al., 2004; Ruef, Aldrich, & Carter, 2003).

When the PSED started, a number of research teams were from outside the US and many adapted the US design for implementation in their own countries (e.g., Delmar & Shane, 2003; Eckhardt, Shane, & Delmar, 2006). The successful launch of the PSED motivated interest in comparing the level of entrepreneurship across countries. The result was the Global Entrepreneurship Monitor (GEM) created in 1997 as a joint research initiative by Babson College and London Business School supported by the Kauffman Center for Entrepreneurial Leadership at the Ewing Marion Kauffman Foundation (Reynolds et al., 2005). Ten countries participated in the first GEM study in 1999: the G-7 (Canada, France, Germany, Italy, Japan, the UK, and the US) along with Denmark, Finland, and Israel. The PSED procedures were revised to emphasize participation in entrepreneurship and cross-national harmonization (Reynolds, 2005). The second GEM study in 2000 added 11 countries: Argentina, Australia, Belgium, Brazil, India, Ireland, Korea, Norway, Singapore, Spain, and Sweden (Reynolds et al., 2000). Over time, more countries joined the GEM effort and some countries stopped participating, presumably because national teams were responsible for funding the data collection efforts in their own country (Reynolds et al., 2005). The latest GEM report covers 50 countries worldwide, seeking to understand and compare entrepreneurial activity across the globe in 2019 (Bosma et al., 2020). The data collected by GEM teams in the various countries have not only helped illuminate the state of entrepreneurship worldwide, but also the enabling conditions at the national level and for specific groups within countries (e.g., women, youth).

SCOTT SHANE: ENTREPRENEUR-OPPORTUNITY NEXUS

The 2009 GAER awardee, Scott Shane, is consistently ranked among the most prolific and influential entrepreneurship scholars (Landstrom et al., 2012). Gupta et al. (2016) identify him as having the most publications on entrepreneurship in major academic journals during the 2000 to 2015 time period.[3] Shane has a reputation of being an "unusually 'complete' entrepreneurship scholar in terms of having made empirical as well as conceptual and methodological contributions" (Davidsson & Wiklund, 2009: 133). The official GAER citation recognized Shane for "publishing significant works that display superior conceptual acumen as well as empirical and methodological sophistication. His research covers virtually all major aspects of the entrepreneurship phenomenon: the individual(s), the opportunity, the organizational context, the environment, and the entrepreneurial process." For several years, Shane offered an intensive week-long PhD seminar in entrepreneurship that attracted young researchers from around the world at a time when doctoral seminars in entrepreneurship were rare at most universities. Shane's seminar gained a strong reputation for "focusing on theory building and key controversies in the entrepreneurship field, with rigorous attention to optimum methodologies for exploring original ideas" (Kelleher, 2009: 1).

Shane started his academic career with a three-country study of firm formation (Shane, Kolvereid, & Westhead, 1991), finding four common factors that predicted the likelihood of starting a new venture—independence, recognition, learning, and roles—even as the level of these four factors was found to vary by country and gender. Starting with his dissertation (see Shane, 1995), his research linked cultural values with innovation at the national level. Hofstede's (1980) cultural measures of individualism and power distance were correlated with the number (per capita) of new patents (Shane, 1992) while individualism, power distance, and uncertainty avoidance were correlated with number of trademarks (Shane, 1993). At the time, Shane was also a strong proponent of dispositional research in management and entrepreneurship (House, Shane, & Herold, 1996). Looking at the rate of entrepreneurship within the

---

[3] A similar study looking at articles published in field journals of entrepreneurship, however, does not find Shane to be among the most prolific authors (Markin et al. 2017).

US over the 1899–1988 period, Shane (1996a) found that the rate of entrepreneurship in the US economy has varied over time and that these variations can be explained by factors such as technological change and protestant ethic.

Shane's early research also looked at international new ventures (McDougall, Shane, & Oviatt, 1994), franchising (Hoy & Shane, 1998; Shane & Hoy, 1996), and venture capitalists (Cable & Shane, 1997; Shane & Cable, 2002). Using information about 138 firms that first offered franchise-offering documents in the US in 1983, Shane (1996b) found that franchising was positively associated with likelihood of survival and growth for the firm. Shane (1996c) examined international expansion among franchisors, observing that US-based franchisors who establish franchisees in other countries should develop a strong capability to protect against and monitor potential franchisee opportunism. Shane (1998) conducted survival analysis on a cohort of 157 new franchisors established in the US between 1981 and 1983, tracking them over time to identify factors that decreased the prospects of cessation of franchising. Notably, Shane's franchising research was informed by agency theory (Eisenhardt, 1989), which focuses on problems that arise when one party (the principal) determines the work for another party (the agent). Over the years, Shane published several articles on franchising (e.g., Azoulay & Shane, 2001; Mitsuhashi, Shane, & Sine, 2008; Shane & Foo, 1999; Shane, Shankar, & Aravindakshan, 2006) and a popular book on the issues and challenges that franchisors face (Shane, 2005).

The year 2000 was a turning point in Shane's academic career as it saw the publication of his two most influential works: Shane (2000) and Shane and Venkataraman (2000).[4] The former was an empirical paper and the latter a conceptual paper, but both were based on the idea of the individual-opportunity nexus that was to inform much of Shane's subsequent work (Shane, 2003). Work on these two papers took place during Shane's time at Massachusetts Institute of Technology (MIT). At the time, MIT was the single-large source of university patents in the

---

[4] As of this writing (May 31, 2020), Web of Science (WoS) reports 1824 citations for Shane (2000) and 4500 citations for Shane and Venkataraman (2000), which translates to an annual average of 61.2 cites for the former and 225 cites for the latter. Researchers consider an average higher than 20 per year as criterion for super-classic status in the field (Durden & Ellis, 1993; Gupta & Dutta, 2018), which suggests that Shane (2000) and Shane and Venkataraman (2000) should be considered super-classics in the entrepreneurship literature.

US. It accounted for 8% of all university patents in the country and had an explicit set of policies to promote new firm formation based on its patents (Shane & Khurana, 2003). Shane (2000) focused on one MIT invention (three-dimensional printing) and used an embedded case study design to examine the eight new venture opportunities exploiting the 3DP™ process. He found that not everyone is equally likely to recognize the same entrepreneurial opportunities which result from technological change (even when they are all exposed to the same invention), with one's recognition of the opportunity shaped by their prior knowledge. Shane (2000) is considered "his single most influential, sole-authored work" with "a profound effect on the field" (Davidsson & Wiklund, 2009: 132). In a subsequent paper that looked at MIT patents from 1980 to 1996, Shane and Khurana (2003) find that career experience impacts new firm formation by affecting expectations about the new venture's liability of newness. Once again, the message was that scholarship on organizational founding should also consider the important role of individual actors.

Shane and Venkataraman (2000) was a conceptual article that sought to stake out a distinctive territory for entrepreneurship research centered on the interface of individuals and opportunities. Building on Venkatara-man's (1997) now-classic work (Javadian & Singh, 2018), Shane and Venkataraman (2000: 218) defined the academic field of entrepreneur-ship as "the scholarly examination of how, by whom, and with what effects opportunities to create future goods and services are discovered, evaluated, and exploited." Shane and Venkataraman (2000) encouraged researchers to focus on three sets of research questions they consider central to the field: (1) why, when, and how opportunities for the creation of goods and services come into existence; (2) why, when, and how some people and not others discover and exploit these opportunities; and (3) why, when, and how different modes of action are used to exploit opportunities to introduce new goods and services to the market.

Shane and Venkataraman (2000: 220) conceived entrepreneurial opportunities as "objective phenomena that are not known to all parties at all times," a position that was soon disputed by those taking a creation view of opportunities (Alvarez & Barney, 2007; Chiles, Bluedorn, & Gupta, 2007). Dissatisfied with the idea that opportunities exist objec-tively 'out there' in ways visible to potential entrepreneurs, scholars taking a creationist position argued that opportunities are generated endoge-nously through entrepreneurial agency (Gupta, Streb, Gupta, & Markin,

2015; Wood & McKinley, 2010). Shane and Venkataraman (2000)'s definition of entrepreneurial opportunities as "those situations in which new goods, services, raw materials, and organizing methods can be introduced and sold at greater than their cost of production" was criticized for requiring that opportunities generate profit (Singh, 2001). Many ventures lose significant amounts of money, and yet operate for years, and may even turn their founders into billionaires (e.g., Uber, WeWorks). Some scholars raised concerns that the opportunity construct was inherently fuzzy (Davidsson, 2015), calling for it to be jettisoned in favor of a multi-construct replacement (Davidsson, 2017).

The ideas discussed in Shane (2000) and Shane and Venkataraman (2000) were expanded and elaborated in Shane and Eckhardt (2003) and Shane (2003). To address the criticisms directed at their original approach to entrepreneurial opportunities, Shane and Eckhardt (2003) proposed two revisions: (a) discovery refers to perception of opportunity rather than the existence of an opportunity, and (b) there is a potential—not a requirement—that the new offering can be sold at greater than the cost of production. Eckhardt and Shane (2010) reaffirmed the objective existence of entrepreneurial opportunities, arguing that while exploitation of opportunity requires human creativity, opportunities themselves exist independent of any given individual. Shane (2012) used the term 'business idea' to capture entrepreneurs' subjective perception of opportunity, and defined opportunity as "technical and market constraints" (Eckhardt & Shane, 2013: 163).

Shane's wide-ranging research on entrepreneurial phenomena includes looking at technological innovation as an important determinant of entrepreneurial opportunity (Eckhardt & Shane, 2011), role of founding team experience on the survival and sales of new ventures (Delmar & Shane, 2006), and usefulness of legitimizing activities (e.g., establishing a legal entity) in increasing likelihood of founding and survival of new ventures (Delmar & Shane, 2004). In a well-cited article, Delmar and Shane (2003) found that business planning among nascent entrepreneurs reduces the likelihood of venture disbanding and strengthens product development and venture organizing activity (see also Shane & Delmar, 2004). Replication efforts have raised concerns about the positive outcomes associated with business planning for new ventures (Honig & Karlsson, 2004; Honig & Samuelsson, 2014), so that the debate about the usefulness of business planning in the entrepreneurial process continues (Davidsson, 2015; Delmar, 2015a, 2015b; Honig & Samuelsson, 2015).

In recent years, Shane has "entered into the novel and controversial territory of" genetic influence on entrepreneurial outcomes (Davidsson & Wiklund, 2009: 133). Nicolaou and Shane (2009) propose four mechanisms through which genes, which they define as "a piece of DNA that is passed from parents to their biological children during reproduction," influence entrepreneurial behaviors through four independent channels: genes affect (a) chemical reactions in the brain, (b) relevant individual differences such as internal locus of control, (c) sensitivity to environmental stimuli related to entrepreneurship, and (d) tendency of people to select into environments conducive to entrepreneurship. Using a survey-based dataset of 870 pairs of monozygotic (MZ) and 857 pairs of same-sex dizygotic (DZ) twins from the UK, Nicolaou, Shane, Cherkas, Hunkin, and Spector (2008) found strong evidence favoring genetic heritability for entrepreneurship, with little effect of family environment and upbringing. Genetic factors were also found to explain variation across people in opportunity recognition (Nicolaou, Shane, Cherkas, and Spector, 2009). Genes may influence the tendency of people to engage in entrepreneurship by affecting the distribution of sensation seeking across people (Nicolaou, Shane, Cherkas, & Spector, 2008). Shane, Nicolaou, Cherkas, and Spector (2010) report that the positive association between personality characteristics of Extraversion and Openness to Experience on the one hand and tendency to become an entrepreneur on the other hand is largely explained by genes. The genetic effects on the tendency to be an entrepreneur seem to be consistent across gender, and part of a broader heritability of occupational choice (Nicolaou & Shane, 2010). Shane and Nicolaou (2013) examine 148 US-based twins, comprising 94 MZ and 54 DZ pairs, to find that 74% of the variance in self-employment income is explained by genetic factors. While there are several challenges to the validity of research relying on twins to determine genetic influence on entrepreneurial outcomes (Arvey, Li, & Wang, 2016), there is also a moral concern about the desirability and public interpretation of such inquiry that makes it controversial (Joseph, 2004).

SUMMARY

This chapter focuses on three GAER honorees, recognized for the strength of their overall research program. The works of these three scholars speak to their dedication to enhancing the conversation in entrepreneurship research, whether it is by challenging widely-held assumptions (David Storey), launching and running large-scale data collection efforts that required sustained resources and funding (Paul Reynolds), and advancing a new framework for delineating the domain of entrepreneurship research (Scott Shane). All three scholars started research entrepreneurship when academic inquiry on entrepreneurial phenomena was still in its infancy. Their commendable efforts have been instrumental in the subsequent development and impressive growth of the field.

REFERENCES

Alvarez, S. A., & Barney, J. B. (2007). Discovery and creation: Alternative theories of entrepreneurial action. *Strategic Entrepreneurship Journal, 1*(1–2), 11–26.

Arvey, R. D., Li, W. D., & Wang, N. (2016). Genetics and organizational behavior. *Annual Review of Organizational Psychology and Organizational Behavior, 3*, 167–190.

Atkinson, J., & Storey, D. (1994). *Employment, the small firm and the labour market*. London: Routledge.

Azoulay, P., & Shane, S. (2001). Entrepreneurs, contracts, and the failure of young firms. *Management Science, 47*(3), 337–358.

Birch, D. (1979). *The job generation process*. Cambridge: MIT Press.

Bosma, N., Hill, S., Ionescu-Somers, A., Kelley, D., Levie, J., & Tarnawa, A. (2020). *Global Entrepreneurship Monitor 2019/2020 Global Report*. Global Entrepreneurship Research Association, London Business School.

Cable, D. M., & Shane, S. (1997). A prisoner's dilemma approach to entrepreneur-venture capitalist relationships. *Academy of Management Review, 22*(1), 142–176.

Capelleras, J. L., Mole, K. F., Greene, F. J., & Storey, D. J. (2008). Do more heavily regulated economies have poorer performing new ventures? Evidence from Britain and Spain. *Journal of International Business Studies, 39*(4), 688–704.

Carter, N. M., Gartner, W. B., & Reynolds, P. D. (1996). Exploring start-up event sequences. *Journal of Business Venturing, 11*(3), 151–166.

Chiles, T. H., Bluedorn, A. C., & Gupta, V. K. (2007). Beyond creative destruction and entrepreneurial discovery: A radical Austrian approach to entrepreneurship. *Organization Studies, 28*(4), 467–493.

Curran, J., & Storey, D. J. (1993). *Small firms in urban and rural locations*. London: Routledge.

Davidsson, P. (2005). Paul D. Reynolds: Entrepreneurship research innovator, coordinator, and disseminator. *Small Business Economics, 24*(4), 351–358.

Davidsson, P. (2015). Entrepreneurial opportunities and the entrepreneurship nexus: A re-conceptualization. *Journal of Business Venturing, 30*(5), 674–695.

Davidsson, P. (2017). Entrepreneurial opportunities as propensities: Do Ramoglou & Tsang move the field forward? *Journal of Business Venturing Insights, 7,* 82–85.

Davidsson, P., & Wiklund, J. (2009). Scott A. Shane: Winner of the Global Award for Entrepreneurship Research. *Small Business Economics, 33*(2), 131–140.

Delmar, F. (2015a). A response to Honig and Samuelsson (2014). *Journal of Business Venturing Insights, 3,* 1–4.

Delmar, F. (2015b). When the dust has settled: A final note on replication. *Journal of Business Venturing Insights, 4,* 20–21.

Delmar, F., & Shane, S. (2003). Does business planning facilitate the development of new ventures? *Strategic Management Journal, 24*(12), 1165–1185.

Delmar, F., & Shane, S. (2004). Legitimating first: Organizing activities and the survival of new ventures. *Journal of Business Venturing, 19*(3), 385–410.

Delmar, F., & Shane, S. (2006). Does experience matter? The effect of founding team experience on the survival and sales of newly founded ventures. *Strategic Organization, 4*(3), 215–247.

Durden, G. C., & Ellis, L. V. (1993). A method for identifying the most influential articles in an academic discipline. *Atlantic Economic Journal, 21*(4), 1–10.

Eckhardt, J. T., & Shane, S. A. (2010). An update to the individual-opportunity nexus. In Z. J. Acs & D. B. Audretsch (Eds.), *Handbook of entrepreneurship research* (Vol. 5, pp. 47–76). New York, NY: Springer.

Eckhardt, J. T., & Shane, S. A. (2011). Industry changes in technology and complementary assets and the creation of high-growth firms. *Journal of Business Venturing, 26*(4), 412–430.

Eckhardt, J. T., & Shane, S. A. (2013). Response to the commentaries: The individual-opportunity (IO) nexus integrates objective and subjective aspects of entrepreneurship. *Academy of Management Review, 38*(1), 160–163.

Eckhardt, J. T., Shane, S., & Delmar, F. (2006). Multistage selection and the financing of new ventures. *Management Science, 52*(2), 220–232.

Eisenhardt, K. M. (1989). Agency theory: An assessment and review. *Academy of Management Review, 14*(1), 57–74.

Freel, M., Carter, S., Tagg, S., & Mason, C. (2012). The latent demand for bank debt: Characterizing "discouraged borrowers." *Small Business Economics, 38*(4), 399–418.

Gartner, W. B. (2014). Organizing entrepreneurship (research). In A. Fayolle (Ed.) *Handbook of research in entrepreneurship* (pp. 13–22). Cheltenham, UK: Edward Elgar.

Gartner, W. B., Shaver, K. G., Carter, N. M., & Reynolds, P. D. (2004). Foreword. In W. B. Gartner, K. G. Shaver, N. M. Carter, and P. D. Reyolds (Eds.), *Handbook of entrepreneurial dynamics: The process of business creation* (pp. ix–xxiii). Thousand Oaks, CA: Sage.

Gupta, V. K., & Dutta, D. K. (2018). The rich legacy of Covin and Slevin (1989) and Lumpkin and Dess (1996): A constructive critical analysis of their deep impact on entrepreneurial orientation research. In G. Javadian, V. K. Gupta, D. K. Dutta, G. C. Guo, A. E. Osorio, & B. Ozkazanc-Pan (Eds.), *Foundational research in entrepreneurship studies*(pp. 155–178).Cham, Switzerland: Palgrave Macmillan.

Gupta, A., Streb, C. K., Gupta, V. K., & Markin, E. (2015). Entrepreneurial behavior during industry emergence: An unconventional study of discovery and creation in the early PC industry. *New England Journal of Entrepreneurship, 18*(2), 61–79.

Gupta, V. K., Ibrahim, S., Guo, G., & Markin, E. (2016). Entrepreneurship research in management and organizational studies: A contribution-based assessment of the literature. *New England Journal of Entrepreneurship, 19*(1), 69–86.

Han, L., Fraser, S., & Storey, D. J. (2009). Are good or bad borrowers discouraged from applying for loans? Evidence from US small business credit markets. *Journal of Banking & Finance, 33*(2), 415–424.

Hofstede, G. (1980). *Culture's consequences: International differences in work-related values.* Beverley Hills, CA: Sage.

Honig, B., & Karlsson, T. (2004). Institutional forces and the written business plan. *Journal of Management, 30*(1), 29–48.

Honig, B., & Samuelsson, M. (2014). Data replication and extension: A study of business planning and venture-level performance. *Journal of Business Venturing Insights, 1–2,* 18–25.

Honig, B., & Samuelsson, M. (2015). Replication in entrepreneurship research: A further response to Delmar. *Journal of Business Venturing Insights, 3,* 30–34.

House, R. J., Shane, S. A., & Herold, D. M. (1996). Rumors of the death of dispositional research are vastly exaggerated. *Academy of Management Review, 21*(1), 203–224.

Hoy, F., & Shane, S. (1998). Franchising as an entrepreneurial venture form. *Journal of Business Venturing, 13*(2), 91–94.

Hughes, A., & Storey, D. J. (Eds.). (1994). *Finance and the small firm.* London: Routledge.

Javadian, G., & Singh, R. P. (2018). Entrepreneurial opportunities as the heart of entrepreneurship research: A reflection on Venkataraman (1997).

In G. Javadian, V. Gupta, D. Dutta, G. Guo, A. Osorio, & B. Ozkazanc-Pan (Eds.), *Foundational research in entrepreneurship studies* (pp. 249–263). Cham, Switzerland: Palgrave Macmillan.

Joseph, J. E. (2004). *Language and identity: National, ethnic, religious*. London: Palgrave Macmillan.

Kelleher, L. (2009). *Entrepreneurial research: Lessons learned from Scott Shane's intensive PhD seminar in entrepreneurship*. Australian Centre for Entrepreneurship Research Exchange Conference, Sydney (Australia).

Kim, P. H. (2006). *Organizing activities and founding processes of new ventures* (Doctoral dissertation). University of North Carolina, Chapel Hill.

Kon, Y., & Storey, D. J. (2003). A theory of discouraged borrowers. *Small Business Economics, 21*(1), 37–49.

Landström, H. (2005). *Pioneers in entrepreneurship and small business research*. Boston, MA: Springer.

Landström, H., Harirchi, G., & Åström, F. (2012). Entrepreneurship: Exploring the knowledge base. *Research Policy, 41*(7), 1154–1181.

MacMillan, I. C. (1991). Editor's note: Delineating a forum for entrepreneurship scholars. *Journal of Business Venturing, 6*(2), 83–87.

MacMillan, I. C. (1993). The emerging forum for entrepreneurship scholars. *Journal of Business Venturing, 8*(5), 377–381.

Markin, E., Swab, R. G., & Marshall, D. R. (2017). Who is driving the bus? An analysis of author and institution contributions to entrepreneurship research. *Journal of Innovation & Knowledge, 2*(1), 1–9.

McCann, B. T. (2017). Prior exposure to entrepreneurship and entrepreneurial beliefs. *International Journal of Entrepreneurial Behavior & Research, 23*(3), 591–612.

McDougall, P. P., Shane, S., & Oviatt, B. M. (1994). Explaining the formation of international new ventures: The limits of theories from international business research. *Journal of Business Venturing, 9*(6), 469–487.

Meeks, M. D. (2004). *Antecedents to the entrepreneurial decision: An empirical analysis of three predictive models* (Doctoral dissertation). University of Colorado, Boulder.

Mitsuhashi, H., Shane, S., & Sine, W. D. (2008). Organization governance form in franchising: Efficient contracting or organizational momentum? *Strategic Management Journal, 29*(10), 1127–1136.

Mueller, P., van Stel, A., & Storey, D. J. (2008). The effects of new firm formation on regional development over time: The case of Great Britain. *Small Business Economics, 30*(1), 59–71.

Nicolaou, N., & Shane, S. (2009). Can genetic factors influence the likelihood of engaging in entrepreneurial activity? *Journal of Business Venturing, 24*(1), 1–22.

Nicolaou, N., & Shane, S. (2010). Entrepreneurship and occupational choice: Genetic and environmental influences. *Journal of Economic Behavior & Organization, 76*(1), 3–14.

Nicolaou, N., Shane, S., Cherkas, L., & Spector, T. D. (2008). The influence of sensation seeking in the heritability of entrepreneurship. *Strategic Entrepreneurship Journal, 2*(1), 7–21.

Nicolaou, N., Shane, S., Cherkas, L., & Spector, T. D. (2009). Opportunity recognition and the tendency to be an entrepreneur: A bivariate genetics perspective. *Organizational Behavior and Human Decision Processes, 110*(2), 108–117.

Nicolaou, N., Shane, S., Cherkas, L., Hunkin, J., & Spector, T. D. (2008). Is the tendency to engage in entrepreneurship genetic? *Management Science, 54*(1), 167–179.

Parker, S. C., Storey, D. J., & Van Witteloostuijn, A. (2010). What happens to gazelles? The importance of dynamic management strategy. *Small Business Economics, 35*(2), 203–226.

Reynolds, P. D. (1987). New firms: Societal contribution versus survival potential. *Journal of Business Venturing, 2*(3), 231–246.

Reynolds, P. D. (2000). National panel study of US business startups: Background and methodology. *Databases for the Study of Entrepreneurship, 4*(1), 153–227.

Reynolds, P. D. (2005). Understanding business creation: Serendipity and scope in two decades of business creation studies. *Small Business Economics, 24*(4), 359–364.

Reynolds, P. D. (2011). Informal and early formal financial support in the business creation process: Exploration with PSED II data set. *Journal of Small Business Management, 49*(1), 27–54.

Reynolds, P., Bosma, N., Autio, E., Hunt, S., De Bono, N., Servais, I., ...Chin, N. (2005). Global entrepreneurship monitor: Data collection design and implementation 1998–2003. *Small Business Economics, 24*(3), 205–231.

Reynolds, P. D., Camp, M. S., Bygrave, W. D., Autio, & Hay, M. (2001). *Global entrepreneurship monitor: 2001 executive report.* Kauffman Center for Entrepreneurial Leadership, Kansas City, MO.

Reynolds, P. D., Carter, N. M., Gartner, W. B., & Greene, P. G. (2004). The prevalence of nascent entrepreneurs in the United States: Evidence from the panel study of entrepreneurial dynamics. *Small Business Economics, 23*(4), 263–284.

Reynolds, P. D., & Curtin, R. T. (2008). *Business creation in the United States: Panel study of entrepreneurial dynamics II initial assessment* (Vol. 16). Hanover, MA.: Now.

Reynolds, P. D., & Curtin, R. T. (2012). *PSED I, II Harmonized transitions, outcomes data set.* Available at https://www.psed.isr.umich.edu/psed/data.

Reynolds, P. D., Hay, M., Bygrave, W. D., Camp, M., & Autio, E. (2000). *GEM 2000 executive report*. Kansas City, MO: Kauffman Foundation.

Reynolds, P. D., Miller, B., & Maki, W. R. (1995). Explaining regional variation in business births and deaths: U.S. 1976–1988. *Small Business Economics, 7*(5), 389–407.

Reynolds, P. D., Storey, D. J., & Westhead, P. (1994a). Cross-national comparisons of the variation in new firm formation rates: An editorial overview. *Regional Studies, 28*(4), 343–346.

Reynolds, P. D., Storey, D. J., & Westhead, P. (1994b). Cross-national comparisons of the variation in new firm formation rates. *Regional Studies, 28*(4), 443–456.

Reynolds, P. D., & White, S. B. (1997). *The entrepreneurial process: Economic growth, men, women, and minorities*. Westport, CT: Quorum.

Ruef, M., Aldrich, H., & Carter, N. (2003). The structure of founding teams: Homophily, strong ties, and isolation among U.S. entrepreneurs. *American Sociological Review, 68*(2), 195–222.

Shane, S. (1992). The effect of cultural differences in perceptions of transaction costs on national differences in the preference for licensing. *Management International Review, 32*(4), 295–311.

Shane, S. (1993). Cultural influences on national rates of innovation. *Journal of Business Venturing, 8*(1), 59–73.

Shane, S. (1995). Uncertainty avoidance and the preference for innovation championing roles. *Journal of International Business Studies, 26*(1), 47–68.

Shane, S. A. (1996a). Explaining variation in rates of entrepreneurship in the United States: 1899–1988. *Journal of Management, 22*(5), 747–781.

Shane, S. A. (1996b). Hybrid organizational arrangements and their implications for firm growth and survival: A study of new franchisors. *Academy of Management Journal, 39*(1), 216–234.

Shane, S. A. (1996c). Why franchise companies expand overseas. *Journal of Business Venturing, 11*(2), 73–88.

Shane, S. A. (1997). Who is publishing the entrepreneurship research? *Journal of Management, 23*(1), 83–95.

Shane, S. A. (1998). Making new franchise systems work. *Strategic Management Journal, 19*(7), 697–707.

Shane, S. (2000). Prior knowledge and the discovery of entrepreneurial opportunities. *Organization Science, 11*(4), 448–469.

Shane, S. (2003). *A general theory of entrepreneurship: The individual-opportunity nexus*. Cheltenham, UK: Edward Elgar.

Shane, S. (2005). *From ice cream to the internet: Using franchising to drive the growth and profits of your company*. Upper Saddle River, NJ: Prentice Hall.

Shane, S. (2012). Reflections on the 2010 AMR decade award: Delivering on the promise of entrepreneurship as a field of research. *Academy of Management Review, 37*(1), 10–20.

Shane, S. A., & Hoy, F. (1996). Franchising: A gateway to cooperative entrepreneurship. *Journal of Business Venturing, 11*(5), 325–327.

Shane, S., & Cable, D. (2002). Network ties, reputation, and the financing of new ventures. *Management Science, 48*(3), 364–381.

Shane, S., & Delmar, F. (2004). Planning for the market: Business planning before marketing and the continuation of organizing efforts. *Journal of Business Venturing, 19*(6), 767–785.

Shane, S., & Eckhardt, J. (2003). The individual-opportunity nexus. In Z. J. Acs & D. B. Audretsch (Eds.), *Handbook of entrepreneurship research* (Vol. 1, pp. 161–194). Boston, MA: Springer.

Shane, S., & Foo, M. D. (1999). New firm survival: Institutional explanations for new franchisor mortality. *Management Science, 45*(2), 142–159.

Shane, S., & Khurana, R. (2003). Bringing individuals back in: The effects of career experience on new firm founding. *Industrial and Corporate Change, 12*(3), 519–543.

Shane, S., Kolvereid, L., & Westhead, P. (1991). An exploratory examination of the reasons leading to new firm formation across country and gender. *Journal of Business Venturing, 6*(6), 431–446.

Shane, S., & Nicolaou, N. (2013). The genetics of entrepreneurial performance. *International Small Business Journal, 31*(5), 473–495.

Shane, S., Nicolaou, N., Cherkas, L., & Spector, T. D. (2010). Genetics, the Big Five, and the tendency to be self-employed. *Journal of Applied Psychology, 95*(6), 1154.

Shane, S., & Venkataraman, S. (2000). The promise of entrepreneurship as a field of research. *Academy of Management Review, 25*(1), 217–226.

Shane, S., Shankar, V., & Aravindakshan, A. (2006). The effects of new franchisor partnering strategies on franchise system size. *Management Science, 52*(5), 773–787.

Singh, R. P. (2001). A comment on developing the field of entrepreneurship through the study of opportunity recognition and exploitation. *Academy of Management Review, 26*(1), 10–12.

Storey, D. J. (1982). *Entrepreneurship and the new firm*. London: Croom Helm.

Storey, D. J. (1991). The birth of new firms—Does unemployment matter? A review of the evidence. *Small Business Economics, 3*(3), 167–178.

Storey, D. J. (1994). *Understanding the small business sector*. London: Routledge.

Storey, D. J. (2004). Racial and gender discrimination in the micro firms credit market? Evidence from Trinidad and Tobago. *Small Business Economics, 23*(5), 401–422.

Storey, D. J. (2014). Understanding the small business sector: Reflections and confessions. In B. Braunerhjelm (Ed.), *20 years of entrepreneurship research: From small business dynamics to entrepreneurial growth and societal prosperity* (pp. 21–33). Stockholm: Swedish Entrepreneurship Forum.

Storey, D. J. (Ed.). (1983). *The small firm: An international survey*. New York: St. Martins.

Storey, D. J., & Johnson, S. (1987). *Job generation and labour market change*. Hampshire, UK: Macmillan.

Storey, D. J., & Jones, A. M. (1987). New firm formation—A labour market approach to industrial entry. *Scottish Journal of Political Economy, 34*(1), 37–51.

Storey, D. J., Keasey, K., Watson, R., & Wynarczyk, P. (1987). *The performance of small firms: Profits, jobs and failures*. London: Croom Helm.

Teixeira, A. A. (2011). Mapping the (in)visible college(s) in the field of entrepreneurship. *Scientometrics, 89*(1), 1–36.

Thiess, D., Sirén, C., & Grichnik, D. (2016). How does heterogeneity in experience influence the performance of nascent venture teams? Insights from the US PSED II study. *Journal of Business Venturing Insights, 5*, 55–62.

Van Stel, A., & Storey, D. (2004). The link between firm births and job creation: Is there a Upas tree effect? *Regional Studies, 38*(8), 893–909.

Venkataraman, S. (1997). The distinctive domain of entrepreneurship research: An editor's perspective. In J. Katz & J. Brockhaus (Eds.), *Advances in entrepreneurship, firm emergence, and growth* (Vol. 3, pp. 119–138). Greenwich, CT: JAI.

Wagner, J. (2006). Are nascent entrepreneurs 'Jacks-of-all-trades'? A test of Lazear's theory of entrepreneurship with German data. *Applied Economics, 38*(20), 2415–2419.

Wood, M. S., & McKinley, W. (2010). The production of entrepreneurial opportunity: A constructivist perspective. *Strategic Entrepreneurship Journal, 4*(1), 66–84.

CHAPTER 9

Conclusion

As an academic field matures, it becomes important to take stock of the work that has been done in an effort to build on the past to shape the future. Such reflective efforts gain additional salience in fields characterized by theoretical pluralism and eclecticism, as is the case with entrepreneurship inquiry. Critical investigations of popular ideas and concepts can reveal blind spots and gaps in the literature and point to ideational ruts and cul-de-sacs that hinder knowledge development. Each individual study, whether published as a journal article or in a book, focuses on specific questions crafted to meet the critical requirements of its audience. As a result, reading published work often constrains our attention on small contributions to knowledge, so that the big task and the big problem for maturing academic fields are to make sure the forest is not obscured by the trees. For this reason, reflecting where we have been, what we have learned, and what remains to be understood is crucial to both advancing our field and helping society address pressing problems and issues (Shepherd, 2015), including grand challenges that confront us as researchers and good citizens (George, Howard-Grenville, Joshi, & Tihanyi, 2016).

Over the past few years, scholars have made tremendous strides in synthesizing and making sense of the academic literature in rapidly expanding fields, such as entrepreneurship (Kraus, Breier, & Dasí-Rodríguez, 2020). Many journals now routinely publish systematic literature reviews, meta-analyses, bibliometric analyses, all of which seek to

© The Author(s) 2020
V. K. Gupta, *Great Minds in Entrepreneurship Research*,
https://doi.org/10.1007/978-3-030-44125-8_9

consolidate previous literature to bring the field closer together. The twin liabilities of smallness and newness have long been part of the vocabulary of entrepreneurship researchers. As the field matures, scholars find themselves facing the curse of bigness, which is about the challenges that come with largeness. It is well known that large firms face issues and challenges that do not trouble small firms. The same is true for academic fields, as they face a different set of issues and problems when they become large and established. A key challenge entrepreneurship research faces today is that while paying attention to past ideas is often claimed, there is often a tendency to see the past as inferior to the present such that recent ideas are considered superior to historic ideas. Indeed, Schildt, Zahra, and Sillanpää (2006: 410) bemoan that research in entrepreneurship appears "to be noncumulative, evidenced by the limited citations of prior published works in the areas" covered in their analyses. The purpose of this book is to highlight that looking back toward the work of the giants and understanding their ideas offer myriad meaningful opportunities for future scholarship.

By any measure, the extant academic literature-related entrepreneurship is humongous, whether one considers it in terms of breadth or depth, which presents its own challenges for researchers. Scholarship on entrepreneurial phenomena is published not only in the field journals, but also in general management journals, as well as in journals of other academic fields (e.g., economics, psychology, and sociology, but also finance, accounting, and geography, among others). Consider GAER laureates like Steven Klepper, John Haltiwanger, and Josh Lerner, with impressive publication records primarily in journals not on the regular reading list of most entrepreneurship researchers. Then, there are also GAER awardees like David Birch and Hernando de Soto, who eschewed journal publications in favor of popular articles, monographs, and books, making it even more challenging for researchers to keep up with new knowledge generated about entrepreneurship.

Given the extensive growth in entrepreneurship research over time, for any one researcher (or a team of researchers) to become familiar with all the intricacies and debates in contemporary entrepreneurship research is now virtually impossible. There was a simpler time, when a researcher could hope to become familiar with the entire entrepreneurship literature fairly quickly. Gartner (2014: 13) shared that in the 1990s "all academic research on entrepreneurship could easily be read within a couple of months." As this book reveals, those simple times are now gone. Davidsson (2016: 18) noted that when he was starting his academic career, "it was possible to have the ambition to more or less 'know the literature'—meaning the entire body of work on entrepreneurship across levels of analysis and disciplinary bases, [but] now it is difficult to keep pace with a single niche thereof."

Consider the proliferation of research that now exists in just one area of entrepreneurship: Entrepreneurial Orientation (EO), which Basso, Fayolle, and Bouchard (2009: 313) describe as "one of the few examples of stabilized concepts in management science." Research on EO started in earnest with Covin and Slevin (1989) and gained momentum with Lumpkin and Dess (1996). Brown, Davidsson, and Wiklund (2001: 953) were quite impressed when they found "no less than twelve" EO studies. By the time Rauch, Wiklund, Lumpkin, and Frese (2009) did their award-winning meta-analysis of the EO-performance relationship, there were 51 studies in the area. It gets even 'better' (or worse, depending on how you look at it). Wales, Gupta, and Mousa (2013) conducted a systematic literature review of EO research based on 158 empirical journal articles. Gupta and Wales (2017) found 121 journal articles that examined performance in the EO literature. A recent review of measurement issues in EO research was based on—hold your breath—551 published articles (White, Choudhary, & Gupta, 2020). Given that EO "remains a vibrant research topic" (Covin & Wales, 2019: 3), one can expect that studies on this topic will continue to appear in academic journals.

Of course, it is not just EO research that has witnessed a virtual explosion in academic scholarship. Similar trends can be seen in other areas of entrepreneurship inquiry. A consequence of this impressive growth in publications is that there now exists a wealth of evidence-based knowledge about many aspects of the entrepreneurial phenomena. This is a positive development, but it also means that an aspiring scholar who wants to contribute to a particular area in entrepreneurship may need to read hundreds of articles just to figure out how they can advance knowledge in that area. Consider, for example, the sheer amount of research one now has to read if one wanted to make a meaningful contribution to the EO literature discussed above. It is therefore unsurprising that research studies are often submitted to journals without the authors fully recognizing the enormity and scope of the prior research on the topic. Articles that synthesize the available body of a knowledge in an area can be helpful (Rousseau, Manning, & Denyer, 2008), but they offer only a partial respite as they reflect someone else's interpretation and understanding of the literature (Tranfield, Denyer, & Smart, 2003).

The stunning growth in the quantity of published research also poses considerable challenge for reviewers and editors. When selecting reviewers, editors need to find scholars with deep knowledge in a particular area, which is quite challenging as the pool of researchers with multiple publications in one area tends to be small. Given the cross-disciplinary nature of research in some areas (e.g., VC research), an ideal reviewer would be someone who keeps abreast of developments across disciplinary boundaries, but such scholars are rare. Wright, Ketchen, and Clark (2020) lament that finding bonafide experts on the topic of a journal submission to start the review process has become increasingly difficult with time. Consequently, any given submission may not receive the same caliber of expert vetting as it would have in the past.

While there are legitimate reasons for scholars focusing on particular research areas (Gartner, Davidsson, & Zahra, 2006), a pitfall is that a thorough and comprehensive knowledge of entrepreneurship is simply not possible when each researcher's expertise and interest is constrained to a particular—but narrow—aspect of a growing literature. As a result, there is a real risk that research claiming to break new ground will miss relevant or similar work already published in journals outside of one's core area. Reviewers or editors may not always catch such omissions during the peer review process because of their own limited reading of the literature. As Gartner (2014: 13) noted, truly "in-depth knowledge of academic scholarship is, now, beyond the 'readability' of any one researcher," no matter how extensively he/she tries to keep up with the ever-expanding literature in entrepreneurship that spans several disciplinary boundaries.

Given these challenges, how do we consolidate and make sense of the progress in entrepreneurship research? This survey of the work of 27 leading scholars, all recipients of the most prestigious award for entrepreneurship research, offers one way to understand the origins and evolution of scholarship on entrepreneurial phenomena. These scholars come from a wide variety of backgrounds, with doctorates in economics (e.g., John Haltiwanger), sociology (e.g., Howard Aldrich), business (e.g., Candy Brush), or other fields. Some GAER awardees spent their entire academic career at one institution (e.g., Arnold Cooper), others moved around considerably (e.g., Sidney Winter), and many were somewhere in the middle (e.g., Paul Reynolds and Scott Shane). There were also those who did not follow traditional academic careers (e.g.,

David Birch and Hernando de Soto). In other words, the life trajectory of the GAER awardees shows there are various paths to reach the towering heights of success in entrepreneurship research, as long as one does quality work that challenges and influences the way the community of scholars thinks about entrepreneurial phenomena.

The main arguments of the GAER awardees diverged widely, sometimes contradicting each other (as we saw, for example, with David Birch and David Storey). The methodological tools they used varied greatly, from mathematical modeling (e.g., Philippe Aghion) to qualitative inquiry (e.g., Kathy Eisenhardt). At first glance, you may even question whether all of them are really examining entrepreneurial phenomena. Yet, as evident from the GAER citation accompanying their award announcement, they are indeed contributing to entrepreneurship research, albeit in different ways, sometimes distant from the paradigms, methodologies, and tools most familiar to many of us.

Smith and Hitt (2005: 572) noted that most of the scholars they classified as "the greatest minds in management and organization research" were trained at—received their doctoral degrees—from US-based "Division 1 Research Schools...and elite private universities." There is a similar pattern here: 22 of the 27 GAER awardees completed their PhDs in the US, with five from Harvard (six, if you count Nancy Hart, part of the Diana Group),[1] three from Stanford, and the rest from other elite institutions, some public (e.g., University of Washington) and some private (e.g., Cornell University). Five awardees were trained at universities outside North America, of which four were European and one from South Africa. While entrepreneurship research may now span the globe (Aldrich, 2012), there continues to be a preponderance of US-based scholars among the core contributors to the entrepreneurship canon (Landstrom, Harirchi, & Astrom, 2012). Bibliographic studies report that US-based scholars are responsible for about half of the published works in entrepreneurship (Luor, Lu, Yu, & Chang, 2014). Landstrom et al. (2012) observe that scholarship originating in the US is equally likely to be cited by American and European researchers, but contributions from Europe are to a larger extent cited only by European scholars. Perhaps, this is why even though scholars from England, Canada, and Germany also contribute to entrepreneurship research, their work in general tends

---

[1] Interestingly, none of the outstanding organizational theorists identified in Smith and Hitt (2005) have doctoral degrees from Harvard.

to be less influential than US-based researchers (which makes the GAER recognition of non-US scholars like David Storey and Bengt Johannisson even more impressive). One cannot also help but notice that researchers from Asian countries, whether developed (e.g., Japan) or emerging (e.g., China), are absent from the list of major contributors to entrepreneurship research identified by Landstrom et al. (2012) as well as the ranks of GAER awardees so far.

There is clearly a need for more openness to voices and ideas from outside the US in the entrepreneurship literature. Consider the case of Germany, which is the fourth-largest contributor to entrepreneurship research (Luor et al., 2014). Yet, if one were to look beyond the classic works of Schumpeter and Weber, German scholarship seems to have had limited influence on academic conversation in entrepreneurship (Landstrom et al., 2012). This is especially surprising when one considers the rich and robust tradition of entrepreneurship inquiry in Germany (Schmude, Welter, & Heumann, 2008) and the strong German private sector, dominated by small-and-medium-sized enterprises (collectively known as *Mittelstand*; Pahnke & Welter, 2019). Substantial entrepreneurial activity also takes place in rapidly-emerging major economies such as China and India (Gupta et al., 2014) and the proportion of growth-minded companies from these countries have been steadily increasing among the world's largest corporations (Gupta, Mortal, & Yang, 2018). Unfortunately, research from emerging economies on entrepreneurial issues remains low (Sinha, Gibb, Akoorie, & Scott, 2020), especially in quality journals (Gupta, Mithani, & Guha, 2019). There is considerable concern that even when scholars from outside US and Europe do submit quality work to academic journals, there is "scant new theory" or novel methodological tools, or even attempts to understand phenomena from different perspectives than the prevailing practices in the US (Barkema, Chen, George, Luo, & Tsui, 2015: 461).

Gartner, the 2005 GAER recipient, encouraged using the historians' toolkit in our research (see Wadhwani, Kirsch, Welter, Gartner, & Jones, 2020). The same could be said about advancing knowledge pertaining to the leading scholars of entrepreneurship. Some commendable efforts have been made over the years to provide biographical coverage of the major figures in entrepreneurship research, such as Landstrom (2005) and Audretsch and Lehmann (2016). Lehmann and Keilbach (2019) present a *Festschrift*, which refers to "a book of essays and papers contributed by the honoree's students and colleagues, where even family members and close friends contribute," to recognize David Audretsch, the 2001 GAER awardee. However, there is still an absence of well-researched books focused on the life journey and career trajectory of particular scholars who have contributed to entrepreneurship research. Such books are commonplace in our 'mother' discipline of economics, for example. From Keynes to Hayek, leading economic scholars and their ideas are discussed at length in books, from both academic and popular press. Such material is sorely missing in entrepreneurship research. Would entrepreneurship scholars—budding and established—not want to know more about the life and career of David Birch, the person behind the idea that small business is responsible for most job creation in society?[2] Similarly, Giacomo Becattini would seem to be of relevance to practitioners and researchers, who may want to better understand the person encouraging us to study districts and clusters. There is a small, but growing, body of autobiographical work among marketing scholars (Aaker, 2005; Levy, 2013; Sheth, 2014). Similar work from, and about, GAER awardees can help us learn from their reflections about the trials and tribulations they faced, the ups and downs of their careers, and how they made their contributions to the advancement of science.

The year 2020 marks the 25th anniversary of the GAER. From David Birch in 1996 to John Haltiwanger in 2020, the GAER recipients are a good reflection of the richness and variety that characterizes entrepreneurship research. In a field where there is an obsession with novel work ('neophilia,' Antonakis [2017] calls it), it is helpful to look back and appreciate the strong set of shoulders upon which to stand and view the path ahead. The GAER scholars have given us an understanding of entrepreneurial phenomena that is far more profound and relevant than is often realized. We shall need their ideas and insights as we march into the future. Yes, there are contradictions, unsupported claims, and disjointed findings, but that is the nature of progress in the social sciences.

As an academic field, we have come a long way from the time in the 1970s when interest in entrepreneurship research first began to take

---

[2] Tatum (2007) describes Birch as having "single-handedly pioneered the study of rapid-growth firms" (companies with an average revenue growth of at least 20% over a four-year period), credits him with coining the term gazelles (Hechavarria, Bullough, Brush, & Edelman, 2019), and describes collaborating with him to create "a new economic index related to entrepreneurialism" (p. 191). Yet, not much is known about Birch beyond that described in Landstrom (2005), which is unfortunate.

off. Building on the scope and wisdom of the outstanding entrepreneurship researchers of the past, such as the ones discussed here, will help produce knowledge we will need to face the challenges and problems of the future. Each of the GAER awardee tackled intriguing questions and did interesting research, from which there is much to be learned. Whether you are a PhD student trying to make sense of the literature, a junior researcher struggling to make a meaningful 'contribution,' or an established scholar already publishing in good journals, the work of GAER awardees should be informative and inspiring to everyone interested in entrepreneurship research. If the past twenty-five years are any indication, the future of scholarship in the field of entrepreneurship is bright, especially if we continue to benefit from the strong shoulders of giants who have made important contributions to the advancing knowledge about entrepreneurial phenomena.

REFERENCES

Aaker, D. (2005). *From Fargo to the world of brands*. New York: Iceni Books.

Aldrich, H. E. (2012). The emergence of entrepreneurship as an academic field: A personal essay on institutional entrepreneurship. *Research Policy, 41*(7), 1240–1248.

Antonakis, J. (2017). On doing better science: From thrill of discovery to policy implications. *Leadership Quarterly, 28*(1), 5–21.

Audretsch, D. B., & Lehmann, E. E. (Eds.). (2016). *The Routledge companion to the makers of modern entrepreneurship*. Oxon, UK: Taylor & Francis.

Barkema, H. G., Chen, X. P., George, G., Luo, Y., & Tsui, A. S. (2015). West meets East: New concepts and theories. *Academy of Management Journal, 58*(2), 460–479.

Basso, O., Fayolle, A., & Bouchard, V. (2009). Entrepreneurial orientation: The making of a concept. *International Journal of Entrepreneurship and Innovation, 10*(4), 313–321.

Brown, T. E., Davidsson, P., & Wiklund, J. (2001). An operationalization of Stevenson's conceptualization of entrepreneurship as opportunity-based firm behavior. *Strategic Management Journal, 22*(10), 953–968.

Covin, J. G., & Slevin, D. P. (1989). Strategic management of small firms in hostile and benign environments. *Strategic Management Journal, 10*(1), 75–87.

Covin, J. G., & Wales, W. J. (2019). Crafting high-impact entrepreneurial orientation research: Some suggested guidelines. *Entrepreneurship Theory & Practice, 4391*, 3–18.

Davidsson, P. (2016). The field of entrepreneurship research: Some significant developments. In D. Bögenhold, J. Bonnet, M. Dejardin, & D. Garcia Pérez de Lema (Eds.), *Contemporary entrepreneurship* (pp. 17–28). Cham, Switzerland: Springer.

Gartner, W. B. (2014). Organizing entrepreneurship. In A. Fayolle (Ed.), *Handbook of research in entrepreneurship: What do we know? What do we need to know?* (pp. 13–22). Cheltenham, UK: Edward Elgar.

Gartner, W. B., Davidsson, P., & Zahra, S. A. (2006). Are you talking to me? The nature of community in entrepreneurship scholarship. *Entrepreneurship Theory and Practice, 30*(3), 321–331.

George, G., Howard-Grenville, J., Joshi, A., & Tihanyi, L. (2016). Understanding and tackling societal grand challenges through management research. *Academy of Management Journal, 59*(6), 1880–1895.

Gupta, V. K., Guo, C., Canever, M., Yim, H. R., Sraw, G. K., & Liu, M. (2014). Institutional environment for entrepreneurship in rapidly emerging major economies: The case of Brazil, China, India, and Korea. *International Entrepreneurship and Management Journal, 10*(2), 367–384.

Gupta, V. K., Mithani, M., & Guha, M. (2019). Creativity, innovation, and entrepreneurship in South Asia. *South Asian Journal of Business Studies, 8*(3), 325–331.

Gupta, V. K., Mortal, S. C., & Yang, T. (2018). Entrepreneurial orientation and firm value: Does managerial discretion play a role? *Review of Managerial Science, 12*(1), 1–26.

Gupta, V. K., & Wales, W. J. (2017). Assessing organisational performance within entrepreneurial orientation research: Where have we been and where can we go from here? *Journal of Entrepreneurship, 26*(1), 51–76.

Hechavarria, D., Bullough, A., Brush, C., & Edelman, L. (2019). High-growth women's entrepreneurship: Fueling social and economic development. *Journal of Small Business Management, 57*(1), 5–13.

Kraus, S., Breier, M., & Dasí-Rodríguez, S. (2020). The art of crafting a systematic literature review in entrepreneurship research. *International Entrepreneurship and Management Journal, 16*, 1023–1042.

Landstrom, H. (2005). *Pioneers in entrepreneurship and small business research*. New York: Springer.

Landstrom, H., Harirchi, G., & Åström, F. (2012). Entrepreneurship: Exploring the knowledge base. *Research Policy, 41*(7), 1154–1181.

Lehmann, E. E., & Keilbach, M. (2019). Preface. In E. Lehmann and M. Keilbach (Eds.), *From industrial organization to entrepreneurship*. A tribute to David B. Audretsch. Cham, Switzerland: Springer.

Levy, S. J. (2013). *One man in his time*. Seattle, WA: Createspace Independent Publishing.

Lumpkin, G. T., & Dess, G. G. (1996). Clarifying the entrepreneurial orientation construct and linking it to performance. *Academy of Management Review,* *21*(1), 135–172.

Luor, T., Lu, H. P., Yu, H., & Chang, K. (2014). Trends in and contributions to entrepreneurship research: A broad review of literature from 1996 to June 2012. *Scientometrics, 99*(2), 353–369.

Pahnke, A., & Welter, F. (2019). The German Mittelstand: Antithesis to Silicon Valley entrepreneurship? *Small Business Economics, 52*(2), 345–358.

Rauch, A., Wiklund, J., Lumpkin, G. T., & Frese, M. (2009). Entrepreneurial orientation and business performance: An assessment of past research and suggestions for the future. *Entrepreneurship Theory and Practice, 33*(3), 761–787.

Rousseau, D. M., Manning, J., & Denyer, D. (2008). Evidence in management and organizational science: Assembling the field's full weight of scientific knowledge through syntheses. *Academy of Management Annals, 2*(1), 475–515.

Schildt, H. A., Zahra, S. A., & Sillanpää, A. (2006). Scholarly communities in entrepreneurship research: A co–citation analysis. *Entrepreneurship Theory and Practice, 30*(3), 399–415.

Schmude, J., Welter, F., & Heumann, S. (2008). Entrepreneurship research in Germany. *Entrepreneurship Theory and Practice, 32*(2), 289–311.

Shepherd, D. (2015). Party on! A call for entrepreneurship research that is more interactive, activity based, cognitively hot, compassionate, and prosocial. *Journal of Business Venturing, 30*(4), 489–507.

Sheth, J. (2014). *The accidental scholar.* Thousand Oaks, CA: Sage.

Sinha, P., Gibb, J., Akoorie, M., & Scott, J. M. (Eds.). (2020). *Research handbook on entrepreneurship in emerging economies: A contextualized approach.* Cheltenham, UK: Edward Elgar.

Smith, K. G., & Hitt, M. A. (2005). Epilogue: Learning how to develop theory from the masters. In K. G. Smith & M. A. Hitt (Eds.), *Great minds in management: The process of theory development* (pp. 572–587). Oxford: Oxford University Press.

Tatum, D. (2007). *No man's land: What to do when your company is too big to be small but too small to be big.* New York: Penguin.

Tranfield, D., Denyer, D., & Smart, P. (2003). Towards a methodology for developing evidence-informed management knowledge by means of systematic review. *British Journal of Management, 14*(3), 207–222.

Wadhwani, R. D., Kirsch, D., Welter, F., Gartner, W. B., & Jones, G. G. (2020). Context, time, and change: Historical approaches to entrepreneurship research. *Strategic Entrepreneurship Journal, 14*(1), 3–19.

Wales, W. J., Gupta, V. K., & Mousa, F. T. (2013). Empirical research on entrepreneurial orientation: An assessment and suggestions for future research. *International Small Business Journal, 31*(4), 357–383.

White, J., Choudhary, S., & Gupta, V. K. (2020). Measurement of entrepreneurial orientation. *Advances in Entrepreneurship, Firm Emergence, and Growth, 22*, In Press.

Wright, M., Ketchen, D. J., Jr., & Clark, T. (2020). Publishing in management: Exhilaration, bafflement, and frustration. In M. Wright, D. J. Ketchen Jr., & T. Clark (Eds.), *How to get published in the best management journals.* Cheltenham, UK: Edward Elgar.

INDEX

Printed by Printforce, the Netherlands